THOMSON
COURSE TECHNOLOGY

Professional • Trade • Reference

SONAR™ 4

SONAR™ 4
IGNITE!

By Brian Smithers

❊ Technical Edit by Cakewalk ❊
❊ Covers Producer and Studio Editions! ❊

MUSKA & LIPMAN
Publishing

SVP, Thomson Course Technology PTR: Andy Shafran
Publisher: Stacy L. Hiquet
Senior Marketing Manager: Sarah O'Donnell
Marketing Manager: Heather Hurley
Manager of Editorial Services: Heather Talbot
Senior Acquisitions Editor: Todd Jensen
Senior Editor: Mark Garvey
Associate Marketing Managers: Kristin Eisenzopf and Sarah Dubois
Project Editor/Copy Editor: Kate Shoup Welsh
Technical Reviewer: Ryan Pietras
Thomson Course Technology PTR Market Coordinator: Elizabeth Furbish
Interior Layout Tech: LJ Graphics, Susan Honeywell
Cover Designer: Mike Tanamachi
Indexer: Sharon Shock
Proofreader: Kim Benbow

ISBN: 1-59200-506-3
Library of Congress Catalog Card Number: 2004109682
Printed in the United States of America
04 05 06 07 08 BH 10 9 8 7 6 5 4 3 2 1

THOMSON

COURSE TECHNOLOGY™

Professional ■ Trade ■ Reference

Thomson Course Technology PTR, a division of Thomson Course Technology
25 Thomson Place
Boston, MA 02210
http://www.courseptr.com

To Barb: You're my inspiration.

Acknowledgments

Thanks to Acquisitions Editor Todd Jensen for his confidence, enthusiasm, and guidance, and to the rest of the Course PTR team, especially Kate Welsh, Mark Garvey, and Brian Proffitt for lending their expertise to the task of making me look good in print. I am indebted to Steve Thomas and the gang at Cakewalk for wading through my seemingly endless torrent of questions along the way, and in particular to Cakewalk's Ryan Pietras for the technical edit.

I would be remiss in not acknowledging David Battino, who gave me my first writing opportunity and who always makes me a better writer, along with my great friend Tony Hill, who prodded me to pick up the phone and call David in the first place. Steve Oppenheimer and his fantastic crew at *Electronic Musician*—David Rubin, Dennis Miller, Gino Robair, Len Sasso, and company—continually challenge and inspire me, and I am grateful to be part of the *EM* extended family.

On a personal note, I would like to thank God for blessing me with the greatest family and the most wonderful friends one could have. Thanks to my loving wife Barb for being my loving wife... and my best friend. Thanks, Mom and Dad, for unconditional love and support, even when I decided not to go into mathematics. Thanks to Andy Hagerman for "shifting my paradigm" and unleashing my inner geek. Finally, my love and gratitude go to Nermal, Hillary, and Leopold for making me laugh even in the middle of post-post-deadline panic and exhaustion.

About the Author

Brian Smithers is a classically trained musician, conductor, and composer who has been performing and teaching music for more than 20 years. Taking the concept of the "Renaissance man" to heart at an early age, he has always maintained a diverse professional and artistic life, performing in everything from jazz combos to symphony orchestras while composing and arranging commercial music. The culmination of this ironic juxtaposition saw him for several years as conductor of a traditional all-acoustic wind band—the world-famous Walt Disney World Band—by day and a music technology writer for *Electronic Musician*, *Music & Computers*, and *Keyboard* by night. An accomplished recording engineer, Mr. Smithers was at the vanguard of the movement to use notebook computers for live remote recording, performance, and production. He founded a Web site that for several years was the only sustaining Internet resource on laptop-based music production. As Course Director of Audio Workstations and Advanced Audio Workstations at Full Sail Real World Education in Winter Park, Florida, Mr. Smithers coordinates and guides the curriculum of what is arguably the largest digital audio workstation lab environment in the world. He teaches Music Technology at Stetson University in DeLand, Florida, where he also trains the student recording staff and engineers the School of Music's annual recordings. He has been a SONAR user since it was Cakewalk 3.0.

Contents at a Glance

Contents

Introduction

This book will get you started making music with one of the most powerful Windows-based music production programs available—Cakewalk's SONAR 4 Producer Edition. It is an equally useful guide to SONAR 4 Studio Edition, Cakewalk's less-expensive but still feature-rich offering. In these pages you will find everything you need to demystify the deep and powerful functions of this popular program, regardless of your prior experience.

SONAR 4 Ignite! takes you step by step through MIDI sequencing, digital audio recording, and mixing your song into a finished product. You'll learn how to set up your project, create tracks, edit MIDI and digital audio clips, and utilize virtual instruments. Finally, you'll see how SONAR's effects plug-ins and exciting surround-sound capabilities enable you to realize a great-sounding mix that's ready for CD or Web distribution.

If you want to make music and you're looking for maximum-strength tools with a minimum learning curve, SONAR 4 Producer Edition and this book will have you jamming in no time. In addition, you'll find extra material on the book's companion Web site, located at http://www.courseptr.com/downloads.

Who Should Read This Book?

This book is intended for novices who are new to music-production software or new to SONAR. Because its capabilities are so vast, SONAR can seem pretty daunting at first, so each chapter deals with a manageable chunk of technology. Each successive chapter builds on the previous ones, taking you to the summit one sure-footed step at a time.

Nearly every step in this book is accompanied by a clear illustration, so you'll never have any doubts about whether you're looking at the right screen or choosing the right tool. The non-technical language helps move you gradually from neophyte to seasoned user with a minimum of trauma; if you're looking for techno-babble that you can use to impress your friends, you won't find any here!

Each task is clearly identified by heading, so you can easily find what you need by checking the table of contents. Although the materials are intended to be taken in order, if you're inclined to skip around or jump straight to what you need, this book will suit your working style and help you find what you're after.

Added Advice to Make You a Pro

You'll soon see that everything in this book is distilled to the essentials that will help you get results, going step by step without lengthy explanations. Be aware, however, that you're jumping into some sophisticated technology, so here and there you'll find special boxes to fill you in on important details.

At the end of the book are three appendixes that delve more deeply into the technology behind SONAR's sequencing and recording capabilities. Discover ways to manage your system's audio setup, learn the ins and outs of MIDI and digital audio and why they're such a complementary team, and find ways to get the best performance out of your computer.

It doesn't matter if you're into classical recording, hip-hop production, or becoming the next Beatles—you've got the power in your hands, so let's get started!

PART I

Meet Sonar

1

Working with Projects and Files

By choosing SONAR to help you make music, you've put virtually all the power of an entire recording studio in your computer. Indeed, SONAR gives you the tools to control your keyboards, record your vocals and guitars, and combine and modify the whole mix to your heart's content. As you do, you'll gradually accumulate numerous files of various types. As long as you know what sort of information is contained within each file and how the files work together, you will always be in command of your creative efforts. In this chapter, you will learn how to:

- Create and open a project
- Import audio into a project
- Document project information
- Save your project in various ways
- Close a project

Creating a New Project

A new song idea usually starts with a new SONAR project. A new project is the musical equivalent of a painter's blank canvas. The project file will eventually hold a complete description of your song—everything from tempo to number of bars, lyrics, effects, MIDI data, and links to external audio and video files. Here's how to create that blank canvas.

1. **Click** on **File**. The File menu will appear.

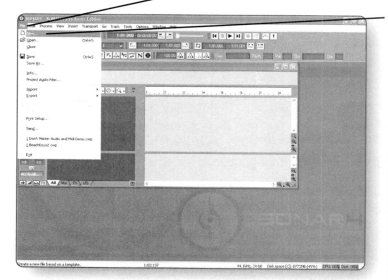

2. **Click** on **New**. The New Project File dialog box will open.

PICK A NAME

If you have Per-Project Audio Folders enabled (we'll discuss that option in Chapter 10, "Managing Audio," in the section "Using Per-Project Audio Folders"), you will be asked to name the new project. Otherwise you will only see a list of templates.

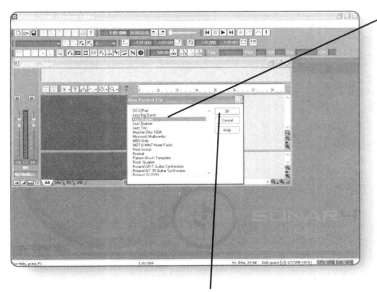

3. Click on the **desired template**. The template name will be highlighted.

TEMPLATES

SONAR 4's templates allow you to choose how you want your new project to look and act, so you can get started making music more quickly. We'll cover templates in detail in Chapter 23, "Getting More Efficient." For now, it's okay to accept the default selection, the Normal template.

4. Click on **OK**. The new project file will appear onscreen.

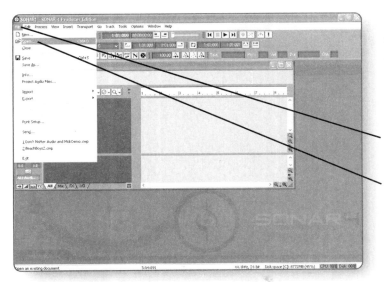

Opening an Existing Project

When you want to do further work on a project you created previously, you simply open the project and pick up where you left off.

1. Click on **File**. The File menu will open.

2. Click on **Open**. The Open dialog box will appear.

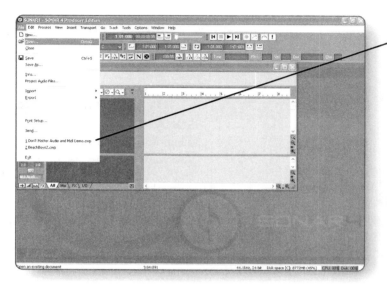

RECENT FILES

SONAR 4 keeps track of the files you've had open recently, listing them as numbered items at the bottom of the File menu. To open a recently used file, click on the File menu, point to the file you want to open, and click on the filename.

3. Navigate to the **file's location**.

4. Click on the **file** that you want to open. The name of the file will appear in the File name box.

5. Click on **Open**. The file will appear onscreen.

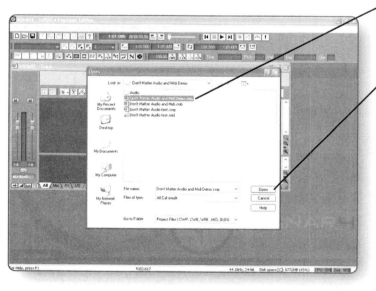

Importing Audio

Once you've got a SONAR project open, you can begin to add audio and MIDI information to start building your song. One way to get audio into SONAR is to import existing audio files. Here's how to do that.

1. Click on **File**. The File menu will open.

2. Point to **Import**. The Import submenu will open.

3. Click on **Audio**. The Import Audio dialog box will appear.

4. Navigate to the **file's location**.

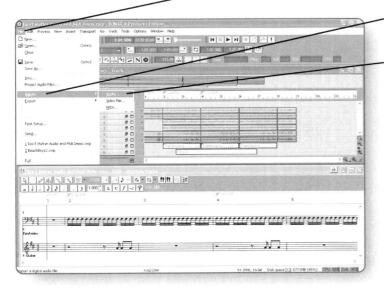

5. Click on the **file** that you want to open. The name of the file will appear in the File name box.

6. Optionally, **click** on the **Play** button to audition the audio file. The audio file will play.

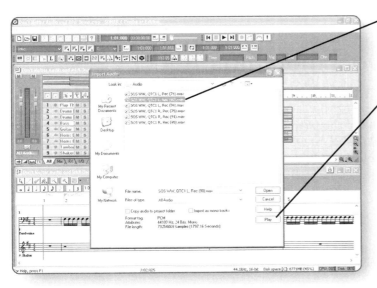

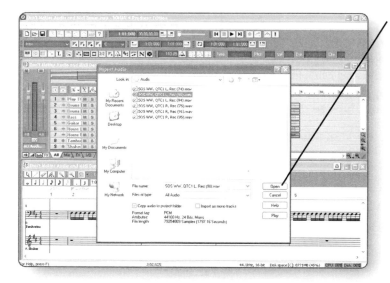

7. **Click** on **Open**. One of two things will occur:

- If no audio track is selected, the audio file will be imported into a new audio track.

- If an audio track is selected, the audio file will be imported into that track.

AUDITIONING AUDIO CLIPS

The Import Audio dialog box will play the selected clip through whatever is designated as your default sound playback device in Windows' Sounds and Audio Devices Control Panel. If you have an audio interface separate from your computer's built-in sound card, you will probably hear the clip through your sound card, not the interface.

Documenting Project Information

One of the powerful things about working in a computer-based DAW such as SONAR 4 is the ability to keep notes about a project within the project itself. SONAR calls this *File Info*. Here's how to view and use it.

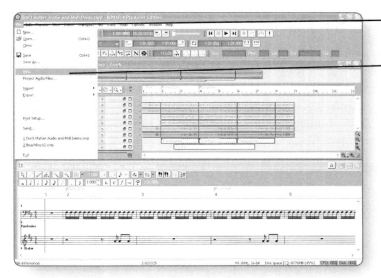

1. Click on **File**. The File menu will appear.

2. Click on **Info**. The File Info dialog box will appear.

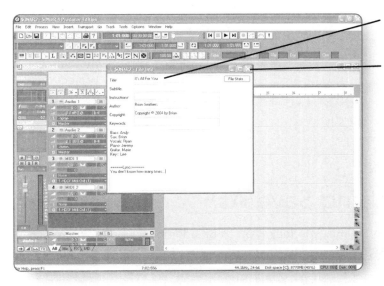

3. Click in any **field** and type to enter text.

4. Click on the **Close button** when you are finished. The dialog box will close, and the information will be remembered.

FILE INFO

The File Info dialog box is a great place to store information such as who wrote the song, who played on it, when it was created, and which version this file represents.

Saving a Project

Of course, there would be no point in slaving over a hot tune just to have it disappear when you turn off the computer, so SONAR 4 makes it easy for you to save your work. Saving your work means preserving all the changes you have made to a project—editing, recording, mixing, and so on—by updating the project file.

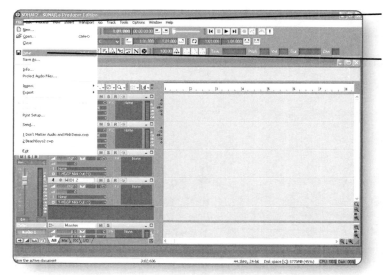

1. Click on **File**. The File menu will appear.

2. Click on **Save**. The current project will be saved with the current filename.

SAVE AND SAVE AS

The first time you save a project, choosing Save may actually open the Save As dialog box, depending on whether you named the project when you created it. The Save As dialog box is explained below.

Using Save As

Sometimes you may want to do additional work on a project without changing the original project file. This is accomplished by using a function called Save As. Save As simply creates a copy of the project file. The copy uses the same audio files as the original, so you don't waste disk space.

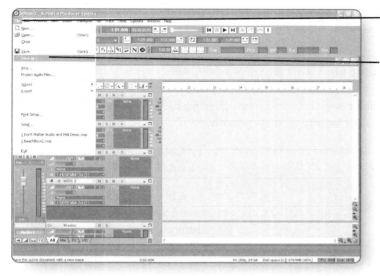

1. Click on **File**. The File menu will open.

2. Click on **Save As**. The Save As dialog box will appear.

3. Navigate to the **folder** where you want to save the project file.

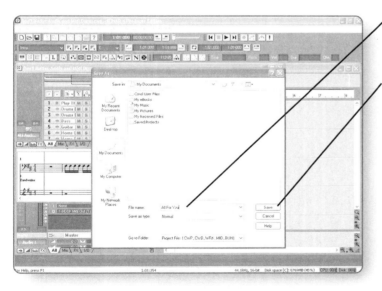

4. Double-click in the **File name** field and **type** a **name** for the new file.

5. Click on **OK**. SONAR closes the dialog box and saves the project, leaving the new version open for further editing.

Closing a Project

You may find yourself wanting to stop work on one project and to start working on another. Although SONAR is capable of having multiple projects open at one time, this can create clutter and potential confusion, so it's usually best to close one project before opening another.

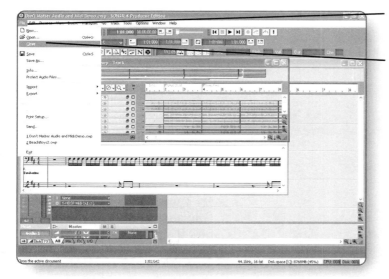

1. Click on **File**. The File menu will open.

2. Click on **Close.** If you have saved the project, it will close immediately. Otherwise, SONAR will prompt you to save the project before closing it.

2

Playing and Listening to SONAR Songs

Before we get too involved in creating new songs, let's explore how SONAR 4 handles playback of a song. After all, what's the point in making a song if you can't listen to it? In this chapter, you will learn to:

- Adjust the volume for playback
- Start and stop playback of a song
- Move forward and backward through a song
- Loop (repeat) a section of a song
- Mute and solo parts of a song

Adjusting Playback Volume

It's extremely important to know how to control how loud your music is going to be. If it's too quiet, you won't be able to make good judgements about how to make it better, especially when we get into mixing in Part V, "Effects and Mixing." If it's too loud, it can damage your ears. Your ears are the whole reason you're making music, so protect them!

ADJUSTING VOLUME

The steps for adjusting volume may vary according to what audio interface or sound card you are using. The following procedure will cover the majority of built-in sound cards, but some may have their own mixers or control panels. Such applets are usually found within the Windows Control Panel, which you can access via the Start menu.

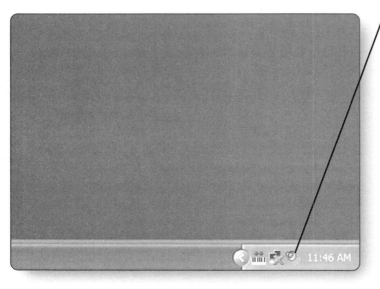

1. **Click** on the **speaker icon** in the **System Tray** section of the **Taskbar**. The volume control slider will appear.

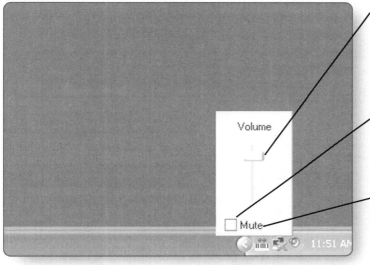

2a. **Drag** the **volume slider** up or down. The volume will increase or decrease, respectively.

OR

2b. **Click** on the **Mute** check box. A ✔ will appear in the box, and all audio playback will be silenced.

2c. **Click** on the **Mute** check box again. The ✔ will disappear, and audio playback will return.

Playing a Song

Now it's time to listen to a song playing back through SONAR. You'll notice that SONAR's basic playback controls resemble those of a tape deck or CD player. Using these familiar controls is one of the things that makes SONAR so user-friendly, but there are also some important differences, as you'll see.

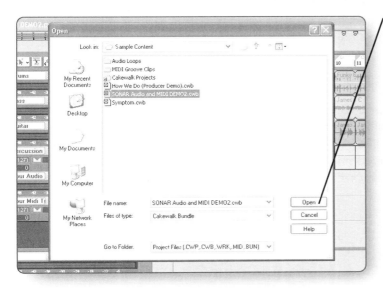

1. **Open** a **SONAR project** following the procedure from Chapter 1, "Working with Projects and Files."

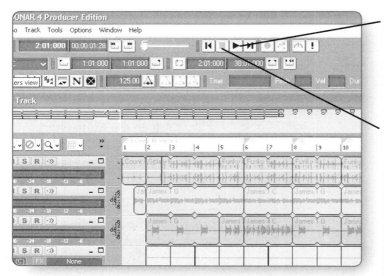

2. Click on the **Play button**. The song will start to play.

3. If necessary, **adjust** the **playback volume** as described in the preceding section.

4. Click on the **Stop button**. The song will stop playing.

PLAY/STOP SHORTCUT

Instead of clicking the Play and Stop buttons, you can simply press the spacebar to start and stop playback.

Moving Forward and Backward

In music creation, there is rarely a time when you'll simply want to listen to a song from start to stop. That's what you want your listeners to do! While you're creating, you need to be able to move from verse to verse to chorus to intro efficiently. Here's how.

Fast Forward and Rewind

Surrounding the Stop and Play buttons on the Transport toolbar are two icons that look very much like the Fast Forward and Rewind buttons on a tape deck or CD player. They are indeed similar, but instead of moving gradually forward and backward they jump directly to the beginning and end of the song.

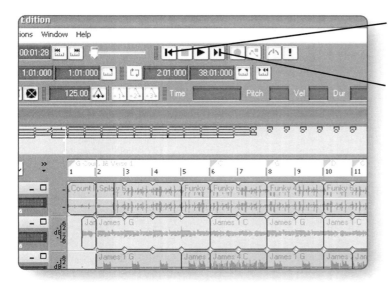

1. **Click** on the **Rewind button**. SONAR will jump to the beginning of the song.

2. **Click** on the **Go to end button**. SONAR will jump to the end of the song.

MORE SHORTCUTS

If you like using the computer keyboard better than the mouse, you can press the W key or Ctrl+Home to rewind, and press Ctrl+End to go to the end of the song.

The Now Time and the Now Slider

SONAR defines the current location within a song by what it calls the Now time. When you start playback, SONAR always starts from Now. The Now time is indicated by a vertical cursor that stretches across the Track pane, and it moves to indicate song position during playback. You can set the Now time directly, either by clicking at the position you want or by moving a slider to the desired point in the song.

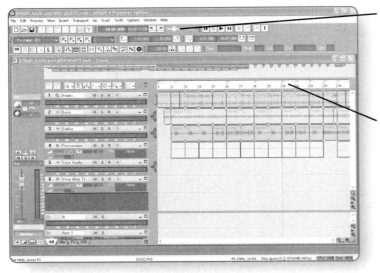

1a. Drag the **Now slider** to the left or right. The Now time will move earlier or later, respectively.

OR

1b. Click in the **Time Ruler**. The Now time will move to wherever you clicked.

STILL MORE SHORTCUTS

You can move the Now time later one bar at a time by pressing Ctrl+PageDown. Pressing Ctrl+PageUp moves the Now time earlier one bar at a time.

Using the Project Navigator

New to SONAR 4 is the Project Navigator, a sort of bird's-eye view of your entire project. A green rectangle indicates what part of the project is currently displayed in the Clips pane, and you can view a different part of the project simply by dragging the rectangle to a new location. You can display the Project Navigator in the Track view above the Track and Clips panes, or you can open it in its own window.

By default, the Project Navigator shows the entire duration of your project (you can customize this if you choose to), but it will not show tracks that are hidden. DXi (virtual instrument) tracks are shown as blank spaces. You can resize the rectangle, effectively zooming the Clips pane in or out, by dragging on its handles. You can even Alt+drag around a segment to make it fill the Clips pane.

Note that repositioning the current Clips pane view does not move the Now time. If you want to start playback from the new position, you will need to click in the Time Ruler or use another of the methods outlined previously to set the Now time.

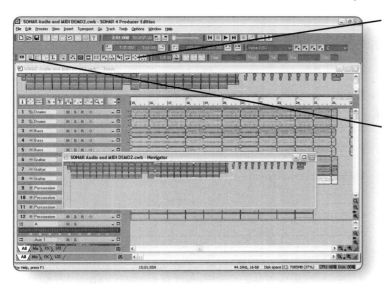

1a. **Click** on the Views toolbar's **Project Navigator button**. The Project Navigator will appear in a separate window.

OR

1b. **Click** on the Track view's **Project Navigator button**. The Project Navigator will appear at the top of the Track view.

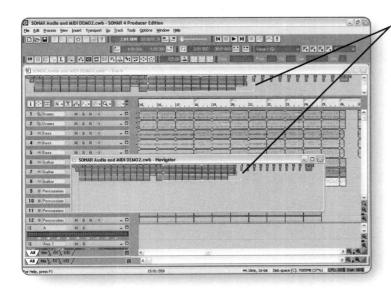

2. **Drag** the **green rectangle** within the Project Navigator. The Clips pane will show whatever is within the rectangle.

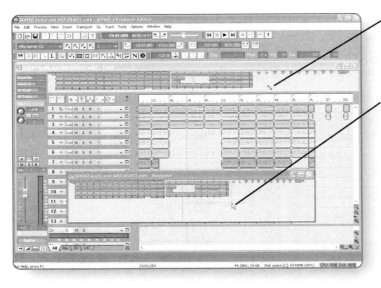

3. Drag one of the **handles** on the green rectangle. The Clips pane will zoom in or out as you resize the rectangle.

4. Alt+drag anywhere within the Project Navigator. When you release the mouse button, the Clips pane will relocate and zoom to show exactly what you selected.

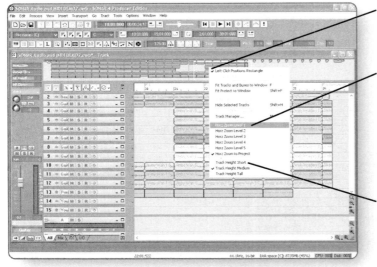

5. Right-click anywhere in the Project Navigator. The context menu will appear.

6. Choose a different **horizontal zoom**. Horz Zoom to Project will show the entire project timeline. The other selections will zoom in, with Level 1 providing the greatest detail.

7. Choose a different **track height**. Track Height Medium is the default.

Looping Playback

As you're working on a song, you may want to have a passage repeat indefinitely so you can practice a part or tweak the mix. Doing this is a simple three-step process: define the beginning and ending points of the loop, engage Loop playback mode, and hit Play. The following steps show you how to do this.

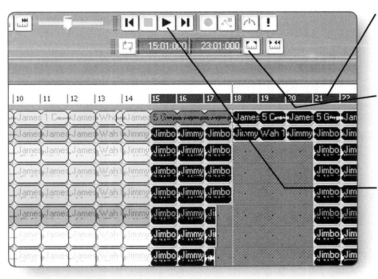

1. Drag in the **Time Ruler** from the **start** of the loop to the **end** of the loop. The selection will be highlighted.

2. Click on the **Set Loop to Selection button**. The selection will be bracketed by yellow loop markers, and the Loop On/Off button will be turned on.

3. Click the **Play button**. The selection will play, looping back to the beginning whenever it reaches the end.

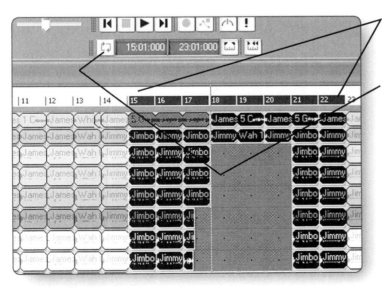

4. Drag a **yellow loop marker**. The Start or End time of the loop will change accordingly.

5. Click the **Loop On/Off button**. SONAR will return to normal playback mode.

Muting and Soloing Parts

There will be times when you want to hear a particular track by itself, and other times when you want to hear the song temporarily without a part. Here's how to mute or solo a part.

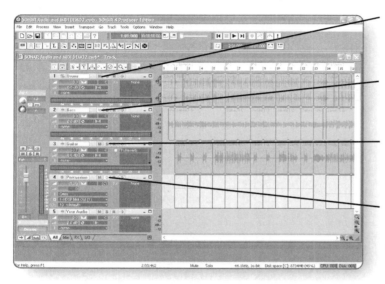

1. **Click** on a track's **Mute button**. That track will not play back with the other tracks.

2. **Click** on the **Mute button** again. The track will now play along with the others.

3. **Click** on a track's **Solo button**. The track will play back all by itself.

4. **Click** on the **Solo button** again. The other tracks will now be heard.

3

Working with Audio and MIDI Clips

The key to mastering a powerful music production program like SONAR 4 is understanding how it organizes musical data. We've already looked at some of the different views SONAR provides of your music, and now we're going to look more closely at a data structure called a *clip*. A clip is a portion of recorded audio or MIDI that can be edited as a single unit. It appears as a rectangle in the right side of the Track view. In this chapter you will learn how to:

- Select clips
- Move and arrange clips
- Copy, paste, and delete clips
- Link clips

Selecting a Clip

You'll find that working with clips is very intuitive and familiar. This is by design—clips are intended to allow you to manage your musical ideas with many of the same functions you use in a word processor. Of course, just as with your word processor, you have to select data before you can do anything with it. The following steps show you how to select one or more clips.

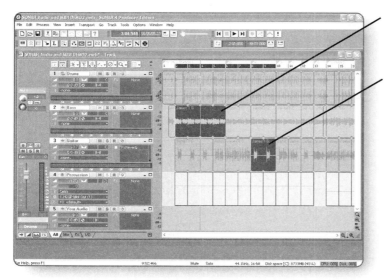

1. Click on the **middle of a clip**. The clip turns a darker color to indicate it is now selected.

2. Ctrl+click on **another clip**. Both clips are selected.

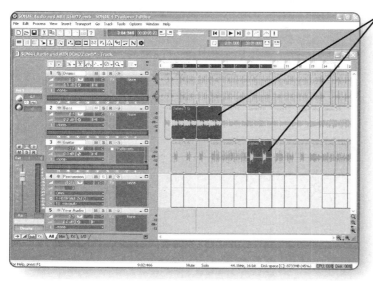

3. Ctrl+click on **either selected clip**. That clip is no longer selected.

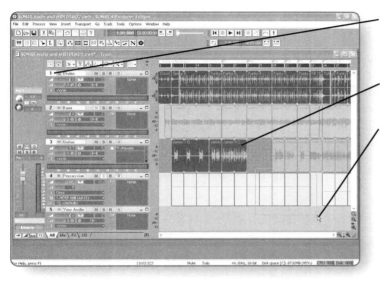

4. Click on a **track number**. All of the clips in that track are selected.

5. Drag around **several clips**. Those clips are selected.

6. Ctrl+drag around **several other clips**. Those clips are added to the previous selection.

Setting Drag and Drop Options

SONAR 4 lets you define exactly what happens when you move and copy clips. Although you can change your mind at any time, the default behavior is defined in the Drag and Drop Options. Here's how to set them the way you want them.

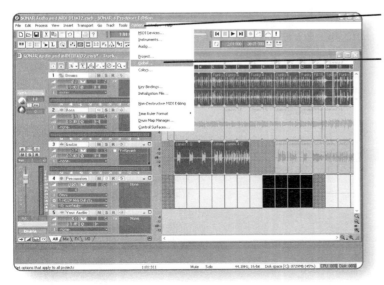

1. Click on **Options**. The Options menu will open.

2. Click on **Global**. The Global Options dialog box will appear.

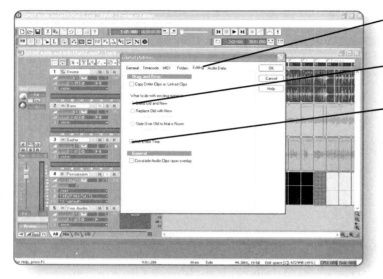

3. Click on the **Editing tab**. The tab will come to the front.

4. Click on an **option button**. The option will be selected.

5. Click a **check box**. A ✔ will appear to indicate the option is active.

6. Click the **check box** again. The ✔ will be cleared, indicating the option is not active. The options work as follows:

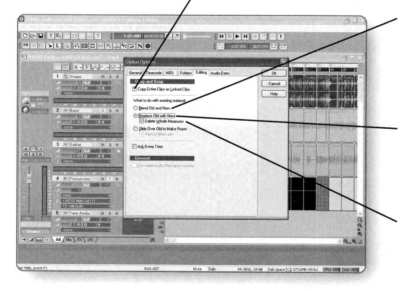

- **Blend Old and New.** This will cause the clip you are moving to merge with any data at the location to which you've moved it, so both will be heard.

- **Replace Old with New.** This will cause any data at the destination to be deleted, leaving only the clip you moved there.

- **Delete Whole Measures.** When you choose to Replace Old with New, this will cause the destination data to be deleted all the way to the next bar line, rather than deleting just enough to fit the moved clip.

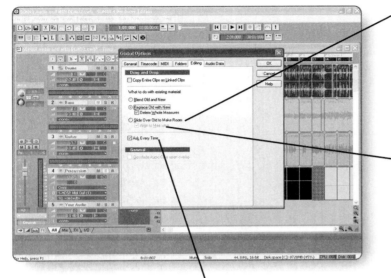

- **Slide Over Old to Make Room.** This will cause all data at the destination *and all data from there to the end of the track* to move to the right (later in time) far enough for the moved clip to fit in.

- **Align to Measures.** When you choose the Slide Over Old to Make Room option, this causes the old data to slide later in whole-measure amounts, rather than just enough to squeeze in the moved clip.

- **Ask This Every Time.** If you ordinarily prefer one of the above options, you can save yourself time by unchecking this box, preventing the Drag and Drop Options dialog box from opening when you move a clip.

Moving a Clip

Once you've selected a clip or clips, you can easily move it to a new location using the same "drag and drop" technique you would use in almost any Windows application. The following steps show you how to do this, along with how to choose the way in which clips will be moved.

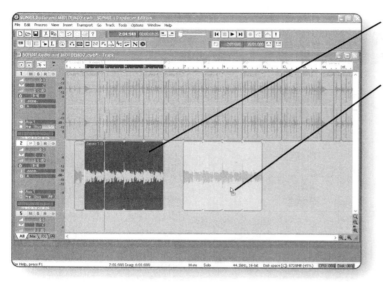

1. Select a **clip or clips** as described earlier. The clips will be highlighted.

2. Drag a **clip** to a point earlier or later in a track or to a different track. The clip will be moved to the new location. Anything at the destination will be moved or replaced according to the Drag and Drop Options you set earlier.

ASK EVERY TIME

If you chose Ask Every Time in the Drag and Drop Options section of the Global Options dialog box (see page 26), you will see the Drag and Drop Options section before the clip is moved. Choose the appropriate options for your current edit and then click OK to complete the move.

Copying and Pasting a Clip

In music as in life, one can never get too much of a good thing. It stands to reason, then, that you will often want to use a musical idea more than once in your song. SONAR 4 lets you copy and paste a clip or a selection of multiple clips, and it even lets you paste a selection repeatedly, saving you time and effort in the production process. Just follow the steps below.

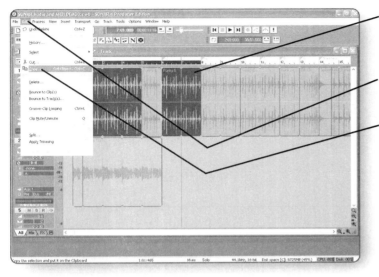

1. **Select** a **clip or clips** as described earlier. The clips will be highlighted.

2. **Click** on **Edit**. The Edit menu will open.

3. **Click** on **Copy**. The Copy dialog box will appear.

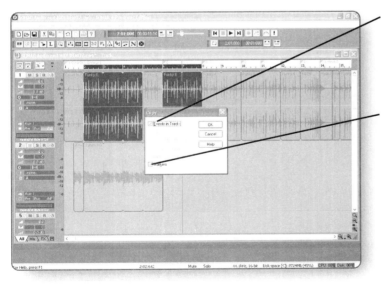

4. If **Events in Tracks** is not already checked, **click** in the **check box**. A ✔ will appear, indicating that events in the track or tracks will be copied.

5. **Click** in other **check boxes** to choose other options as needed. A ✔ will appear for each option you have chosen.

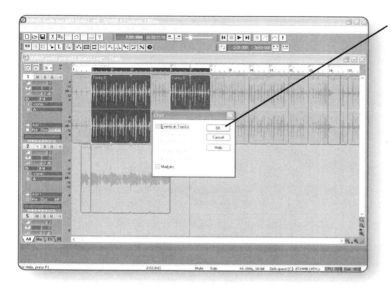

6. **Click** on **OK**. The dialog box will close, and the selected clips will be copied.

WHY DOESN'T ANYTHING HAPPEN?

You won't actually see any result from simply copying a clip. The clip is copied to the Windows *clipboard*, where it remains available to be pasted once or several times. If you want to remove a clip from its current location and load it into the clipboard to be pasted, follow the procedure above using the *Cut* command instead of the Copy command.

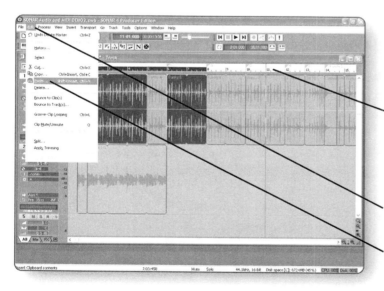

7. **Click** in the **Time Ruler** to place the Now time where you want to paste the selection. The cursor will indicate the Now time's new position.

8. **Click** on **Edit**. The Edit menu will open.

9. **Click** on **Paste**. The Paste dialog box will appear.

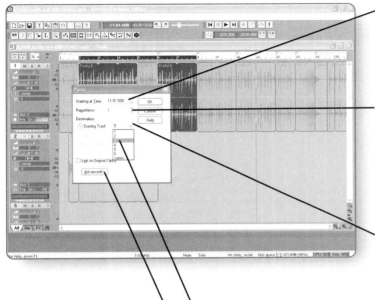

10. If necessary, change where the clips are to be pasted by **clicking** in the **Starting at Time field** and **typing** a **new time**. The time you type will be displayed.

11. Click the **plus (+)** or **minus (−) buttons** next to the **Repetitions field** to set the number of times you want to paste the selection. The Repetitions field will display the number you set.

12. Click on the **down arrow** at the right of the **Starting Track field**. The list of available starting tracks will open.

13. Click on the **number of the track** into which you want to paste the clips. The Starting Track drop-down list box will close and display the track number you chose.

14. Click on **Advanced**. The Paste dialog box will expand to display the advanced options.

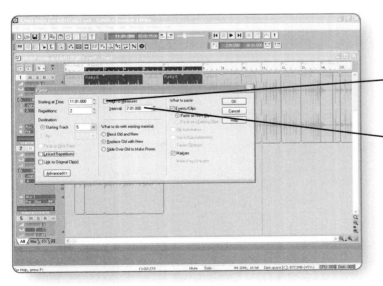

15. Choose the appropriate **advanced options**. These options include

- **Align to Measures.** Each repetition of the pasted clips will start on a bar line.

- **Interval.** Each repetition of the pasted clips will start this far after the previous one started. This value always starts at the length of the selection currently in the clipboard.

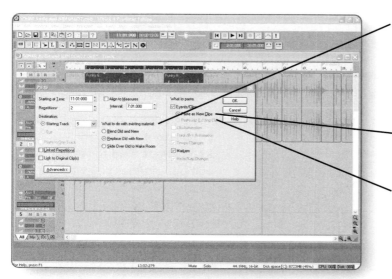

- **What to do with existing material.** These options mean exactly what they did in the Drag and Drop Options section discussed earlier.

- **Paste as New Clips.** The data will be pasted as distinct clips.

- **Paste into Existing Clips.** The pasted data will be incorporated into any clips that exist at the destination.

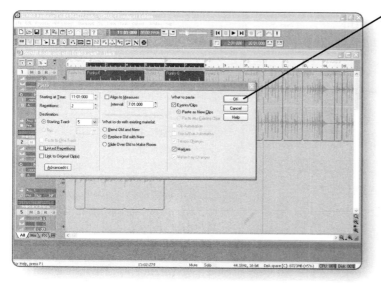

16. **Click** on **OK**. The dialog box will close, and the selection will appear where you pasted it.

DRAG AND DROP

You can also copy a clip once using drag and drop. Just hold down the Ctrl key as you move a clip, and SONAR will make a copy of the clip and leave the original in place.

Deleting a Clip

Even Beethoven needed an eraser; fortunately, SONAR 4 allows you to delete clips easily. Of course, you'll want to be sure you're deleting exactly what you want—nothing more and nothing less—so follow the steps below.

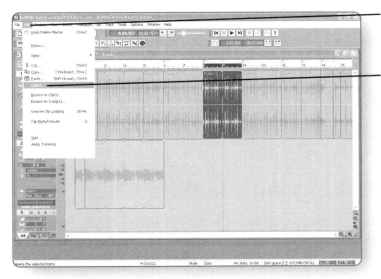

1. Select any **clip or clips** you want to delete and click on Edit. The Edit menu will open.

2. Click on **Delete**. The Delete dialog box will appear.

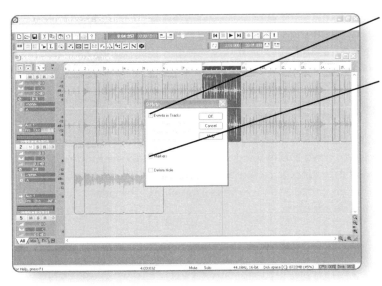

3. If necessary, **click** on the **Events in Tracks check box**. A ✔ will appear.

4. Click to choose **additional options** as appropriate. A ✔ will appear for each chosen option.

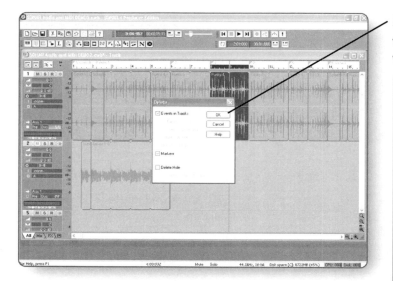

5. Click on **OK**. The dialog box will close, and the selected clips will be removed from the tracks.

DELETE HOLE

Choose Delete Hole to make everything that follows the deleted data move to the left (earlier) to fill in the gap. Specify Shift by Whole Measures to fill in the gap while maintaining the same bar and beat relationships within the moved data.

Working with Linked Clips

Wouldn't it be terrible to copy and paste a cool bass clip about a million times and later decide you wanted to change one note of the clip... and have to re-paste it a million times? SONAR 4 can save you from this kind of heartache! All you need to do is create *linked clips*. Linked clips are automatically updated with any changes you make to any one of them. Had you done that with your bass clip, you could change that one note in any of the linked copies, and the note would be changed throughout the entire song. If this sounds cool and powerful, read on and see how to make it happen.

Pasting Clips as Linked Clips

You create linked clips during the pasting process. You can choose to have the new copies linked only to each other without effecting or being affected by changes to the original, or you can choose to have the original and the new copies all be interdependent.

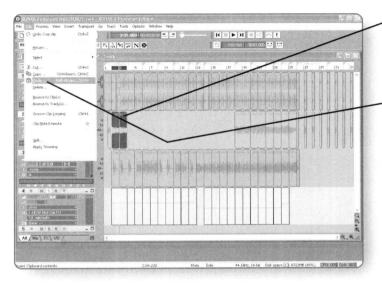

1. **Copy** one or more **clips** as described previously. The clips will be held in the clipboard, ready to be pasted.

2. **Click** on **Paste** in the **Edit menu**, as described previously. The Paste dialog box will appear.

3. **Click** on **Advanced**. The Paste dialog box will expand to show the Advanced options:

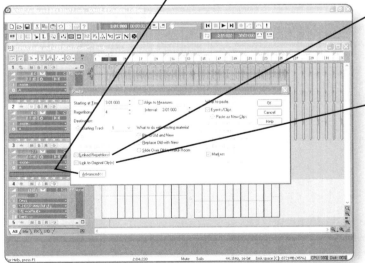

- **Linked Repetitions.** Check this option to make the copied clips interdependent without affecting the original.

- **Link to Original Clip(s).** Check this option *in addition to* Linked Repetitions to make all of the copied clips and the original interdependent.

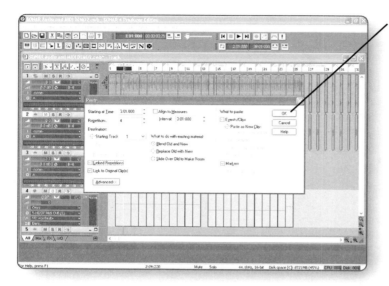

4. Click on **OK**. The dialog box will close, and the linked clips will be pasted.

DRAGGING, DROPPING, LINKING

You can link clips using drag-and-drop copying by checking the Copy Entire Clips as Linked Clips option in the Drag and Drop Options section.

Selecting Linked Clips

It's easy and convenient to select a group of linked clips so they can be copied, moved, or deleted as a unit. Here's how.

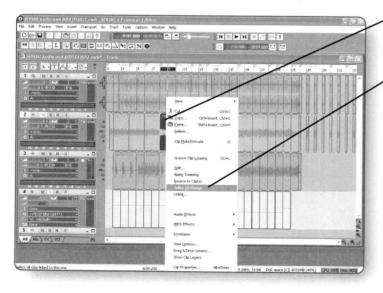

1. Right-click on any one of a group of **linked clips**. The context menu will appear.

2. Click on **Select All Siblings**. All of the linked clips will be selected and ready to be copied, moved, or deleted.

Unlinking Linked Clips

SONAR 4 knows that we all change our minds sometimes, so linking clips is not necessarily a permanent arrangement. Follow these steps to break the link between clips.

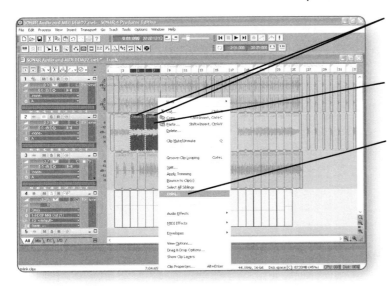

1. Select one or more of a group of **linked clips**. The clips will be highlighted.

2. Right-click on any one of the **selected clips**. The context menu will appear.

3. Click on **Unlink**. The Unlink Clips dialog box will appear.

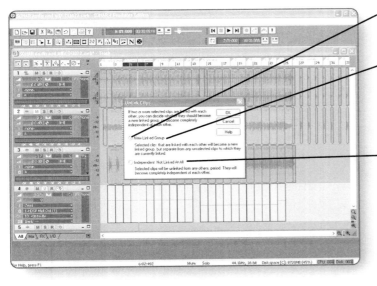

4. Click on the desired **option**. The option will be selected.

- **New Linked Group.** The selected clips will no longer be linked to the original group, but they will be linked to each other.

- **Independent, Not Linked At All.** The selected clips will not be linked to each other or to the original group.

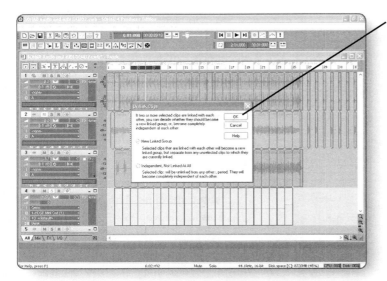

5. Click on **OK**. The dialog box will close and the clips will be unlinked.

4

Customizing SONAR's Look and Feel

Call it computer *feng shui*, call it cute, or call it crazy. Whatever you call it, the fact is that you're going to spend a lot of time looking at your computer screen when you're making music in SONAR 4, and you'd better like what you see. Cakewalk has thoughtfully provided ways for you to customize SONAR's work environment so it looks and acts the way that is most comfortable and productive for you. In this chapter you will learn how to:

- Show and hide various toolbars
- Customize the appearance of the Track view
- Create, resize, rename, and sort tracks
- Zoom in and out
- Arrange views and save view layouts
- Change SONAR's colors

Showing and Hiding Toolbars

SONAR 4 features a variety of toolbars, each one providing important one-click functions for specific situations. You've already worked with the Transport toolbar in Chapter 2, "Playing and Listening to SONAR Songs." If you display all of the toolbars all of the time, your screen will be quite cluttered, so here's how to pick and choose just the ones you need.

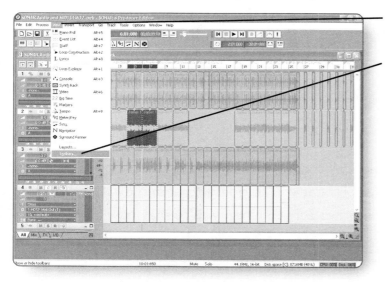

1. Click on **View**. The View menu will open.

2. Click on **Toolbars**. The Toolbars dialog box will appear.

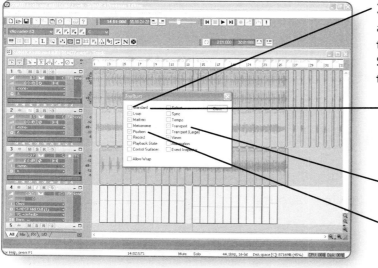

3. Click a **check box** to choose a toolbar. A ✔ will appear, and the toolbar will be displayed. Some of the most common toolbars are

- **Standard.** Includes basic Windows functions such as Open, Save, Cut, Copy, and so on.

- **Transport.** Start, Stop, Rewind, Record, and so on.

- **Position.** Displays the Now time and Now time slider.

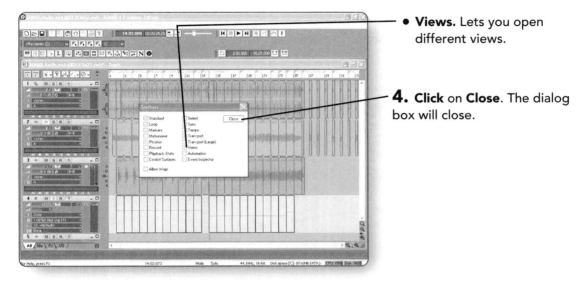

- **Views.** Lets you open different views.

4. Click on **Close**. The dialog box will close.

Customizing the Track View

SONAR 4's Track view is the default view of your music and is your primary workspace. It is the one view that cannot be closed without closing the current project, although it can be modified in numerous ways or minimized. You'll notice that the Track view is divided into two spaces: the Track pane on the left and the Clips pane on the right. Next we'll explore ways to make the Track view display exactly what you need to see as you work—no more and no less.

Creating and Naming Tracks

As is typical of recording/sequencing programs, SONAR 4 organizes your musical ideas into *tracks*. As you saw while playing songs in Chapter 1, "Working with Projects and Files," tracks represent a sequence of audio or MIDI information arranged along a timeline. Events that are seen in parallel in tracks take place simultaneously at playback. SONAR lets you create as many tracks as you need to hold and coordinate your musical ideas. When you need another track, here's how to make one.

1. **Right-click** in any **open space** in the **Track pane**. The context menu will appear.

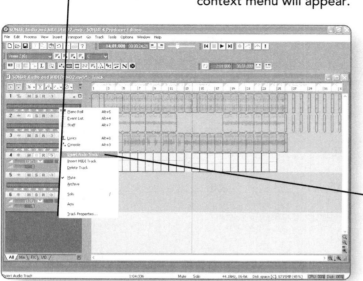

NO OPEN SPACE

If there is no open space in the Track pane, you can click on any track number or any blank space on a track's title bar.

2. **Click** on **Insert Audio Track**. An audio track will be created and displayed below any existing tracks.

3. **Right-click** in any **open space** in the **Track pane**. The context menu will appear.

4. **Click** on **Insert MIDI Track**. A MIDI track will be created and displayed below any existing tracks.

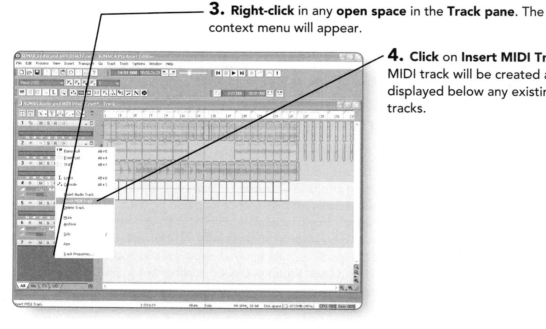

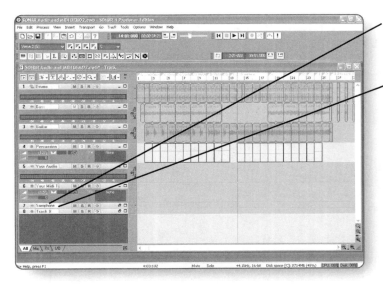

5. Double-click on any **track name**. The existing name will be highlighted.

6. Type a **new name** for the track. The new name will be displayed in the track name field.

7. Press Enter. The new name will be applied to the track.

Deleting Tracks

In your efforts to keep your Track view neat and tidy, you'll want to get rid of any unused tracks. Here's how to delete them.

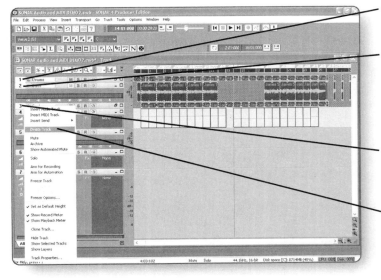

1. Click on a **track number**. The track is selected.

2. Optionally, **Ctrl+click** on the **track number** of any **additional tracks** you want to delete. Those tracks will be added to the selection.

3. Right-click on the **track number** of any **selected track**. The context menu will appear.

4. Click on **Delete Track**. The selected tracks will be deleted.

Changing the Order of Tracks

Once you've got a complex arrangement going, you're going to want to bring some order to the chaos. Fortunately, SONAR 4 lets you reorganize your tracks whenever the whim strikes you. For example, you might want your keyboard parts all to be next to each other for ease of editing. Here's how to rearrange the Track view.

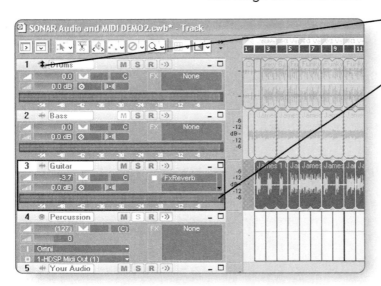

1. Click on a track's **track type icon**. The cursor will appear as a two-headed vertical arrow.

2. Drag the **track** up or down. A black outline will show the track's new position.

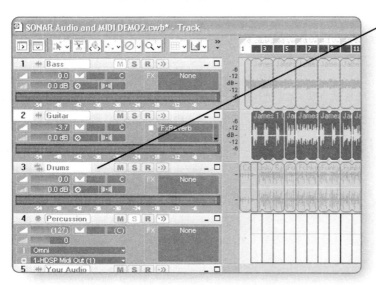

3. Drop the **track** at its new position. The track will appear at that position, and all tracks will be renumbered accordingly.

TRACK NUMBERS

Notice that the track numbers always start at 1 and run in sequence down the Track pane. The numbers are for reference only, and do not travel with individual tracks.

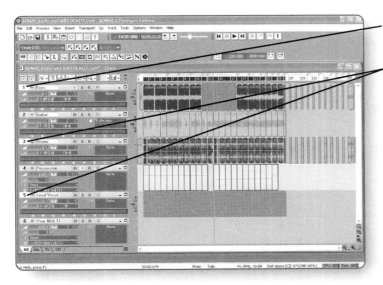

4. Click on a **track number**. The track is selected.

5. Ctrl+click on the **track numbers** of additional **non-adjacent tracks**. The tracks are added to the selection.

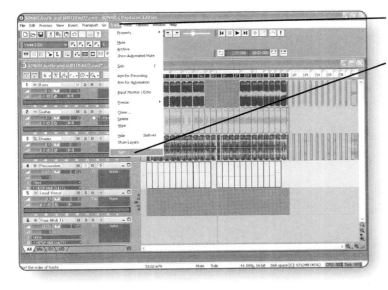

6. Click on **Track**. The Track menu will open.

7. Click on **Sort**. The Sort Tracks dialog box will open.

8. Click on the **Selected option button**. The option is highlighted.

9. Click on the **Descending option button**. The option is highlighted.

10. Click on OK. The dialog box will close, and the selected tracks will be moved to the top of the Track pane.

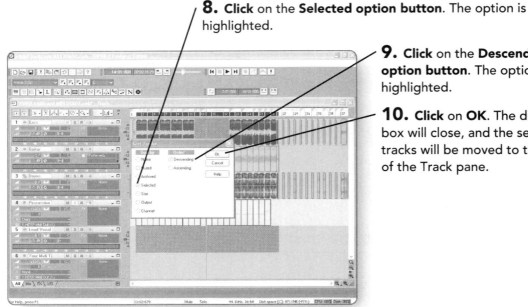

Fitting Tracks to the Window

SONAR 4 has a couple of really cool display functions that give you a clear overview of your song quickly. The following steps show you how to get all of your tracks to fit neatly into the available vertical window space and how to get your whole song, from beginning to end, to fit neatly into the available horizontal window space.

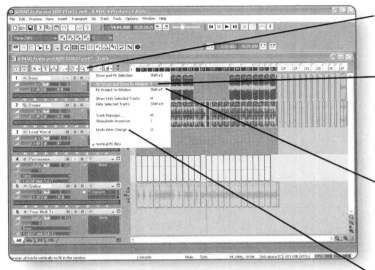

1. Click on the **down arrow** at the right of the **Zoom tool**. The View Options menu will open.

2a. Click on **Fit Tracks and Buses to Window**. All tracks will be resized vertically so they fit in the window.

OR

2b. Click on **Fit Project to Window**. All tracks will be resized vertically and horizontally so the entire project fits in the window.

3. Click on **Undo View Change**. Tracks will return to their previous sizes.

MAXIMUM ZOOM

Sometimes a project will have enough tracks or be long enough that SONAR can't fit it all into the window. In this case, all tracks will be minimized and zoomed out as far as possible.

Setting Track View Options

The Clips pane has a number of visual cues to help you sort through the information presented there efficiently and accurately. By following these steps you can choose which options you need and want.

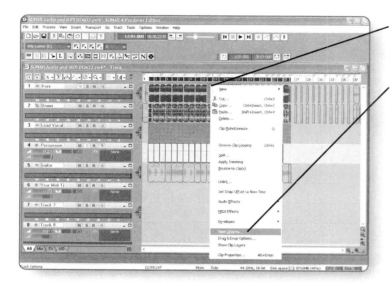

1. Right-click on any **open space** in the **Clips pane**. The context menu will open.

2. Click on **View Options**. The Track View Options dialog box will appear.

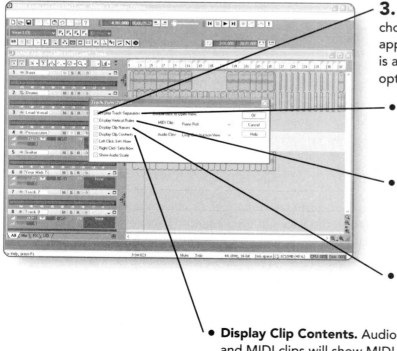

3. Click on a **check box** to choose an option. A ✔ will appear to show that the option is active. The most important options include the following:

- **Display Track Separators.** These horizontal lines help you see which track you're working in.

- **Display Vertical Rules.** These vertical lines show the beginnings of measures so you can place clips accurately in time.

- **Display Clip Names.** If a clip has a name, it will be visible within the clip.

- **Display Clip Contents.** Audio clips will show waveforms, and MIDI clips will show MIDI notes.

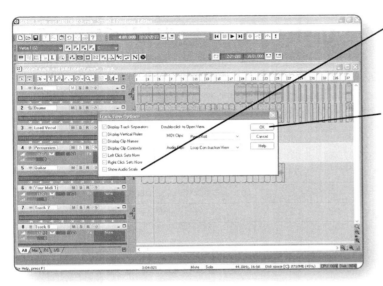

- **Show Audio Scale.** The divider between the Tracks pane and the Clips pane will show the level of audio waveforms in decibels.

4. **Click** on **OK**. The dialog box will close, and the chosen options will be applied.

Resizing the Track and Clip Panes

Sometimes you just need to see more of your clips, and other times you need to have a clear view of every track parameter. Luckily, SONAR 4 lets you decide how the Track and Clips panes share the available screen space.

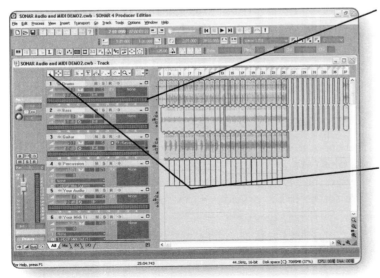

1. **Click** and **hold** anywhere along the **left** or **right edge** of the **pane divider**. The cursor will appear as a two-headed arrow.

2. **Drag** the **divider** to the left or to the right. The Track and Clips panes will resize accordingly.

3. **Click** on the **Show/Hide Inspector button**. The Inspector pane will close, leaving more horizontal space for the Clips pane.

Using the Zoom Controls

One of the most common functions you'll use while working in SONAR is zooming in and out between a close-up view and a bird's-eye view of your song. In the lower-right corner of the Track view are the vertical and horizontal zoom controls. Get to know them well!

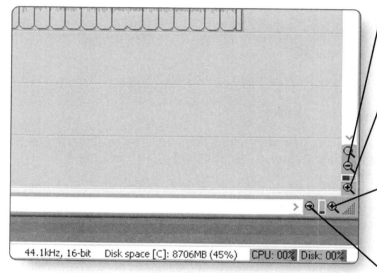

44.1kHz, 16-bit   Disk space [C]: 8706MB (45%)   CPU: 00%   Disk: 00%

1. **Click** on the **minus (−) button** on the **vertical zoom control**. The Track view will zoom out to show less vertical detail.

2. **Click** on the **plus (+) button** on the **vertical zoom control**. The Track view will zoom in to show more vertical detail.

3. **Click** on the **plus (+) button** on the **horizontal zoom control**. The Track view will zoom in to show more horizontal detail.

4. **Click** on the **minus (−) button** on the **horizontal zoom control**. The Track view will zoom out to show less horizontal detail.

DRAGGING AND ZOOMING

You can also zoom by clicking on the small bar between the plus (+) and minus (−) buttons and dragging. Drag toward the plus (+) button to zoom in. Press the letter U to return to the previous zoom level.

Using Layouts

SONAR allows you to save different sets and arrangements of edit views, so you can recall a particular working arrangement quickly and efficiently. These arrangements are called *layouts,* and each project's layout is saved with the project and recalled when the project is opened. You can also save as many layouts as you want in the global layouts list and apply them to any open project. Once you've got your views arranged the way you want them, follow these steps to save the arrangement as a layout.

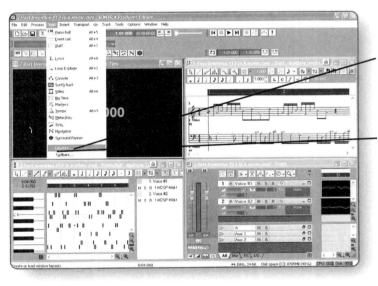

1. Click on **View**. The View menu will open.

2. Click on **Layouts**. The Window Layouts dialog box will appear.

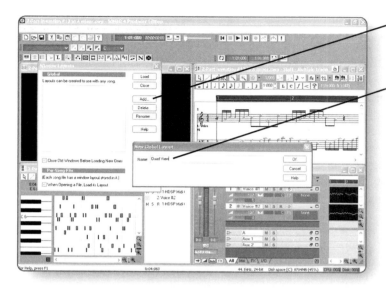

3. **Click** on **Add**. The New Global Layout dialog box will appear.

4. **Type** a descriptive **name** for the **new layout**, and then **click** on **OK**. The dialog box will close, and the new layout will appear in the global layouts list.

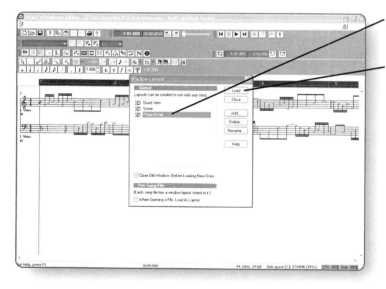

5. **Click** on a **layout name**. The layout will be selected.

6. **Click** on **Load**. The layout will be applied to the current project.

Changing SONAR's Appearance

Although at first glance the appearance of a musical tool might not seem terribly important, the fact is that when you're working in a graphical editing environment, looks *do* matter! If you work in a particularly bright or dark space, work a lot on a notebook computer, or have any visual impairment or colorblindness, you'll especially appreciate the ability to tailor SONAR's colors to suit your eyes.

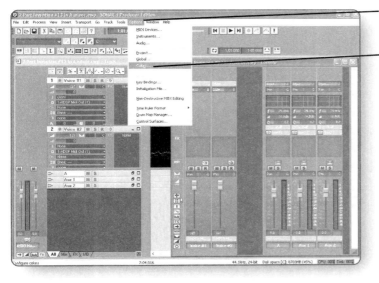

1. **Click** on **Options**. The Options menu will open.

2. **Click** on **Colors**. The Configure Colors dialog box will appear.

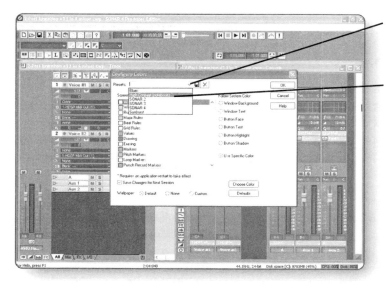

3. **Click** on the **down arrow** at the right of the **Presets field**. The Presets list will open.

4. **Click** on the **name** of a **colors preset**. The Presets list will close, and the preset will be applied to the current project.

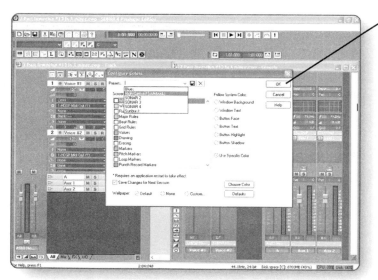

5. **Click** on **OK**. The dialog box will close.

PART II

Using Audio Loops

5

Importing and Using Audio Loops

A lot of modern music production involves the use of musical elements that repeat anywhere from a few times in a row to throughout the duration of a song. A classical musician might call such a repetitive figure an *ostinato*, but in the contemporary vernacular it's called a *loop*. There are even whole libraries of loops that you can purchase for use in your own projects. SONAR 4 Producer and Studio Editions give you the tools necessary to work with loops efficiently and creatively. In this chapter you will learn how to:

- Use the Loop Explorer view
- Find and audition loops
- Bring loops into your project
- Repeat loops
- Turn clips into loops

Using the Loop Explorer View

A *loop* is simply a clip that is designed to be repeated over and over. The Loop Explorer view is your window into your collection of loops and the tool for finding the ones you want and importing them into your project.

Opening the Loop Explorer View

If the Loop Explorer view looks suspiciously like Windows Explorer, that's no coincidence. The window is designed to take advantage of what you already know about navigating through your files and folders.

1a. **Click** on **View**. The View menu will open.

2a. **Click** on **Loop Explorer**. The Loop Explorer view will appear.

OR

1b. **Click** on the **Loop Explorer icon** on the **Views toolbar**. The Loop Explorer view will open.

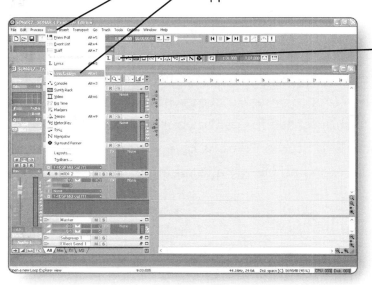

Customizing the Loop Explorer View

The default view of the Loop Explorer may not include all the information you need to pick out the loops you want, so here's how to tweak it to your way of thinking.

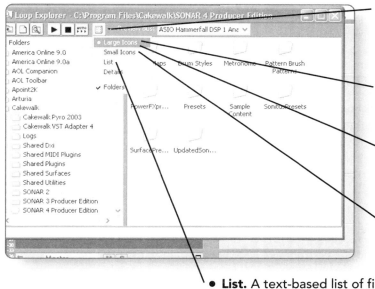

1. Click on the **down arrow** at the right of the **Views button**. The Views drop-down list box will open.

2. Click on a **view option**. The window will show that view. The available views include

- **Large icons.** Files will be displayed as large icons, similar to the default My Computer view.

- **Small icons.** Similar to the Large icons setting, but more icons fit within the window.

- **List.** A text-based list of files sorted by name.

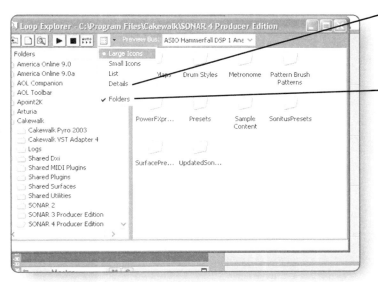

- **Details.** Similar to the List option, but with additional information, such as file date, file size, and file type.

- **Folders.** This option causes the left-hand pane (Tree view) to be hidden or displayed.

DETAILS, DETAILS

You can sort the Details view by any displayed attribute, making it easy to find a loop you created last month, the most recent version of a loop, or a particularly large loop. Simply click at the top of a column to sort by that attribute. Click again to reverse the order of the list.

Locating and Auditioning a Loop

Although the Loop Explorer may look like Windows Explorer, it's got a couple of tricks up its sleeve for picking out your loops. It lets you navigate files and folders using standard techniques like those we discussed in Chapter 1, "Working with Projects and Files," and then it lets you listen to a loop to be sure it's the one you want. The following steps show you how to take advantage of this.

1a. Click on a **folder** in the **Tree view (left) pane**. The folder's contents will be displayed in the Contents view (right) pane.

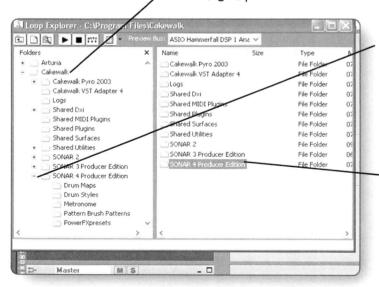

OR

1b. Click on the **plus (+)** or **minus (−)** to the left of a **folder** in the **Tree view pane**. The Tree view will expand to show the folder's subfolders.

OR

1c. **Double-click** on a **folder** in the **Contents view pane**. The folder's contents will be displayed in the Contents view pane.

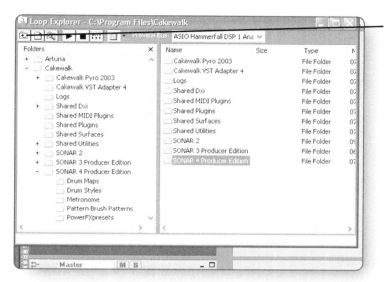

2. Optionally, **click** on the **Move up icon**. The Contents view pane will display the contents of the folder that contains the current folder.

3. Click on the **down arrow** at the right of the **Preview Bus drop-down list**. The Preview Bus drop-down list will open.

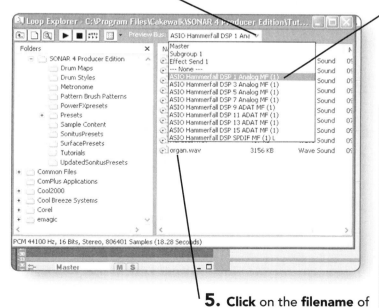

4. Click on the **output** through which you want to audition loops. The output will be chosen, and you will hear loops auditioned through this output.

PREVIEW OUTPUT

You will ordinarily want to choose your sound card's main stereo output, the one through which you listen to SONAR songs. This is usually the default selection in the Preview Bus drop-down list, so you may not need to change this setting.

5. Click on the **filename** of the **loop** you want to audition. The loop will be selected.

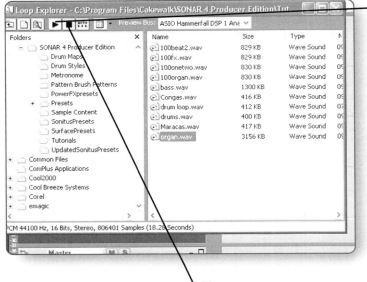

6. Click on the **Play button**. The loop will play through the selected output.

7. Click on the **Stop button**. The loop will stop playing.

HOW LONG IS MY LOOP?

Since you are, after all, in the Loop Explorer view, any file you audition will loop indefinitely as it plays back, allowing you to hear what it sounds like when it repeats. Sometimes this can make it difficult to tell how long the loop actually is, but at the bottom of the Loop Explorer view the Status Bar shows you the length of the selected loop in seconds.

WHEN IS A LOOP NOT A LOOP?

Unfortunately, there's no way to tell in the Loop Explorer view whether a particular audio file is a loop or a plain old clip. Don't worry—in a few pages you'll learn how to make *any* clip into a loop.

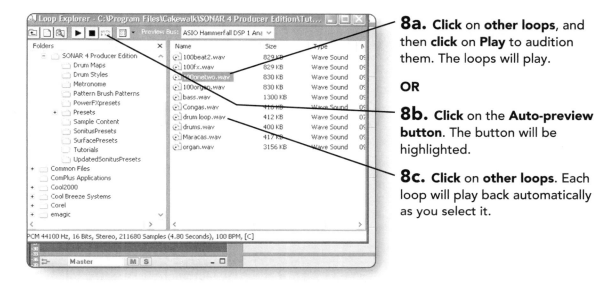

8a. **Click** on **other loops**, and then **click** on **Play** to audition them. The loops will play.

OR

8b. **Click** on the **Auto-preview button**. The button will be highlighted.

8c. **Click** on **other loops**. Each loop will play back automatically as you select it.

Bringing a Loop into a Project

Okay, so you've found one or more loops you want to use in your song. Now you need to get them into your project. SONAR uses a simple drag-and-drop procedure for importing loops, as outlined in the following steps.

SAMPLE FILES

The rest of this chapter uses a set of loops that are included with SONAR 4 as examples. Although the steps will work with any loops you may want to use, you will probably want to follow along with the sample files the first time through, and then apply what you learn to other materials. The sample loops are installed within your SONAR 4 Producer Edition's Tutorials folder, which is ordinarily found at C:\Program Files\Cakewalk\ SONAR 4 Producer Edition\Tutorials.

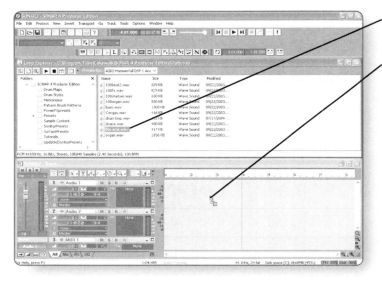

1. **Click** on the **filename** of a **loop**. The loop is selected.

2. **Drag** the **loop** into the **Clips pane** and **drop** it in an **audio track**. The loop will be imported into the project and placed where you dropped it.

SAVING A STEP

If you drop a loop into any part of the Clips pane other than an audio track, an audio track will be automatically created to hold the loop. Knowing this can save you from having to create audio tracks manually!

3. **Click** on the **filename** of a **loop**. The loop is selected.

4. **Ctrl+click** on the **filenames** of one or more **additional loops**. The loops are added to the selection

5. **Drag** the **loops** into the **Clips pane** and **drop** them. The loops will be placed in existing or newly created audio tracks at the time position where you dropped them.

ORDER, ORDER!

The loops will always be placed into tracks in the order in which they were listed in the Loop Explorer, whether you have sorted them by name, date, type, or size. Of course, once you've imported them, you can always rearrange them using the techniques discussed in Chapter 3, "Working with Audio and MIDI Clips."

Working with Loops

Because a loop is a special kind of clip, everything you learned in Chapter 3 about working with clips applies to loops as well, with the exception of linking. Additionally, loops make it ultra-simple to repeat musical ideas through a process that's almost like painting loops!

1. **Drag** the loop **maracas.wav** from the Loop Explorer into an **audio track**. The loop will be added to the project and will appear wherever you dropped it in the track.

2. **Drag** the **loop** to the very **beginning** of a **different audio track**. The loop will be moved to measure one of the second track.

3. **Ctrl+drag** the **loop** to **measure five**. The loop will be copied.

4. **Copy** the **loop** to **measure nine**. You will now have three copies of the loop, at measures one, five, and nine.

5. **Select** and **delete** the **loop** in **measure five**. You will now have only two copies of the loop.

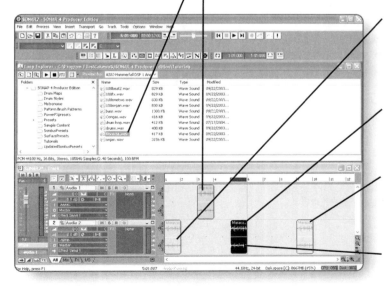

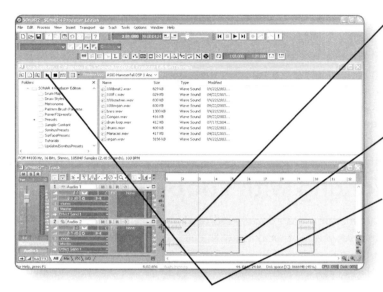

6. **Point** to the **right edge** of the **loop**. The cursor will turn into a little rectangle with a double-headed arrow, indicating that it is ready to adjust the right edge of the loop.

7. **Drag** the **right edge** of the **loop** to the right. The loop will "roll out" as far as you drag it.

8. **Play** the **song** from the beginning. You will hear the maracas loop repeat several times in perfect time.

Making a Clip into a Loop

So by now you're asking yourself, "If a loop is a special type of clip, can I turn any clip into a loop?" The answer is yes! Any clip can be made into a loop by following the steps outlined here.

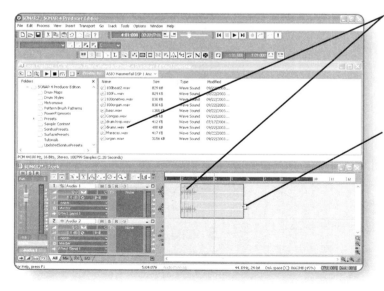

1. **Drag** the clip **drums.wav** from the Explorer view into any **audio track**. The clip will be added to the project, and it will appear wherever you dropped it in the track.

2. **Grab** the **right edge** of the **clip** and **drag** it to the right. The clip will be extended.

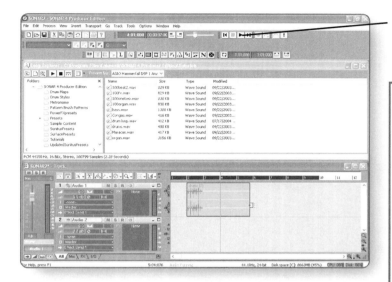

3. Play the **song**. The clip will not repeat during playback because it is not yet a loop.

A CLIP, NOT A LOOP

Unlike maracas.wav, drums.wav is a plain, ordinary clip and not yet a loop. Two visual clues give this away. First, notice that the corners of the maracas clip are angled to indicate that it is a loop. Second, when you roll out a clip that isn't a loop, the waveform pattern doesn't repeat itself—in most cases, you will only see straight lines extending to the right.

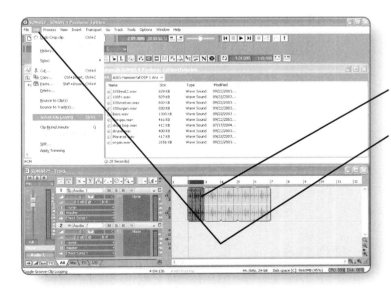

4. Press Ctrl+Z. The last edit (rolling out the drums clip) will be undone.

5. Click on the **drums clip**. The clip will be selected.

6. Click on **Edit**. The Edit menu will open.

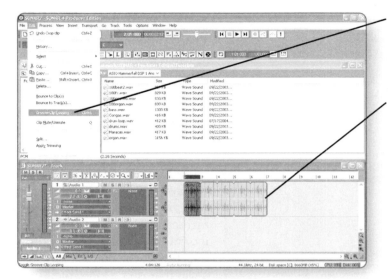

7. **Click** on **Groove-Clip Looping**. The clip's corners will be angled, indicating that it is now enabled for looping.

8. **Roll out** the **drums loop**. This time it will repeat itself for as long as you rolled it.

LOOP SHORTCUT

You can also enable looping by using the context menu. Right-click on a clip and choose Groove-Clip Looping from the context menu. Even faster is to select a clip and press Ctrl+L. What's "groove-clip looping?" That's what the next chapter is all about!

6

Using Groove Clips

As if loops weren't already cool enough, SONAR 4 also supports *groove clips*, a type of clip that takes looping even further. A groove clip knows its own tempo and pitch, enabling it to adapt to the tempo and pitch of your songs. This allows you to manipulate audio clips in ways that were unheard of even in mega-bucks studios just a couple of years ago. In this chapter you will learn how to:

- Work with groove clips
- Set and change tempos
- Set and change project pitch

Working with Groove Clips

SONAR 4 includes a variety of different groove clips for you to use in your songs. Additionally, SONAR allows you to import Sonic Foundry ACID™–style loops, opening up dozens of commercial loop libraries for your use. Here's how to get them into your project.

You can import groove clips like regular audio clips as you did in Chapter 1, "Working with Projects and Files," or you can drag groove clips into the Clips pane directly from the Loop Explorer view as you did with loops in Chapter 5, "Importing and Using Audio Loops." The advantage of dragging them in is that you can drag them directly to whatever track and time you wish without having to designate the location ahead of time.

Because groove clips are special loops and loops are special clips, it stands to reason that everything you know about arranging clips and loops applies to groove clips, doesn't it? Of course, groove clips give you a bit more than simple clips or loops, and we'll get to that soon. Before we get too fancy, though, let's get some groove clips arranged in the Clips pane.

SAMPLE GROOVE CLIPS

The following steps use several groove clips from the SONAR 4 Producer Edition\Tutorials folder as examples. The steps apply equally to any groove clips, but you may wish to follow along with these same clips the first time through.

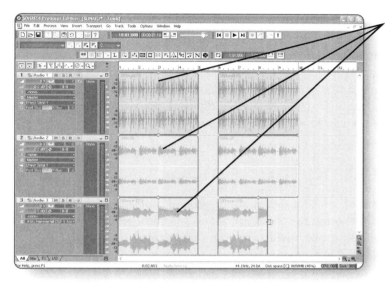

1. Import one or more **groove clips** as described previously. The clips will appear in the Clips pane. In this example, I have imported the clips 100beat2.wav, 100fx.wav, and 100organ.wav to measure one.

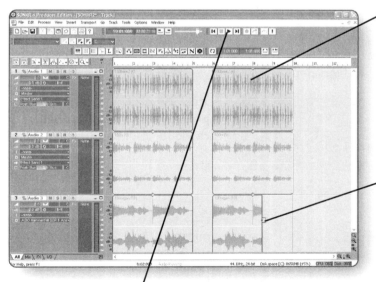

2. Copy the **clips** using either the Copy/Paste or drag-and-drop techniques discussed in Chapter 3, "Working with Audio and MIDI Clips." The clips will be copied to wherever you place them. In this example, I have copied the three clips to measure six.

3. Roll out one or more **groove clips** as discussed in Chapter 5. The clips will repeat when you play the song. In this example, I have rolled both copies of all three clips by two bars.

4. Click on **Play**. The groove clips will play back, looping where you rolled them and matching each other perfectly in time. If you have followed the example, you will hear four bars of the three loops playing together followed by one bar of silence and four more bars of all three loops.

> ## BAD TIMING?
>
> If you chose your own clips and any one of them doesn't match the timing of the others, it is probably not a real groove clip. We'll learn how to fix this in Chapter 7, "Creating and Editing Groove Clips," but for now you should simply replace it with a different clip.

Setting the Tempo

If one of the cool things about groove clips is that they are smart enough to follow your song's tempo, you should probably know how to set your song's tempo, right? In fact, SONAR 4 allows you to change tempo as often as you want, and no matter how crazy you get your groove clips will follow along. Here's how to map out your tempos.

1. If necessary, display the Tempo toolbar by **right-clicking** on any **empty space** in the toolbars area and **checking Tempo**. The Tempo toolbar will be displayed.

2a. **Click** on the **Tempo** number box. The current tempo field will be highlighted.

2b. **Type** a **new tempo** and **press Enter**. The tempo will be changed.

OR

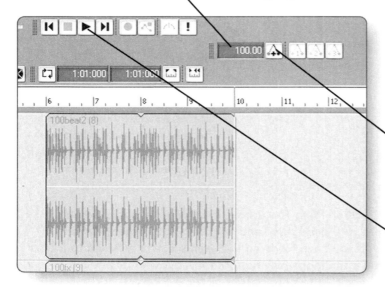

2c. **Click** on the **plus (+)** or **minus (−)** buttons at the right of the **Tempo number box**. The tempo will increase or decrease in whole-number increments.

3. **Click** on **Play**. The song will play at the new tempo.

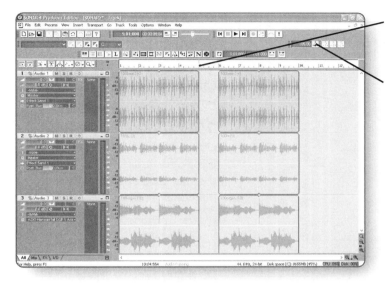

4. **Click** in the **Time Ruler** at **measure five**. The Now time will move to measure five.

5. **Click** on the **Insert Tempo button**. The Tempo dialog box will appear.

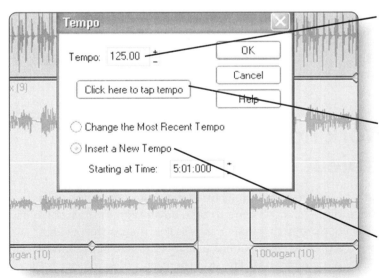

6a. **Type** a **new tempo** in the dialog box's **Tempo number box**. The new tempo will be displayed.

OR

6b. **Click** on the **Click here to tap tempo button** at your desired tempo. SONAR will calculate the tempo of your mouse clicks and enter the time in the Tempo number box.

7. **Click** on the **Insert a New Tempo option button**. The option will be selected.

8. Optionally, **type** a **time** in the **Starting at Time number box**. The box will show your entry.

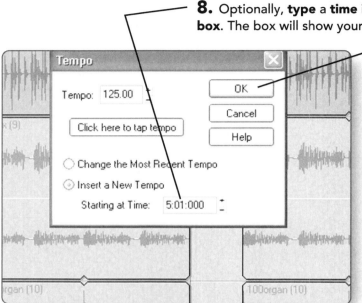

9. Click on **OK**. The tempo change will be inserted at the time you chose.

10. Click on **Play**. The groove clips will play back at the original tempo for four bars, and after the measure of silence they will play back at the new tempo.

THINK AHEAD, NOW

The Starting at Time field always starts with the current Now time, so if you set the Now time before opening the Tempo dialog box (as we just did), you won't need to type in a location for the tempo change.

Working with Project Pitch

Okay, so you've successfully dealt with the tempo coolness of groove clips—now it's time to take advantage of their ability to follow your project's pitch changes. This means that even though a groove clip contains a nasty bass line in D, SONAR will make it a nasty bass line in F-sharp and then a nasty bass line in E-flat if that's what your song requires. How do you communicate all this pitch information? By following these steps, naturally!

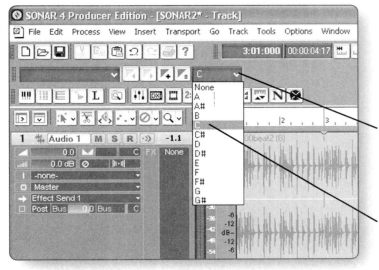

1. If necessary, display the Markers toolbar by **right-clicking** on any empty space in the **toolbars** area and **checking Markers**. The Markers toolbar will be displayed.

2. Click on the **down arrow** at the right of the **Default Groove-Clip Pitch drop-down list box.** The Default Groove-Clip Pitch list will open.

3. Click on a **default pitch**. The list will close and display your choice. In the example, I have chosen C.

KEY AND PITCH

When dealing with groove clips, there is an important difference between the terms *key* and *pitch*. Although a musician considers them related terms, in SONAR you can choose a key signature for your song, and it will have no effect on your groove clips. The pitch of a groove clip is set by comparing its *reference note* to the project's default pitch (which you just set) and any pitch markers (which you are about to create), regardless of key signature.

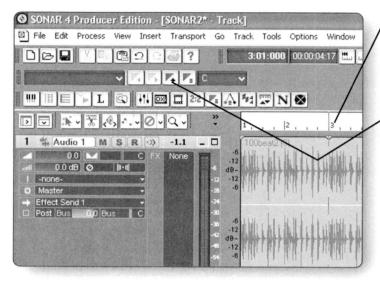

4. **Click** in the **Time Ruler**. The Now time will be set to wherever you clicked. In the example, I have set the Now time to measure three.

5. **Click** on the **Insert marker button** on the **Markers toolbar**. The Marker dialog box will appear.

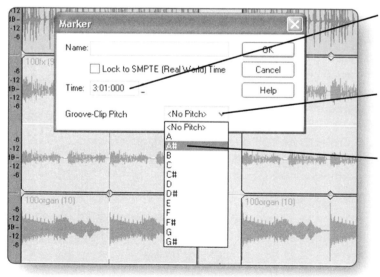

6. Optionally, **type** a **new location** in the **Time field**. It will display the location where the pitch marker will be placed.

7. **Click** on the **Groove-Clip Pitch drop-down list box**. The list will open.

8. **Click** on the **new pitch**. The list will close and display your choice. In the example, I have chosen A-sharp.

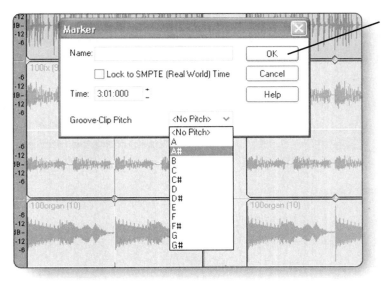

9. Click on **OK**. The dialog box will close, and a pitch marker will be placed at the location you specified.

10. Click on **Play**. The groove clips will play back, changing pitch at the marker you created.

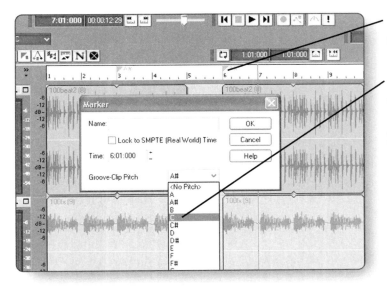

11. Ctrl+drag the new **pitch marker** to a new location. The Marker dialog box will open.

12. Optionally, **change** the **Groove-Clip Pitch** setting to a new value. The field will display your choice. In the example, I have chosen C.

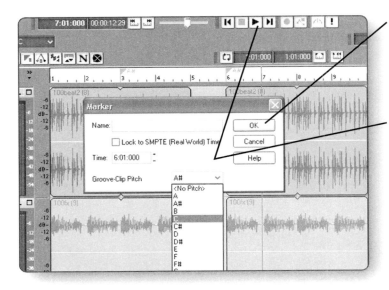

13. **Click** on **OK**. The dialog box will close, and a new marker will appear at the location to which you dragged the copy of the original marker.

14. **Click** on **Play**. The song will play back, changing pitch at each marker.

7

Creating and Editing Groove Clips

SONAR 4 does more than let you use ACID-ized groove clips—it lets you fine-tune them and even create them from scratch. The key to this power is found in the Loop Construction view, so that's where we'll spend time next. In this chapter you will learn how to:

- Use the Loop Construction view
- Set and change groove clip parameters
- Turn a clip into a groove clip
- Manipulate the sound of a groove clip
- Fine-tune the time-stretching of a groove clip

Opening the Loop Construction View

The Loop Construction view lets you control all of a groove clip's parameters, from whether and how it changes key to how it changes tempo. Note that the Loop Construction view can only be opened when you already have audio selected. Unlike the Loop Explorer view, it doesn't include any provision for finding and opening a file—it just works with the clip you have selected when you open it.

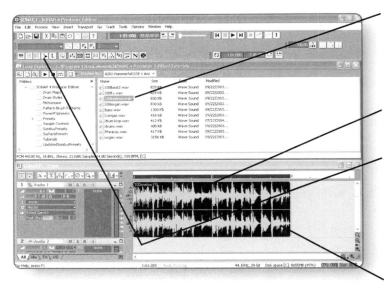

1. If necessary, **import** a **groove clip** as discussed in Chapter 6, "Using Groove Clips." The groove clip will appear in your project

2. Select the **groove clip**. The clip will be highlighted.

3a. Click on the **Loop Construction view button**. The Loop Construction view will appear with the selected clip displayed.

OR

3b. Double-click on the **groove clip**. The Loop Construction view will appear with the selected clip displayed.

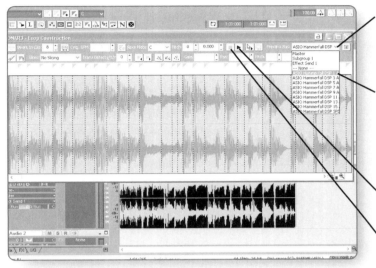

4. **Click** on the **down arrow** at the right of the **Preview Bus drop-down list box**. The drop-down list will open.

5. **Click** on the **audio output** through which you want to audition groove clips. The list will close, and your choice will appear in the box.

6. **Click** on the **Preview Loop button**. The groove clip will play.

7. **Click** on the **Stop Preview button**. Playback will cease.

Following Project Pitch (or Not!)

In Chapter 6 you saw how to create pitch markers within your song so that groove clips could transpose themselves automatically and follow your song's harmonic progression. The Loop Construction view lets you enable this ability within a groove clip. As you'll see, sometimes this isn't desirable, so you can also disable pitch following. The following steps show you how to turn this ability on or off.

SAMPLE LOOPS

Once again, we turn to the sample loops Cakewalk thoughtfully provided with SONAR 4 in the Tutorials folder. For this example, it's highly recommended that you follow along with the sample loop once before you start experimenting.

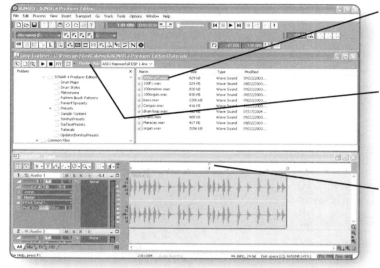

1. **Import** a percussion-based **groove clip**, such as 100beat2.wav. The clip will appear in your project.

2. **Set** the **default project pitch** as previously discussed. The chosen default pitch will be displayed in the Default Project Pitch field.

3. **Insert** a **pitch marker** halfway through the clip. The marker will appear where you create it.

4. **Play** the **song** and **listen** to what happens. The percussion will change pitch when it reaches the pitch marker.

WHAT'S WRONG?

That doesn't sound very natural, does it? We expect pitched instruments to follow the song's harmonic progression, but your drummer doesn't retune her drums every time you play a different chord, does she? In general, you will want Follow Project Pitch to be enabled for pitched instruments and disabled for non-pitched percussion instruments and special effects.

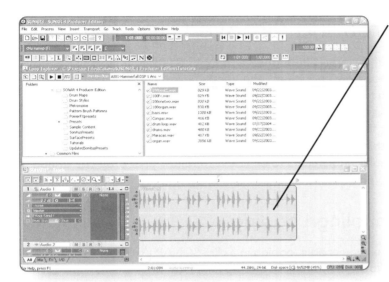

5. Double-click on the **groove clip**. The Loop Construction view will appear.

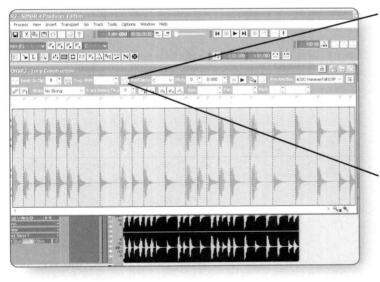

6. Click on the **Follow Project Pitch button**. The button will no longer be highlighted, and the Root Note field will be grayed out.

7. Play the **song**. The groove clip will no longer change pitch at the pitch marker.

8. Click on the **Follow Project Pitch button**. The button will be highlighted, and pitch following will once again be enabled.

Creating Groove Clips

As if it weren't enough that SONAR 4 lets you manipulate the space-time continuum, the Loop Construction view also lets you turn ordinary, run-of-the-mill audio clips into groove clips. (Okay, Einstein, that bit about space-time is a little overstated, but the control SONAR gives you over pitch and time is nothing short of magic!) In the steps that follow, you'll take a regular audio clip and enable it to follow your project's tempo and pitch changes.

Enabling Looping

When you enable looping in a clip, SONAR does two things. First, it allows you to roll out the clip in a track so it repeats itself as we did in Chapter 5, "Importing and Using Audio Loops." Second, it uses information you provide about the number of beats in the clip to adjust the playback speed of the clip to the project tempo. The following steps show you how to turn looping on and provide the info SONAR needs to change the clip's tempo.

1. Drag a regular non-looping **clip** like drums.wav into an **audio track**. The clip will appear where you place it, with square corners indicating it is not a loop. . . yet.

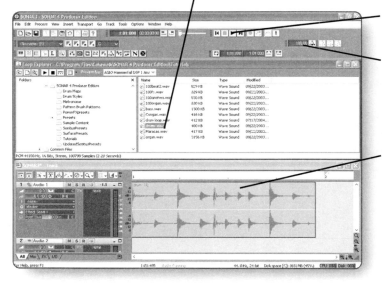

2. Click on **Play**. The clip will play back.

3. Change the **tempo** and **play** the **clip** again. The clip will play back exactly as it did before, because, again, it's not yet a groove clip.

4. Double-click the **clip**. The Loop Construction view will appear.

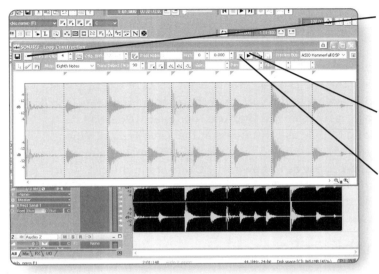

5. **Click** on the **Enable Looping button**. Beat-slicing markers will appear in the waveform, and the corners of the clip itself will be angled instead of square.

6. **Click** on **Preview Loop**. The loop will now play at the project tempo.

7. **Click** on **Stop Preview**. The loop will stop playing.

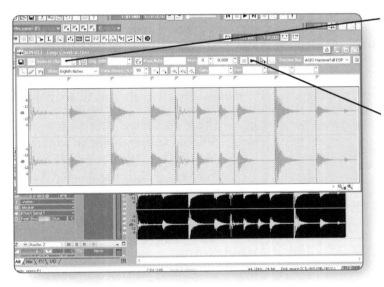

8. **Enter** a **new number** in the **Beats in Clip field** and **press Enter**. The number of beat-slice markers will change to reflect the new number of beats.

9. **Preview** the **loop**. It will play back faster or slower, depending on the number you entered.

BEATS ME

SONAR uses the Beats in Clip value to calculate the playback speed of the loop. For example, if you tell SONAR the clip represents eight beats, it will play it at one speed, and if you say it represents four beats, it will play it twice as fast because four beats takes half as long to play as eight beats at the same tempo. When you enable looping for a clip, SONAR makes a real good guess as to how many beats are in the clip, so if the numbers make your head hurt, relax and let SONAR do the work!

Enabling Stretching

Stretching a clip is similar to looping it, except that you can't roll the clip out as you can with a loop. A stretched clip does adapt to the project tempo, although it does so by comparing its original tempo with the project tempo rather than basing the calculation on the Beats in Clip value. This would be a better way to stretch something that's not clearly rhythmic but needs to cover a specific musical time. Here's how to set it up.

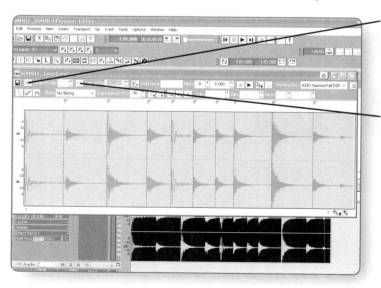

1. If necessary, **click** on the **Enable Looping button** to turn looping off. The button will not be highlighted, and the clip itself will have square corners.

2. Click on the **Enable Stretching button**. The button will be highlighted.

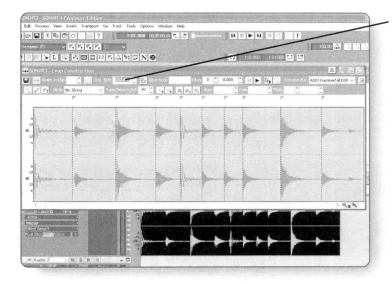

3. **Enter** a new **tempo** in the **Original (Orig.) BPM** field and **preview** the **clip**. The clip will play at a tempo that depends on the relationship between the original BPM setting and the project tempo.

FASTER AND SLOWER

If the value in the Orig. BPM field is higher than the project tempo, the clip will play back slower than normal speed. If the value in the Orig. BPM field is lower than the project tempo, the clip will play back faster than normal speed. If the original BPM value is the same as the project tempo, the clip will play back at its natural speed.

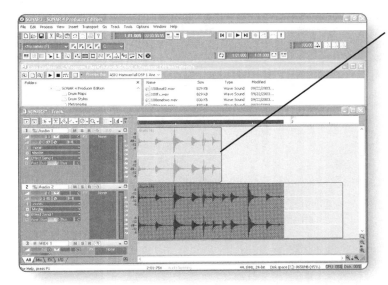

4. In the Clips pane, **drag** the **right edge** of the **clip** to the **left**. The clip will be shortened.

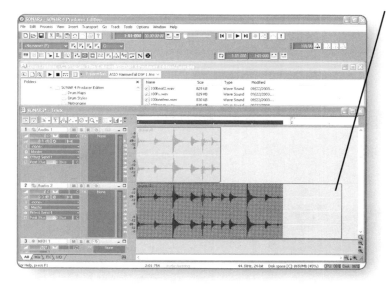

5. Drag the **right edge** of the **clip** to the **right**. The clip will be lengthened, but it will not repeat like a loop.

Setting a Clip's Root Note

SONAR transposes groove clips by comparing a clip's root note with the default project pitch and any pitch markers. You can change this behavior by changing the clip's root note value as follows.

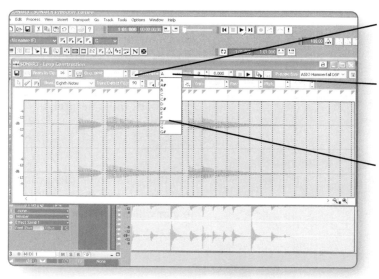

1. If necessary, **click** on **Follow Project Pitch**. The button will be highlighted.

2. **Click** on the **down arrow** at the **Root Note drop-down list box**. The drop-down list will open.

3. **Click** on the desired **root note**. The list will close and display your choice.

ROOT NOTES

It's not really necessary to identify a groove clip's root note accurately, but it is a good idea. In the short run, all you need to know is the relationship between a clip's root note and the current pitch marker. If they're the same, the clip will play back at its original pitch, and everything else is relative. In the long run, however, you'll be much happier and more efficient if you take the time to label your groove clips according to their true original root notes.

Changing the Sound of a Groove Clip

A new feature of SONAR 4 is the ability to change the sound of a groove clip on a slice-by-slice basis. You can change the pitch, volume, or pan, of each slice individually to create your own personal sound.

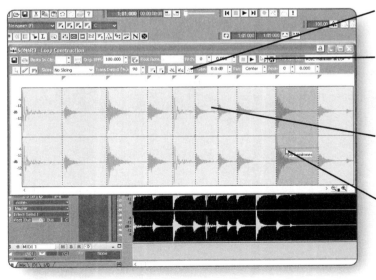

1. **Click** on the **Enable Slice Auto-preview button**.

2. If necessary, **click** on the **Show/Hide Pitch Envelope button**. The Pitch Envelope will be displayed.

3. **Click** on **slices** one by one until you find one you want to transpose.

4. **Drag** the **Pitch Envelope** for that slice **up** or **down** to transpose it.

5. Optionally, **repeat** the **process** to change the gain or pan of a slice.

Fine-Tuning a Groove Clip's Timing

According to the laws of nature, the tempo and pitch of an audio sample are intertwined—when one goes up, so does the other. That's why when SONAR lets you manipulate groove clips, you sometimes hear odd artifacts and sonic misbehaviors, especially at extreme tempo changes. The Loop Construction view lets you fine-tune the beat slices so that this misbehavior is minimized. You will still find that doubling the tempo of a groove clip makes it sound different, but following these steps will help you achieve the best-sounding results.

1. **Import** the **clip drums.wav** to the beginning of an **audio track**. The clip will appear in the track.

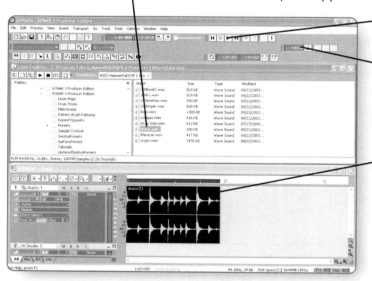

2. **Play** the **clip**. The clip will play once and stop.

3. **Change** the **tempo** to **90 BPM** and **play** the **clip** again. The clip will sound exactly the same, because it is not a loop or a groove clip.

4. **Double-click** the **clip**. The clip will open in the Loop Construction view.

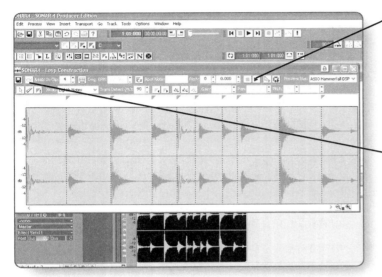

5. **Preview** the **clip** in the Loop Construction view. The clip will play repeatedly, because the Loop Construction view loops clips when it previews them regardless of whether looping is enabled.

6. **Click** on **Enable Looping**. A series of slicing markers will appear within the clip.

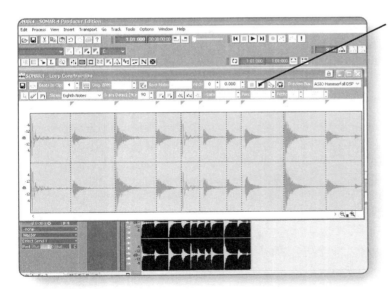

7. **Preview** the **looped clip**. The clip will play back slower, at the project tempo of 90 BPM.

NOT BAD—YET

The clip—now a loop—does a pretty good job of adapting to the project's tempo, which is a good deal slower than the clip was to begin with. SONAR usually does a good job of automatically determining the right way to change a clip's tempo. No doubt you notice a couple of telltale signs, though, especially at the very end of the clip right before it loops. It sounds almost as if the drummer knocked over the hi-hat, doesn't it? We'll fix it, but to illustrate how the slicing process works the first thing we're going to do is make it sound *worse!* Have faith—it will get better.

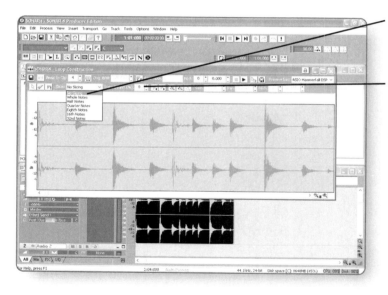

8. Click on the **down arrow** at the **Slices drop-down list box** and **choose No Slicing.**

9. Click in the **Transient Detection (Trans. Detect %)** number box, **type 0** (zero), and then **press Enter**. All of the slicing markers will disappear.

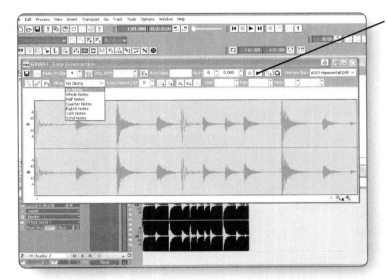

10. **Preview** the **clip**. It will sound awful due to the complete lack of slicing markers.

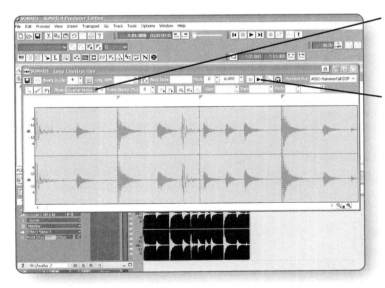

11. **Set** the **Slices value** to **Quarter Notes**. Slicing markers will appear at beats 2, 3, and 4 (B2, B3, and B4).

12. **Preview** the **clip**. It will sound a little better, but not great.

SLICES

The Slices value places slicing markers exactly at musical subdivisions, from whole notes to 64th notes. This is a good starting point for slicing a rhythmic loop like this one.

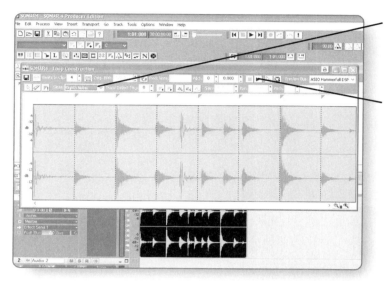

13. Set the **Slices value** to **Eighth Notes**. Four more slicing markers will appear at eighth-note subdivisions.

14. Preview the **clip**. It will sound better still, but some glitches remain.

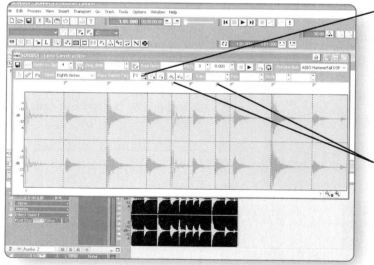

15. Click between the **plus (+)** and **minus (−) buttons** at the right of the **Trans Detect (%) number box** and drag upward to increase the value. As it reaches 73%, slicing markers will appear at the sixteenth notes just before and just after B3.

16. Drag the **B3 slicing marker** and the **next slicing marker** prior to B4 slightly to the **right** so they line up with the peaks of the waveform. The markers will appear where you place them.

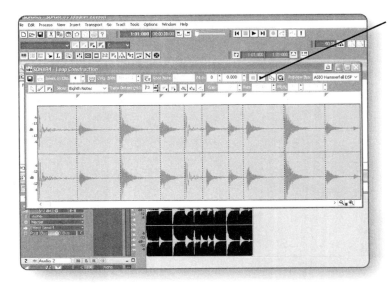

17. Preview the **clip**. It will sound almost perfect, but there's still a glitch in the final hi-hat note.

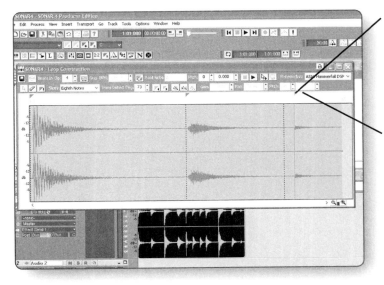

18. Double-click in the top half of the Loop Construction view's **timeline** right above the last sixteenth note. A slicing marker will be created where you double-clicked.

19. If necessary, **drag** the **new slicing marker** so it aligns exactly with the sixteenth note's peak. The marker will be relocated.

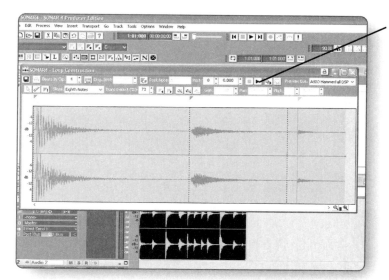

20. Preview the **clip**. It will finally sound correct, and as promised even better than it did with SONAR's default slicing way back in Step 7!

SLICE, DETECT, TWEAK

For best results, start by setting the Slice size to a note value that covers most of a loop. Then get the subtler details by bumping up the Trans Detect (%) value. Make your final tweaks manually.

PART III

Creating Your Own Audio

8

Recording Your Own Audio

So far, you've seen that loops and groove clips are powerful tools for creating music, and that they can speed up the process of developing a song considerably. If you're a saxophonist like me, however—or a singer or a guitarist or any other kind of skilled performer—loops only get you part of the way there. Sooner or later you're going to want to put your own "voice" into your song, and that means audio recording. Never mind later, let's do it sooner—as in now! In this chapter you will learn how to:

- Choose audio inputs and outputs
- Prepare an audio track for recording
- Record audio
- Use punch record and loop record

Choosing Audio Inputs and Outputs

One of the most important concepts in SONAR 4—or, for that matter, any music-production situation—is *signal flow*. Although this is a pretty straightforward term—it really does refer to audio and MIDI signals flowing into, through, and out of your system—it is one of those "minutes to learn, lifetime to master" concepts. Throughout the rest of this book your understanding of signal flow will grow step by step. We've already managed the "out of" part by playing back songs, clips, loops, and groove clips. Now we'll handle the "into" part by getting new audio and eventually new MIDI information into SONAR. When we get to mixing, you'll see the internal signal flow, the "through" part.

For this chapter, we will assume that you have a microphone, guitar, keyboard, or other instrument properly connected to your audio card's physical input jack or jacks. Naturally what you see onscreen will reflect your particular audio card and will therefore be slightly different from what you see on these pages. If you have technical difficulties, start by consulting your audio card's documentation. Appendix A, "Setup and Troubleshooting," also has some tips for troubleshooting audio problems, and the SONAR 4 manual and help system are full of useful information.

PROTECT YOUR EARS!

Whenever you are dealing with audio devices, you are pointing amplified sound at your ears. Ordinarily, this is a good thing and a benign thing. However, any system capable of giving you satisfyingly high-quality playback is also capable of blasting your ears with accidental loud sounds, such as *feedback*. Feedback happens when a sound runs through the same signal path repeatedly, getting amplified more and more each time until it produces an ear-splitting squawk or squeal. The most common cause of feedback is when a sound going into a microphone comes out speakers and is picked up again by the microphone. This is one reason performers wear headphones when recording. Although this isn't a common occurrence and can be avoided by skillful and careful engineering practices, if it does happen you will want to stop it immediately. Turn off the microphone, turn off the track's record-arm button, turn down the volume of your speakers, or stop SONAR's audio engine as explained later. Protect your ears!

1. Click on the **I/O tab** in the Track pane. The I/O tab will come to the front.

2. Click on the **down arrow** at the right of the **track input drop-down list**. The input drop-down list will open.

3. Click on the **name** of the **input** from which you wish to record. The list will close, and the input will be displayed in the track's input field.

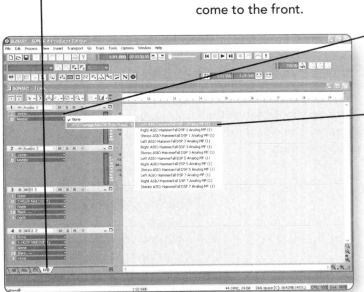

INPUT NAMES

SONAR lists inputs in pairs, so if, for example, you have a stereo (two-input) sound card called the "Feldspar 9000J," you will see something like Left Feldspar, Right Feldspar, and Stereo Feldspar listed as your available input options. If you have a mono (one-channel) source plugged into your sound card, you will need to choose one of your mono track inputs, most likely Left Feldspar. If you're recording from a stereo source, you would simply choose Stereo Feldspar.

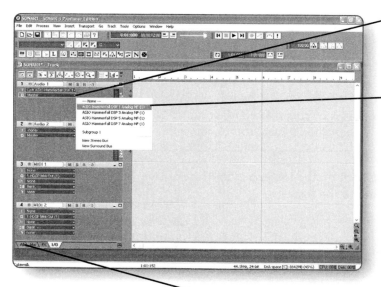

4. Click on the **down arrow** at the right of the **track output drop-down list**. The output drop-down list will open.

5. Click on the **name** of the **output** to which you ordinarily listen. The list will close, and the output you chose will be displayed in the track's output field.

6. Click on the **All** tab in the Track pane. The All tab will come to the front.

NO MASTER

If you're working from SONAR's Normal template, you will see that the track output is already set to Master. Although this seems like a perfectly reasonable output, go ahead and choose your audio card's primary stereo output as the track's output. We'll discuss exactly what that Master is when we discuss mixing.

> ## I/O VERSUS ALL
>
> Notice that the input and output you just chose in the I/O tab are both displayed in the All tab as well. This is because the Mix, FX, and I/O tabs are all *subsets* of the information displayed in the All tab. The subset tabs are useful for helping you find the specific parameters you need quickly. They are also an efficient way to squeeze a limited amount of information about a whole bunch of tracks into the window all at once.

Preparing an Audio Track for Recording

Once you've chosen your track's input and output, there are just a couple more things you need to do before you can successfully record audio into SONAR 4. You need to be sure you or the artist you're recording can hear what's being recorded, and you need to "arm" the track for recording so SONAR will actually commit it to disk.

Arming a Track for Recording

Every recording device, whether it's based on hardware or software, requires you to specify what tracks are going to be recorded at any given time. This is known as *record-arming* a track. Essentially, it tells SONAR to direct what's coming in on that track to the hard disk for storage and eventual playback. It doesn't get any simpler than this, as you'll see in the next steps.

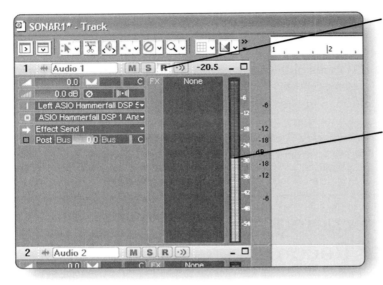

1. Click on the **Record (R) button** on the track to which you wish to record. The Record button will turn red, and the track itself will turn a different color to indicate it is armed.

2. Play your **instrument** or **sing** into the microphone. The track's input meter will show the level of the input signal. If you don't see any signal, consult your sound card's documentation.

3. If necessary, **adjust** the **track input level** by increasing or decreasing the output volume of your instrument or microphone pre-amp. The input meter will reflect any changes.

SETTING LEVELS

The answer to the question, "How loud should I make my input?" would take almost an entire book by itself in order to sort out the technical hows and whys and the different schools of thought, and to filter through all the misinformation. The simplest solution is that, because SONAR's meters are *peak* meters by default, you should set your input so that when you sing or play your loudest, the input meter approaches *but never hits* the top of the scale. Notice that the scale in the Track Inspector is larger, and therefore gives you more precise information than the meter in the Track pane. SONAR has no way of adjusting the volume of an input, so to make the input louder, you need to sing louder, play harder, or turn up the volume of your instrument or microphone pre-amp.

Starting and Stopping SONAR's Audio Engine

When feedback or digital distortion occurs, it can be uncomfortable and even dangerous, so you need to be able to fix it quickly. For this purpose, SONAR has a button that can turn off its audio engine, stopping all audio activity and interrupting the feedback so you can remedy it. Here's how to turn SONAR's audio engine off and back on.

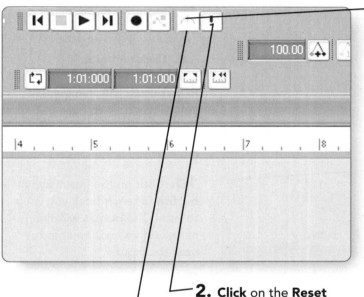

1. With at least one audio track record-armed, **click** on the **Audio Engine button**. The button will be grayed out, indicating that the audio engine is off, and no sound will be recorded or played.

> ### RESET
>
> When you are in the middle of recording or playing, the Audio Engine button will already be grayed out, and you will need to use the Reset button instead.

2. Click on the **Reset button**. Playback or recording will stop, and the audio engine will be turned off.

3. Click on the **Audio Engine button** again. The button will be illuminated, and the words "Audio Running" will appear in the status bar at the bottom of the screen.

Enabling Input Echo

If you can hear yourself in your headphones, you can probably skip this section. Appendix A will give you a more detailed explanation of when and why you need Input Echo, but for now it's sufficient to say that if you have record-armed a track and you can't hear yourself, you will need to turn Input Echo on. Here's how to do exactly that.

1a. **Select** one or more **tracks**.

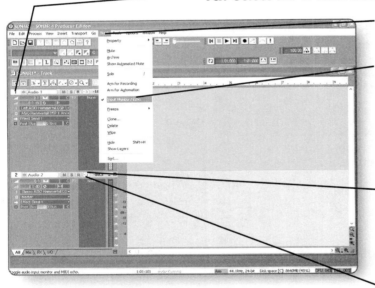

1b. **Click** on **Track**. The Track menu will open.

1c. **Click** on **Input Monitor/Echo**. The track's Input Echo button will illuminate, and you will be able to hear the input.

OR

1d. **Click** on the **Input Echo button** for each track you want to hear. The button will illuminate, and you will be able to hear the input.

2. **Click** again on the **Input Echo button**. The button will be grayed out, and you will no longer hear the input.

Making Your First Audio Recording

If you haven't read this chapter from the beginning, please do so now. It will save you frustration and reduce the risk of ugly and potentially dangerous distortion and feedback. If you have read the preceding steps already, then you are *finally* ready to record audio! It's really pretty simple if you've prepared properly.

1. Double-click the **track name field** and **type** in an informative **name**. The name you type will be displayed, and all audio files recorded to this track will use that name.

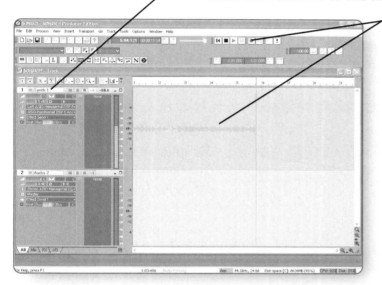

2. Click the **Record button**. Recording will begin, the Now time will advance, and a waveform representing your input will be drawn in the recording track.

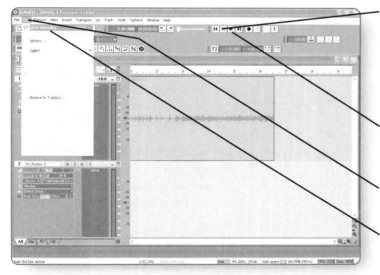

3. Click the **Stop button**. Recording will stop, the Now time will reset to its previous position, and an audio clip will appear, showing the waveform of what was just recorded.

4. Click the **Play button**. The clip you just recorded will play back.

5. Click on **Edit**. The Edit menu will open.

6. Click on **Undo Recording**. The clip you recorded will disappear. Nobody gets it perfect on the first take!

Using Punch Record

One of the great innovations in recording technology was the ability to *punch in* and replace just a portion of a recording. This allowed engineers to retain the good parts of a "take" and replace only the parts that had mistakes or imperfections. SONAR's Auto Punch record mode brings this same innovation to your desktop.

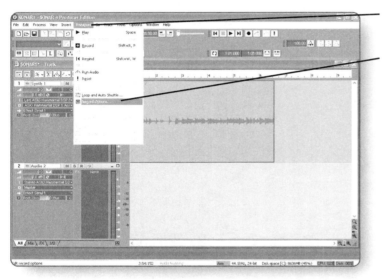

1. **Click** on **Transport**. The Transport menu will open.

2. **Click** on **Record Options**. The Record Options dialog box will appear.

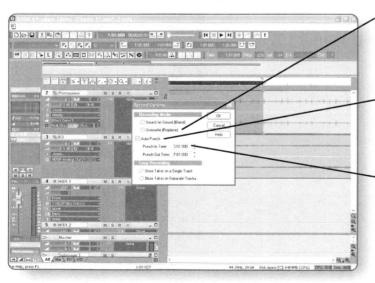

3. **Click** on **Overwrite (Replace)**. This will cause newly-recorded audio to replace the previous take.

4. **Click** on **Auto Punch**. This will cause SONAR to record between the punch-in and punch-out times.

5. **Double-click** in the **Punch In Time field** and type the location at which you want to punch in. The value you enter will be displayed.

6. Double-click in the **Punch Out Time field** and type the location at which you want to punch out. The value you enter will be displayed.

7. Click on **OK**. The dialog will close, and two red markers will appear in the Time Ruler, reflecting the punch-in and punch-out times you chose.

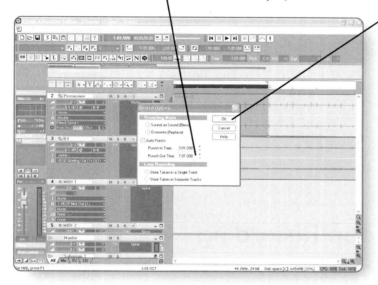

A QUICKER WAY

You can also set the punch-in and punch-out times by dragging in the Time Ruler, right-clicking there, and clicking Set Punch Points within the context menu. Doing this automatically engages Auto Punch mode, but you still need to specify Overwrite (Replace) from the Record Options menu.

8. Click in the **Time Ruler** to set the Now time to some convenient point prior to the punch region. The Now time will reflect the point you chose.

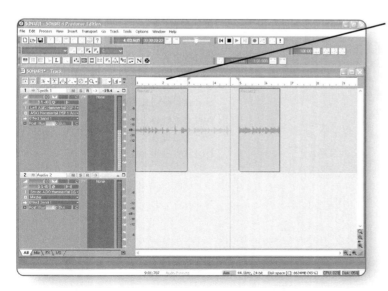

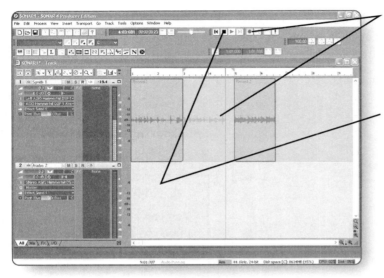

9. **Click** on the **Record button**. Playback will begin at the Now time, and recording will begin at the punch-in marker and end at the punch-out marker.

10. **Click** on the **Stop button**. Playback will stop, and a new clip will appear between the punch markers.

Loop Recording

Sometimes in the search for that elusive perfect take, you'll want to try recording a passage several times in a row. Loop record mode allows you to do this without interruption. Simply set up the time you want to loop, hit Record, and repeat the passage until you get a keeper. These steps show you how.

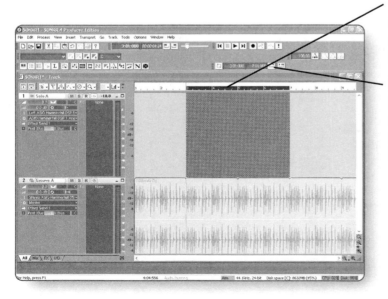

1. **Drag** in the **Time Ruler** from the start of the loop to the end of the loop. The selection will be highlighted.

2. **Click** on the **Set Loop to Selection button**. The selection will be bracketed by yellow loop markers, and the Loop On/Off button will be turned on.

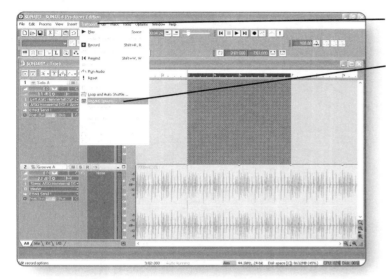

3. **Click** on **Transport**. The Transport menu will open.

4. **Click** on **Record Options**. The Record Options dialog box will appear.

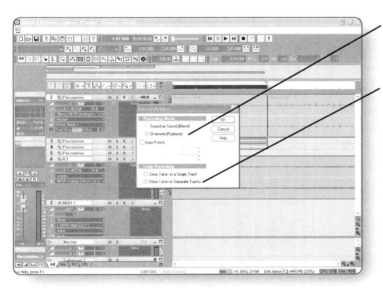

5. **Click** on **Overwrite (Replace)**. The option will be highlighted.

6. **Click** on **Store Takes in Separate Tracks**. The option will be highlighted.

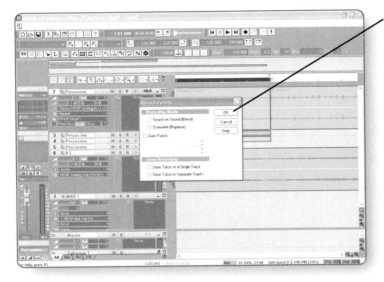

7. **Click** on **OK**. The dialog box will close.

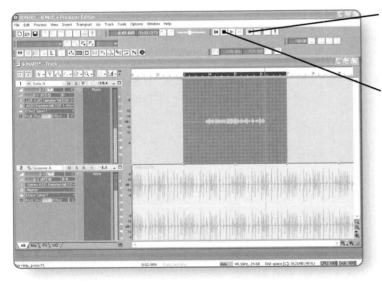

8. **Click** the **Record button**. Recording will begin, looping from the end back to the beginning until you stop it.

9. **Click** the **Stop button**. Recording will stop, and the various takes will appear in newly-created tracks.

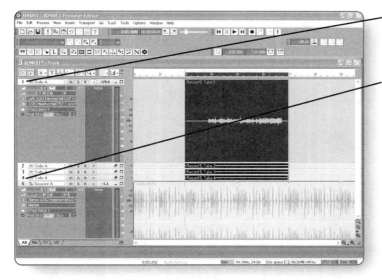

10. **Click** on the **track number** of the record-armed track. The track number will be highlighted.

11. **Shift+click** on the **track number** of the last newly created track. The number of that track, and of any tracks between it, and the record-armed track will be highlighted.

12. **Press** the **H key**. SONAR will show only the selected tracks.

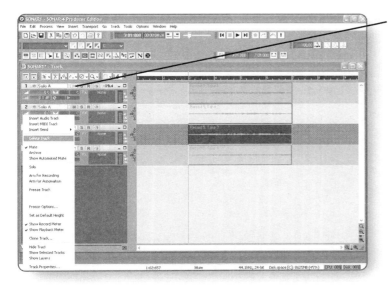

13. **Click** the **Mute button** of all but one of the loop-recorded tracks. The mute buttons will turn yellow to indicate the tracks' muted status.

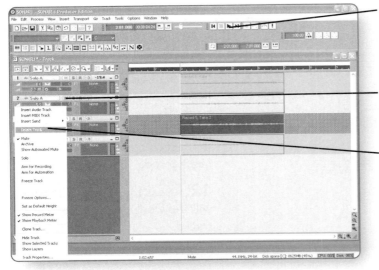

14. **Click** on the **Play button**. The selection will play, looping from the end back to the beginning.

15. **Click** the **Mute buttons** to listen to each track separately so you can choose the best take.

16. Once you have chosen the best take, **delete** the **unused tracks** as discussed in Chapter 4, "Customizing SONAR's Look and Feel." You will be left with only the good take.

CAN'T CHOOSE JUST ONE?

If you find that you like part of one take and part of another, you can combine the best of both by editing them together. That's what the next chapter is all about!

9

Editing Audio

One of the real breakthroughs of the computer-music revolution is the ability to dissect and manipulate audio recordings down to the level of a single sample. Some folks blame this editing magic for the proliferation of talentless-but-cute pop stars who are fixed and tuned and polished by skilled engineers in order to sell records, and there may be some truth to that! At the same time, giving creative musicians more efficient tools with which to make music is never a bad thing. In this chapter you'll experience the power of digital audio editing as you learn how to:

- Scrub clips to find audio events
- Use SONAR's grid for precise editing
- Split audio clips
- Select partial clips
- Slip-edit audio clips
- Create fades and crossfades
- Use destructive processes on clips

Scrubbing Audio

No, the term "scrubbing" doesn't have anything to do with cleaning up your audio tracks. It's a throwback to the days of editing magnetic tape. Because tape doesn't provide any visual reference like SONAR's clip waveforms, engineers would find precise spots on tape by manually moving the tape back and forth across the playback head slowly until they heard what they were looking for. Until you get to be an expert at *seeing* what you want to hear in the waveform, SONAR's Scrub tool will let your ears be your guide.

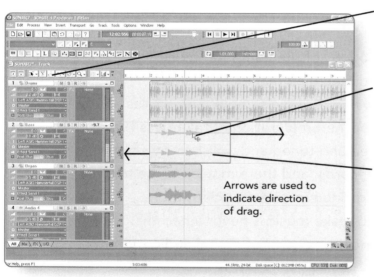

Arrows are used to indicate direction of drag.

1. **Click** on the **Scrub tool icon**. A small speaker icon (the Scrub tool) will appear next to the mouse pointer.

2. **Drag** the **Scrub tool** slowly from **left** to **right** across an audio clip. The audio clip will play.

3. **Drag** the **Scrub tool** from **right** to **left**. The audio clip will play in reverse.

FASTER, SLOWER, IN BETWEEN

Variable playback speed is a key aspect of the Scrub tool. Scrub quickly to hear different segments of a clip in real time. When you have found the spot you want to edit, scrub back and forth slowly until you have found exactly the right spot.

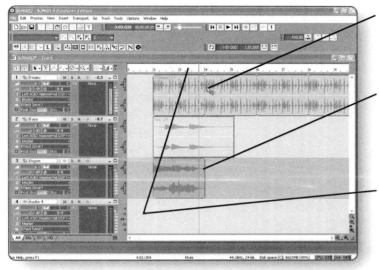

4. **Drag** the **Scrub tool** across a different audio clip. You will hear that clip, because the Scrub tool is clip-specific by default.

5. **Drag** the **Scrub tool** across an audio clip on a muted track. You will not hear anything, because the Scrub tool respects the Mute button setting.

6. **Drag** the **Scrub tool** in the Time Ruler. You will hear the entire arrangement at that point, because the Scrub tool is no longer clip-specific when you drag in the Time Ruler.

Using Snap to Grid

SONAR 4 allows you the option of conforming certain edit functions to a timing grid. The grid can be based on musical bars and beats, on minutes and seconds, or on other SONAR events such as markers. What this means is that, depending on how you set the Snap to Grid options, you could move a clip exactly to a marker, move a clip exactly one beat earlier, select exactly one second of a clip, or split a clip precisely one minute into a song. Of course, sometimes you don't want to be constrained by a grid, so you can easily turn Snap to Grid off. These steps walk you through the most common scenarios.

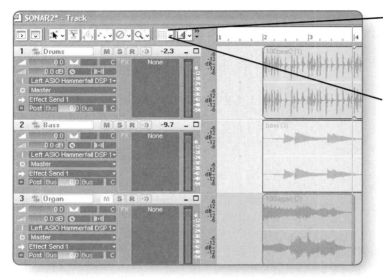

1a. **Click** on the **Snap to Grid button**. The button will be highlighted, indicating that Snap to Grid is enabled.

1b. **Click** on the **down arrow** next to the **Snap to Grid button**. The Snap to Grid dialog box will appear.

OR

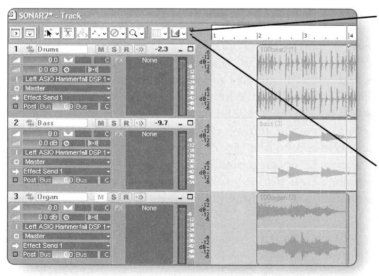

1c. If the Snap to Grid button is not visible, **click** on the **More Buttons arrows** at the right end of the Track view toolbar and **click** on the **Snap to Grid option** in the list that opens. The list will close, and Snap to Grid will be enabled.

1d. **Click** again on the **More Buttons arrows** and **choose Snap to Grid Options**. The Snap to Grid dialog box will appear.

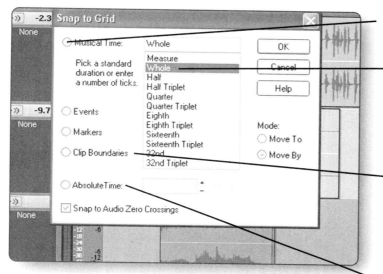

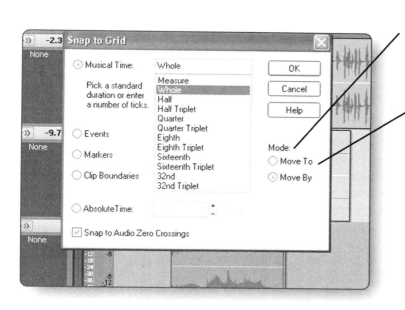

2. Click on an **option**. The most common options include

- **Musical Time.** This option sets the grid to musical values such as a measure, a quarter note, or an eighth note, allowing you to make rhythmic edits.

- **Clip Boundaries.** This option makes the beginning and end of any clip into a grid point, allowing you to drag one clip against another with no space and no overlap.

- **Absolute Time.** This option sets the grid to clock values such as minutes or seconds, allowing you to make precise time-based edits.

- **Mode.** This option only applies to moving and copying clips within a Musical Time or Absolute Time grid.

  - **Move To** snaps the moved clip to the nearest grid point, so, for example, the clip will start exactly at a particular quarter note or a specific second.

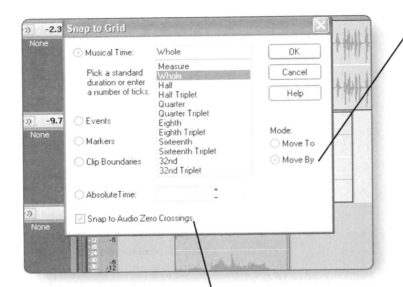

- **Move By** constrains the *distance* a clip moves to a multiple of a grid value, so, for example, a clip will end up exactly one measure earlier or ten seconds later. In Move By mode, if the clip started just before or after a grid point, it will end up exactly the same distance away from the nearest grid point when it has been moved.

- **Snap to Audio Zero Crossings.** This preference forces the Now time, selection boundaries, and slip-edits to snap to the nearest point at which the waveform crosses the zero volt line, helping to avoid clicks and pops at clip boundaries. This preference is independent of all other options in the Snap to Grid dialog box, and it takes precedence over the chosen grid value.

SNAP TO AUDIO ZERO CROSSINGS

As a rule, you should leave Snap to Audio Zero Crossings on all the time. It will save you a lot of time and trouble fixing the sort of nasty little clicks and pops that you would otherwise hear at the beginnings and ends of audio clips.

Splitting Audio Clips

If you want to combine the best parts of several vocal takes or cut the chorus out of a song, you'll need to chop up the audio clips before you can rearrange them. SONAR gives you two different ways to split audio clips—the Split command and the Scissors tool. The Split command lets you split several clips at once, and the Scissors tool lets you cut a segment from the middle of a clip just by dragging. Here's how they work.

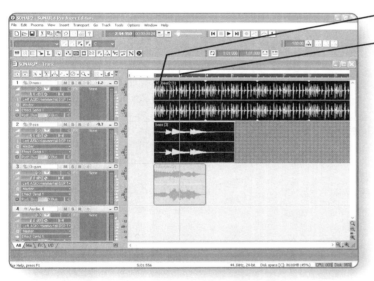

1. **Select** one or more **clips**.

2. **Click** in the **Time Ruler** at the point where you want to split the clips. The Now time will be set to that position.

3. **Press** the **S key** on your keyboard. The clips will all be split at the Now time.

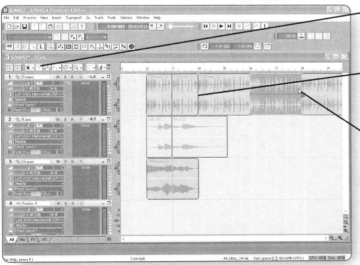

4. **Click** on the **Scissors tool button**. A scissors icon will appear with the mouse pointer.

5. **Click** on an **audio clip**. The clip will split into two clips at the position at which you clicked.

6. **Drag** within an **audio clip**. When you release the mouse button, the clip will be split at the beginning and end of where you dragged.

Selecting Partial Clips

In Chapter 3, "Working with Audio and MIDI Clips," you worked with whole clips—selecting them, copying them, pasting them, and even deleting them. Sometimes, however, careful editing requires working with smaller sections of audio; fortunately, SONAR allows you to select partial clips. You can then copy, paste, and delete the partial clips. Selection of partial clips conforms to the grid if it's enabled, so you can select just the fourth bar of a clip or exactly ten seconds of an ambience loop.

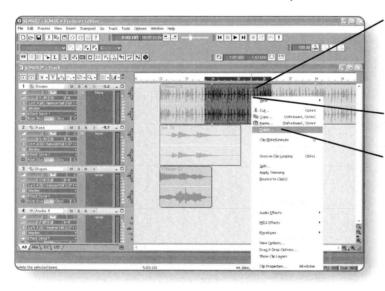

1. **Press** and **hold** the **Alt key** and **drag** within an audio clip. The portion of the clip over which you Alt+dragged will be selected.

2. **Right-click** on the **selection**. The context menu will open.

3. **Click** on **Delete**. The Delete dialog box will appear.

4. If necessary, **click** on the **Events in Tracks check box**. A ✔ will appear.

5. **Click** to **choose** additional **options** as appropriate. A ✔ will appear for each chosen option.

6. **Click** on **OK**. The dialog box will close, and the selected clips will be removed from the tracks.

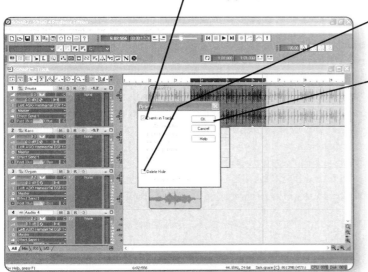

DELETE HOLE

Choose Delete Hole to make everything that follows the deleted data move to the left (earlier) to fill in the gap. Specify Shift by Whole Measures to fill in the gap while maintaining the same bar and beat relationships within the moved data.

THE SAME, ONLY DIFFERENT

Choosing Cut, Copy, or Paste from the Edit menu or context menu will achieve the same results as we discussed in Chapter 3, except that the selected partial clip will be the object of the action rather than the entire clip.

Slip-Editing a Clip

The term *slip-editing* refers to the process of trimming a clip non-destructively. In SONAR, this is accomplished simply by grabbing one end of a clip and dragging it to make the clip shorter. The technique is the same one you used to roll out loops and groove clips, but slip-editing is usually used to reduce the length of a clip. You can lengthen a clip, but if the clip is not looped, you may only add silence to the end of the clip. Note that when slip-editing, you will see the clip jump to grid values—this is intended to help you make grid-based edits if you wish, but it does not restrict you from placing the clip boundary off the grid if you like. The only Snap to Grid option that applies strictly to slip-editing is Snap to Audio Zero Crossings.

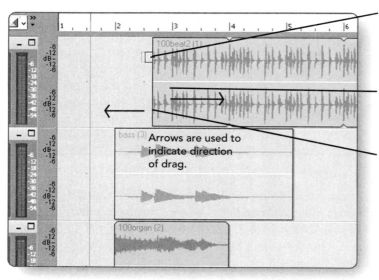

Arrows are used to indicate direction of drag.

1. Position the **mouse pointer** at one end of an audio clip. The pointer will change to a slip-editing icon.

2. Drag the **end** of the **clip inward**. The clip will grow shorter.

3. Drag the **end** of the **clip outward**. The clip will grow longer.

SLIP-EDITING

You can change your mind all day long about the length of a clip, because slip-editing is entirely non-destructive. If you lengthen a clip beyond its original length, however, you will see a straight line instead of a waveform, indicating silence where there is no real sound.

Using Fades and Crossfades

The best way to think of what fades and crossfades can do for you is to listen to a good DJ, either the radio kind or the club kind. DJs are always fading a song in after they talk over the intro, fading a song out because they need to read the weather, and fading one song out while they fade another one in—that's a *crossfade*—so nobody gets the notion to leave the dance floor. On a smaller scale, fades and crossfades are also essential tools for creative *splicing* of different takes and other sonic surgery. If you have chosen not to enable Snap to Audio Zero Crossings, fading the ends of and crossfading the seams between clips is highly recommended.

Fading In and Out

Fading a clip in or out in SONAR couldn't be simpler, as you'll see in these steps. It's always a good idea when a clip is fairly exposed to fade it in and out to remove any abrupt changes to and from silence. You might also want to fade out applause early at the end of a live track—three minutes of applause is gratifying on stage, but annoying on CD!

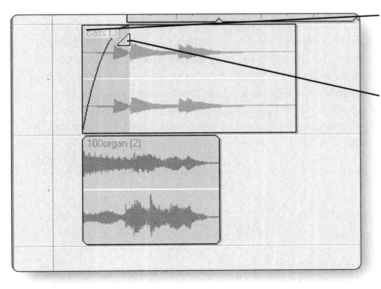

1. **Position** the **mouse pointer** at the upper-left corner of an audio clip. The pointer will turn into a triangle (the Fade tool).

2. **Click** and **drag** from the **corner inward**. The left end of the clip will be shaded, and a line will appear indicating the changing volume of the clip as it fades in.

3. **Play** the **clip**. The clip will start from silence and gradually get louder until it reaches full volume at the end of the shaded area.

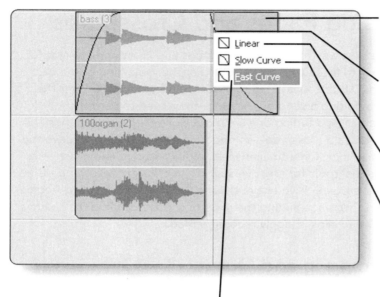

4. Drag the **upper-right corner** of the **clip inward**. This will create a fade-out.

5. **Right-click** at the **top** of the **fade curve**. The Fade Curve menu will appear. Its options include

- **Linear.** The fade takes place at a steady pace over its entire length.

- **Slow Curve.** The fade-in or fade-out starts slowly and then accelerates, with most of the volume change occurring toward the end of the fade.

- **Fast Curve.** The fade-in or fade-out starts quickly and then slows down, with most of the volume change occurring toward the beginning of the fade.

Creating Crossfades

Crossfading clips is as easy as fading them in or out. It's an important function for any kind of meticulous editing, because it lets you make the transition from one clip to another smooth and gradual. It's a great way to cover up any glitches or changes in volume from one take to another. It can also be used to blend the end of one song seamlessly into the start of another.

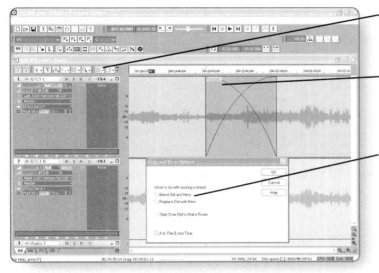

1. Click on the **Enable/Disable Automatic Crossfades button**. The button will be highlighted.

2. Drag a clip so that it overlaps another. The Drag and Drop Options dialog box will appear.

3. Click on **Blend Old and New**, and then click OK. The dialog box will close, and fade-in and fade-out curves will appear where the clips overlap.

SAVING TIME

If you are doing this sort of thing a lot, you can save yourself time by setting the default Drag and Drop Options (in Global Options, Editing) to Blend Old and New and deselecting Ask This Every Time.

Setting Default Fade Curves

SONAR lets you choose default curves for fades and crossfades. You can always edit the curve via the Fade Curve menu as discussed previously, but if you find yourself using one curve more than the others, you can save yourself time by setting it as the default curve.

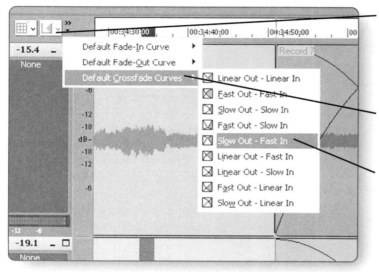

1. Click on the **down arrow** to the right of the **Enable/Disable Automatic Crossfades button**. The Fade Options menu will appear.

2. Point to the **fade type** for which you wish to set a default. A submenu will open.

3. Click on the desired **fade curve**. The menu will close, and the chosen curve will become the default for that fade type.

SUGGESTED DEFAULT FADES

Although circumstances and your ears will dictate the best curve for any given situation, you might want to start with the following defaults: Slow fade-in, Fast fade-out, and Slow Out-Fast In crossfade.

Editing in Multi-Lane Tracks

SONAR 4 introduces a powerful new way to edit together a composite—*comp* for short—of the best parts of several takes. You can actually load several takes together into the same track and show them on separate *lanes* side by side. Better still, you can crop them to the same point and crossfade them easily.

1. Select one or more **tracks**.

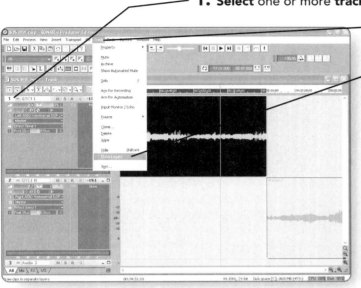

2. Click on **Track**. The Track menu will open.

3. Click on **Show Layers**. A ✔ will appear next to the option, and the menu will close. Multi-lane tracks will be enabled only for the tracks you selected.

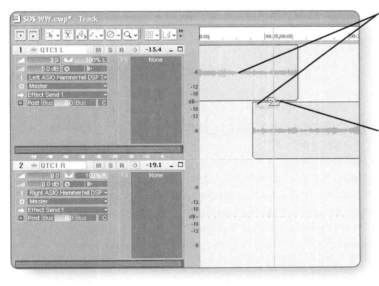

4. Drag two **clips** into the same track, **choosing Blend Old and New** when the Drag and Drop Options dialog box appears. The two clips will appear side by side in the same track.

5. Point to the **place** where the two clips touch. The cursor will turn into the Smart Cropping tool.

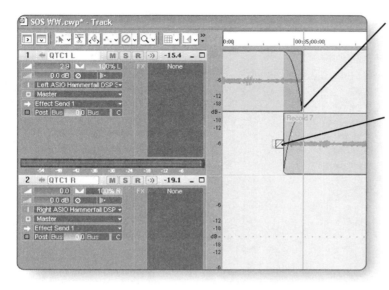

6. **Click** where you want the **clips** to be **cropped**. The end of the earlier clip and the beginning of the later clip will be cropped to the same position.

7. If you have Automatic Crossfades enabled, you can **drag** the **end** of **either region** so it overlaps the other, and the two will be automatically crossfaded for the duration of the overlap.

BACK TO NORMAL

When you are done using multi-lane editing on a track, you can deselect Show Layers to return to normal view. The edits you have made will be retained even when the track is shown normally.

Processing Audio

SONAR features a number of powerful audio-processing functions. Some of these take the form of non-destructive real-time audio effects, such as reverb and delay, which we'll cover in Chapter 16, "Using Audio Effects." First, though, let's turn our attention to a special category of processes that must be performed *offline*, meaning that they must take place before playback. You could also call these *file-based* processes, because they operate directly on the audio data contained in audio clips.

DANGER, DANGER!

These processes are *destructive,* changing the actual data in audio clips. You can use Undo if you change your mind during editing, but after you close a project, the changes are permanent. A cautious approach is to *clone* a track (as discussed in Chapter 10, "Managing Audio") before applying destructive processes.

Normalizing Audio

To normalize an audio clip is to raise its volume to the highest possible level without distortion. SONAR looks through the clip to find its highest peak, measures the distance from that peak to just below the onset of distortion, and then raises the volume of the entire clip by that amount. It is not necessary to normalize all of your clips, but if a clip is too soft, normalizing is a quick fix.

1. **Select** a whole or partial **clip**. The selection will be highlighted.

2. **Click** on **Process**. The Process menu will open.

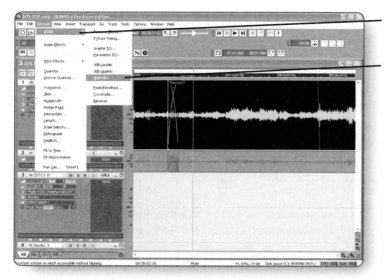

3. **Point** to **Audio**. The Audio submenu will open.

4. **Click** on **Normalize**. The menu will close, and the selection will be normalized.

ABNORMALIZATION

Normalization is no panacea. When you make the clip louder, you make any background noise in the clip louder, too. The best solution is always to record your audio at proper levels to begin with.

Reversing Audio

Back in the '60s and '70s, there was a popular and controversial recording technique called *backward masking*. Rock stars were accused of putting subliminal messages in their records by mixing in phrases that had been played in reverse. Of course, whether anybody could understand the messages well enough to be influenced by them was another matter, but musicians, engineers, and fans were fascinated by the unnatural sound of backward voices and instruments. SONAR makes child's play out of reversing audio.

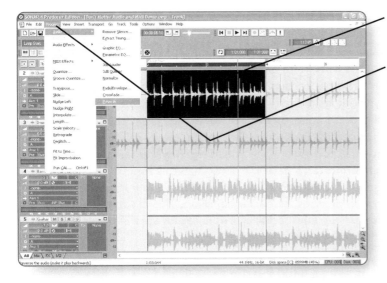

1. Select all or part of an **audio clip**.

2. Click on **Process**. The Process menu will open.

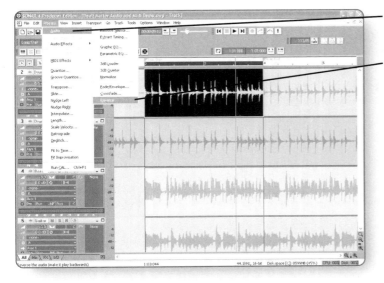

3. Point to **Audio**. The Audio submenu will open.

4. Click on **Reverse**. The menu will close, and the selected audio will be reversed.

TRY THIS AT HOME

Of course, this is a great tool for finding out exactly what they were saying in those "subliminal" messages by reversing the backward masking!

Removing Silence

SONAR can automatically find and remove the silent parts of a clip. One reason for doing this is that silence is rarely really silent! The background noise when musicians aren't playing may seem insignificant in a single part, but when there's background noise on each of several tracks it can add up and be noticeable. Removing the "silent" parts of those tracks keeps the noise from accumulating. Anyone familiar with the engineering term *gate* will recognize this function. Another reason for removing silence is to split a clip into multiple clips between phrases for easier handling. This is especially useful in dialog or narration editing, but it has its uses in music production as well.

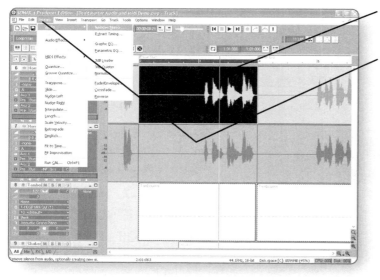

1. **Select** all or part of an **audio clip**.

2. **Click** on **Process**. The Process menu will open.

3. Point to **Audio**. The Audio submenu will open.

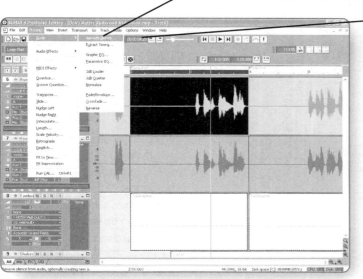

4. Click on **Remove Silence**. The Remove Silence dialog box will appear.

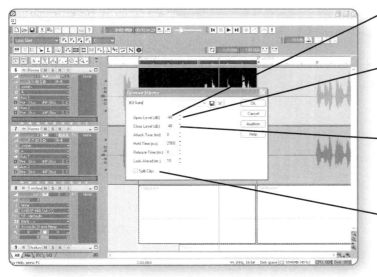

5. Enter values for the various parameters. Key options include

- **Open Level.** As a sound rises above this volume, it will no longer be considered silence and will be kept.

- **Close Level.** As a sound dips below this volume, it will be considered silence and will be removed.

- **Split Clips.** If this option is checked, the clip will be divided up into smaller clips wherever silence is removed.

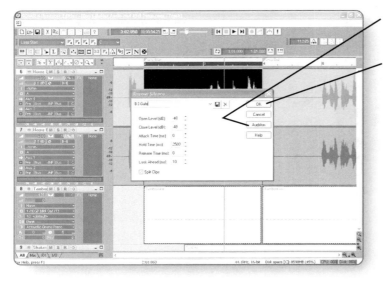

6. Optionally, **click** on **Audition** to preview the effect.

7. Click on **OK**. The dialog box will close, and the silence will be removed.

HOLD IT

Hold Time sets a minimum length for a clip, so you don't end up with too many tiny clips. Look Ahead extends the resulting clip earlier in time in order to catch the subtlety of a sound's attack. Your ears will tell you when this is necessary.

10

Managing Audio

When working with audio in SONAR, you can find yourself accumulating a lot of tracks and eating up a lot of space on your hard disk. Keeping your project file and your hard disk well organized is the key to managing your virtual studio. You already know that naming your tracks and projects wisely is a step in the right direction. In this chapter you will learn more about managing audio, including how to:

- Archive, clone, and wipe audio tracks
- Store each project's audio in its own folder
- Retrieve hard disk space by applying trimming and consolidating audio
- Clean up your audio folders

Archiving Audio Tracks

In Chapter 2, "Playing and Listening to SONAR Songs," you learned how to mute and solo tracks to control what parts of a project you could hear. Archiving a track can be considered a special case of muting. When you mute a track it is silenced, but it is still active. You can un-mute a track during playback. It's as though it were running alongside the rest of the tracks ready to jump in at any moment. When you archive a track it is essentially made inactive. You can't reactivate it without stopping playback, and it doesn't use any system resources at all. An archived track is a great place to store tracks that you aren't using but that contain alternate takes or other elements you might need later.

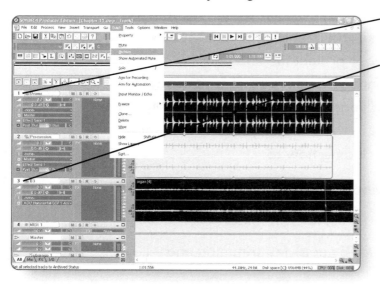

1. **Click** on a **track number**. The track will be selected.

2. Optionally, **Shift+click** or **Ctrl+click** on one or more additional **track numbers**. The tracks will be added to the selection.

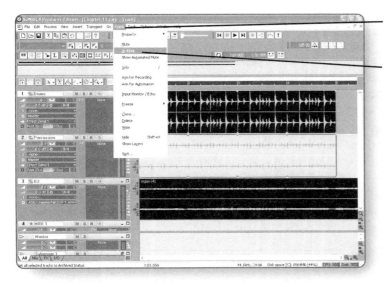

3. Click on **Track**. The Track menu will open.

4. Click on **Archive**. The menu will close, and the letter A will appear on the Mute button of the track(s). The track(s) will also turn a darker color to indicate archive status.

5. Select one or more **archived tracks**. The tracks will be highlighted.

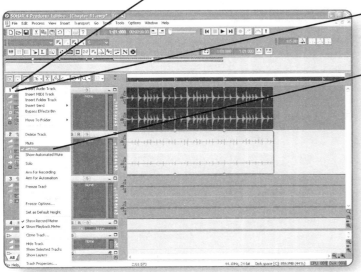

6. Right-click on the **track number** of a selected track. The context menu will open.

7. Click on **Archive**. The menu will close, and the selected tracks will return to normal status.

ARCHIVING TRACKS

You can change the archive status of a track from either the Track menu or the context menu. Note that if a track was muted when it was archived, it will still be muted when you un-archive it.

Cloning a Track

Cloning a track is exactly what it sounds like—making an identical copy, including all clips, effects, and settings. By itself, all it does is reinforce the original track, making it slightly louder without changing the sound at all. Delay the clone slightly and pan it to one side, though, and the interaction becomes more complex. You can vary the effects and edits on the clone and do all sorts of things to add variety to the sound. Another great use for a clone is as a safety copy before you start doing complex or destructive edits to the original. Just clone a track, archive the original or the clone (because they're identical, it doesn't matter which), and go wild!

1. **Select** one or more **audio tracks**.

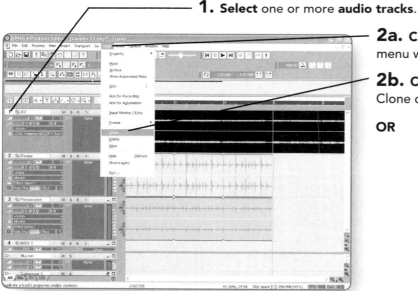

2a. **Click** on **Track**. The Track menu will open.

2b. **Click** on **Clone**. The Track Clone dialog box will appear.

OR

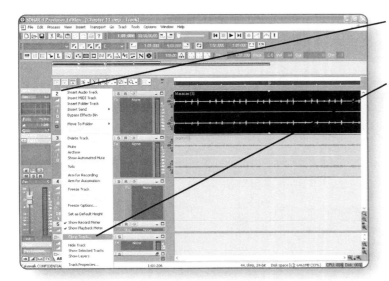

2c. Right-click on the **track number** of a selected track. The context menu will open.

2d. Click on **Clone Track**. The Track Clone dialog box will appear.

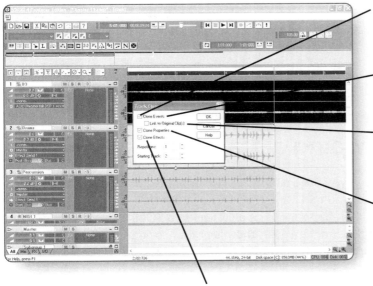

3. Click on the desired **options**. A ✔ will appear next to selected options, which include

- **Clone Events.** This option will cause all clips to be cloned.

- **Link to Original Clips.** This option will cause all cloned clips to be linked to the source track's clips.

- **Clone Properties.** This option will cause track name and I/O settings to be cloned.

- **Clone Effects.** This option will cause track effects to be cloned.

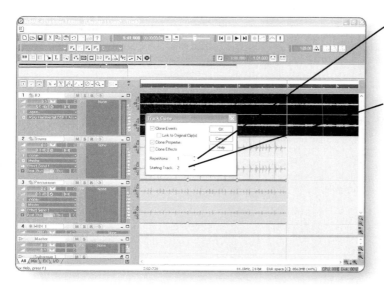

4. **Type** the desired **number** of repetitions in the **Repetitions field**. This is how many clones will be created.

5. **Type** a **number** for the desired **target track**. Existing tracks from that number down will move downward to make room.

A QUICK WAY TO SET UP FOR RECORDING

A quick way to set up a track for recording additional takes is to clone just the track properties. The cloned track will be blank, but its input and output will be set the same as the track in which you recorded the previous take.

Wiping a Track

Even you have an idea or performance that turns out to be less than you had hoped for now and then, right? There's no shame in it—it happens to us all. Thanks to SONAR's Wipe Track command, however, there's not any evidence of that fact! Wiping a track removes all clips from a track while leaving the track itself and all of its I/O settings intact.

1. **Select** one or more **tracks**.

2. **Click** on **Track**. The Track menu will open.

3. **Click** on **Wipe**. The track will be cleared of all clips.

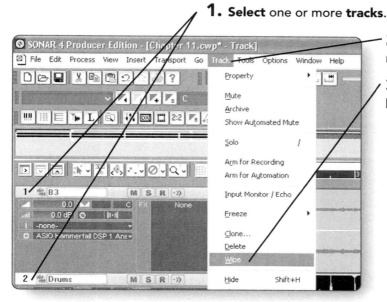

Using Per-Project Audio Folders

By default, SONAR 4 puts all audio files from all projects in a single folder called Audio Data within the Cakewalk Projects folder. Because each project knows exactly which audio files it needs, this doesn't affect SONAR's performance, but it can make backing up a project and managing your hard disk more difficult than it has to be. It's a good idea to have SONAR put each project in its own folder with a subfolder for that project's audio files. Here's how to take advantage of that option.

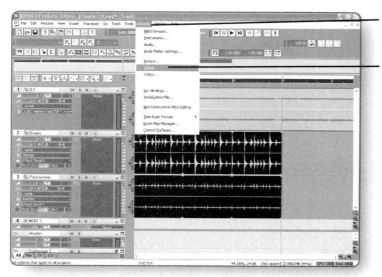

1. Click on **Options**. The Options menu will open.

2. Click on **Global**. The Global Options dialog box will appear.

3. Click on the **Audio Data** tab. The tab will come to the front.

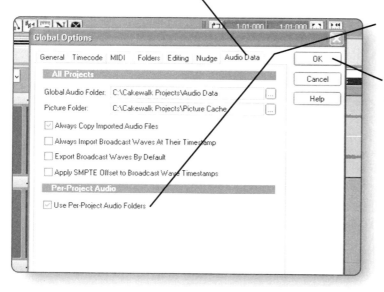

4. Click on **Use Per-Project Audio Folders**. A ✔ will be placed by that option.

5. Click on **OK**. The dialog box will close.

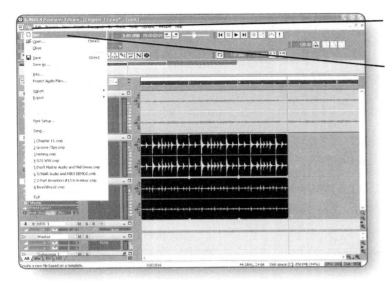

6. Click on **File**. The File menu will open.

7. Click on **New**. The New Project dialog box will open.

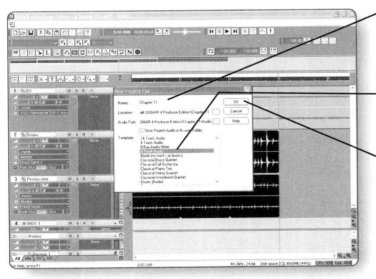

8. Type a **name** for the new project. The Location and Audio Path fields will update to reflect the name you typed.

9. Choose a **template**. The template name will be highlighted.

10. Click on **OK**. The dialog box will close, and the new project will appear onscreen.

Consolidating Project Audio

If you haven't been using per-project audio folders, or if you've imported audio into your project, the audio from any given project may be both intermingled with audio from other projects and scattered among several folders on your hard disk. In order to organize your data better, you can use the Consolidate Project Audio command. It collects all audio files from an open project into a single subfolder of the Audio Data folder.

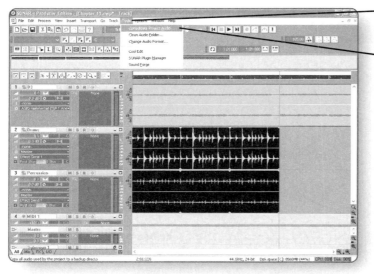

1. Click on **Tools**. The Tools menu will open.

2. Click on **Consolidate Project Audio**. The Consolidate Project Audio dialog box will appear.

3. Click on **OK**. The dialog box will close, and SONAR will place copies of the project's audio files into a single folder.

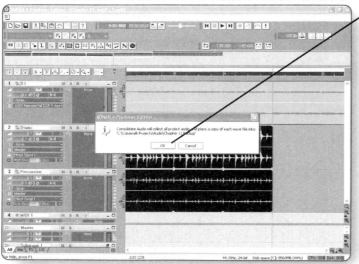

DON'T FORGET THE PROJECT FILE!

Be aware that the folder that now contains all of the project's audio files does not include the project file itself. If you back up the consolidated folder *and* the project file you will have a complete backup of your project.

Applying Clip Trimming

Because SONAR's slip-editing is nondestructive, it leaves a lot of unused audio data on your hard disk. This is great if you change your mind about an edit, but it's a big waste of space once you get to a point in a project where you're committed to the arrangement. You can reclaim this wasted space by permanently deleting the audio that has been trimmed away. That's what the Apply Trimming command does, and here's how to use it.

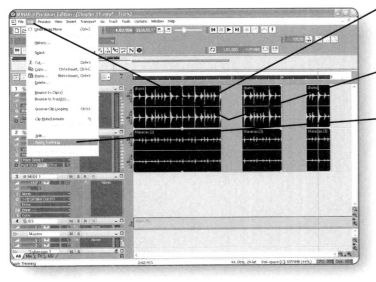

1. Select the **clips** from which you want to delete slip-edited data.

2. Click on **Edit**. The Edit menu will open.

3. Click on **Apply Trimming**. The trimmed audio will be deleted.

> ### SAVING SPACE
>
> When it's time to archive a project, you may want to select all of your clips (Edit, Select All) and then apply trimming to them all. That will ensure that you're not wasting storage space on a lot of data you don't want.

Cleaning Audio Folders

Sooner or later—actually, there's no later about it when you're dealing with audio files—you're going to find your hard disk overflowing with audio files, and you'll want to clean off any unused data to make room for more creativity. It's best to let SONAR handle this for you, because each project file knows exactly what files it owns. The Clean Audio Folder command will search your system for project files, and then build a list of audio files that don't belong to any project. You can then delete these files and reclaim the wasted drive space.

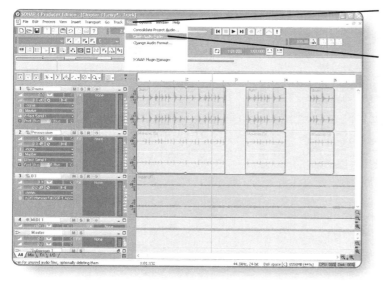

1. **Click** on **Tools**. The Tools menu will open.

2. **Click** on **Clean Audio Folder**. The Clean Audio Folder dialog box will appear.

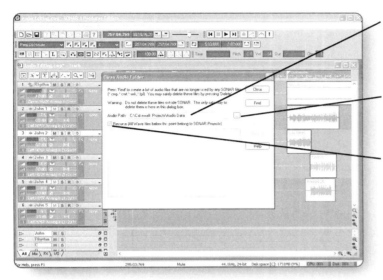

3a. **Type** the **name** of the folder you want to search.

OR

3b. **Click** on the **Browse** button and navigate to the folder you want to search.

4. Optionally, **click** on **Recurse**. A ✔ will appear next to the option.

SEARCHING HIGH AND LOW

SONAR will search your entire hard drive for project files, but it will only search the folder you choose for audio files to delete. *Recurse* tells SONAR to look for audio files in sub-folders of the chosen folder.

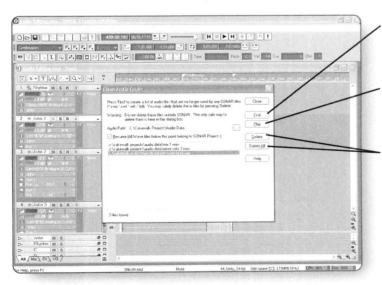

5. **Click** on **Find**. SONAR will search the specified folder and display a list of orphaned files.

6. Optionally, **click** on **Play** to audition files. The selected file will play.

7. **Click** on **Delete** or **Delete All.** The selected file or all files, respectively, will be deleted from your hard disk.

PART IV

Working with MIDI

11

Using the Cakewalk TTS-1

MIDI is a powerful language for controlling synthesizers, and SONAR 4 gives you every bit of control the MIDI language allows. One of the great things about MIDI is that it uses a common set of instructions that can be applied to any MIDI-capable synthesizer, regardless of its brand, model, or vintage. That means that all of the tools and functions in the next few chapters will work on whatever synthesizers you already own. To keep things consistent, though, I'll use the new Cakewalk TTS-1 that is included with SONAR 4. It's a software synthesizer—sometimes called a *virtual instrument*—that runs directly within SONAR. Depending on your level of experience with MIDI synthesizers, you will probably find it useful to follow along using the TTS-1 and then later apply the lessons to other instruments. In this chapter, you will learn how to:

- Use the Synth Rack to start the TTS-1
- Assign MIDI track outputs
- Change patches on the TTS-1
- Control the tempo of a project

Opening the Tutorial Project

Cakewalk has included several tutorials with SONAR, and you should go through them to help solidify all of the concepts you're learning. I'm going to use the first tutorial project as an example in this chapter, but of course everything here applies to any project.

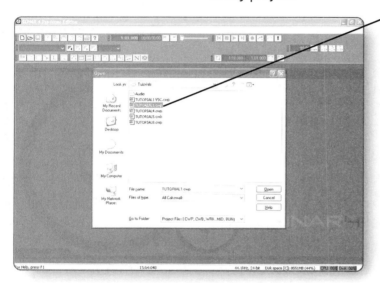

1. Open the first tutorial project, **TUTORIAL1.cwp**. You'll find it in the folder C:\Program Files\Cakewalk\SONAR 4 Producer Edition\Tutorials.

> **STUDIO EDITION**
>
> If you have SONAR 4 Studio Edition, the path will be C:\Program Files\Cakewalk\SONAR 4 Studio Edition\Tutorials.

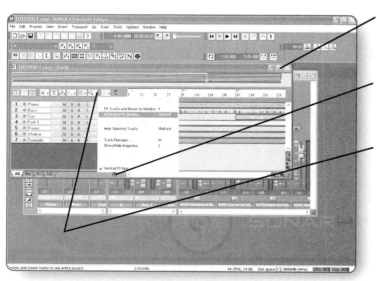

2. Click the **Maximize button**. The Track view will expand to fill the window.

3. If necessary, **click** on the **Show/Hide Bus pane button** to close the Bus pane.

4. Click on the **down arrow** to the right of the Zoom tool. The View Options menu will open.

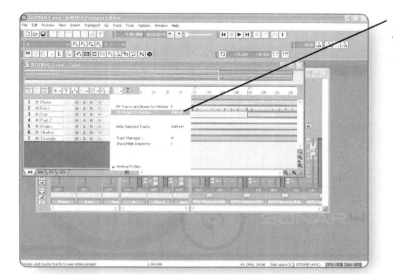

5. **Click** on **Fit Project to Window**. The tracks will be resized to fill the window.

Using the Synth Rack

The Synth Rack is SONAR's tool for starting and managing virtual instruments. It gives you a unified set of tools for starting or deleting any of the available DXi synthesizers, and it lets you open their editing interfaces for mad tweaking.

Opening the Synth Rack

Although it's possible to insert software synthesizers directly on tracks, it's usually more useful to create them from the Synth Rack. All of the software synthesizers you are currently running will appear in the Synth Rack, regardless of how you create them initially.

1. **Click** on **View**. The View menu will open.

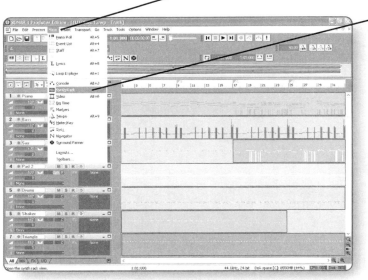

2. **Click** on **Synth Rack**. The Synth Rack dialog box will appear.

Starting the TTS-1

The TTS-1 is a General MIDI 2 synthesizer that uses Roland's acclaimed Sound Canvas sound set. The following steps apply equally well to any of the numerous third-party software synthesizers available.

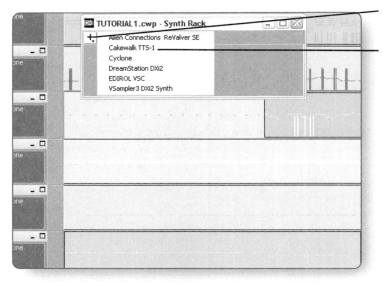

1. **Click** on the **Insert button**. The Insert menu will open.

2. **Click** on **Cakewalk TTS-1**. The Insert DXi Synth Options dialog box will appear.

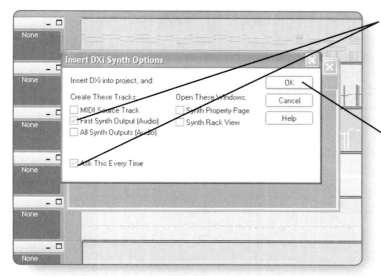

3. **Click** on the **First Synth Output (Audio)** and **Ask This Every Time options** to choose them, and deselect all others. A ✔ will appear next to only those two options.

4. **Click** on **OK**. The dialog box will close, and the TTS-1 will appear in the Synth Rack.

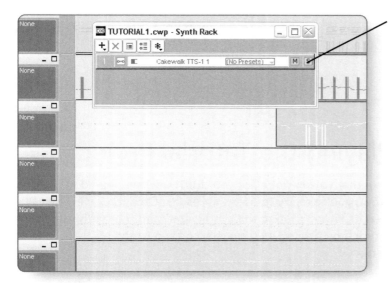

5. **Click** on the Synth Rack's **Close button**. The Synth Rack will close.

CLOSING THE SYNTH RACK

It's okay to close the Synth Rack or the editing page of any soft synth. Although an application's Close button ends the program completely, it doesn't work the same way for windows within SONAR, except for the Track view. You can always reopen the Synth Rack from the View menu, and you can reopen any synth from the Synth Rack.

Assigning MIDI Track Outputs

In order to hear the results of MIDI notes in a track, you must assign the output of the track to that instrument. This causes MIDI data to be sent from the track to a synthesizer, where the synthesizer responds by playing those notes.

1. **Click** on **the I/O tab** in the **Track pane**. The I/O tab will come to the front

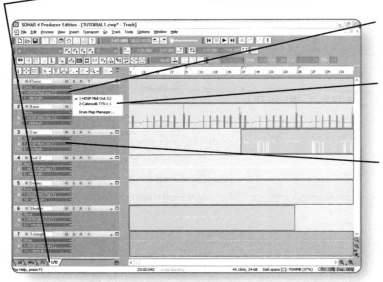

2. **Click** on the **down arrow** at the right of a track output field. The track output menu will open.

3. **Click** on **Cakewalk TTS-1.** The menu will close, and the track output field will display "Cakewalk TTS-1 1."

4. **Repeat Steps 2** and **3** for each track. All outputs will show "Cakewalk TTS-1 1."

Playing the Tutorial Project

Now that you've got all of your MIDI tracks assigned to the TTS-1, you're ready to hear the results. Each track will now feed its information to the synthesizer, and the synthesizer will respond by playing its sounds according to the MIDI instructions.

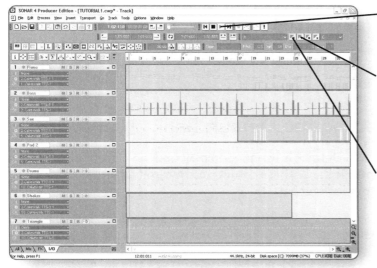

1. **Click** on the **Play button**. The tutorial project will play through the TTS-1.

2. **Click** on the **Next Marker button**. The Now time will skip immediately to the next marker, and playback will continue from that point.

3. **Click** on the **Previous Marker button**. The Now time will skip immediately to the previous marker, and playback will continue from that point.

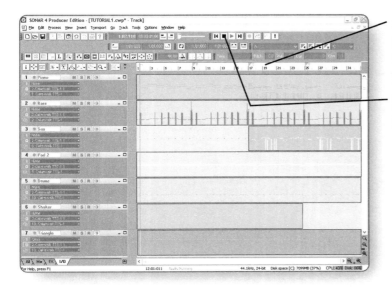

4. **Click anywhere** in the **Time Ruler**. The Now time will skip immediately to that point, and playback will continue.

5. **Click** on the **Stop button**. Playback will stop.

Changing Patches

The various instrument sounds that a synthesizer can make are organized into *banks* and *patches*. A patch is an individual timbre, and a bank is a collection of 128 patches.

Setting the Default Bank and Patch

Each MIDI track is assigned to play back on a specific patch of a specific bank. These settings are located near the track output assignment.

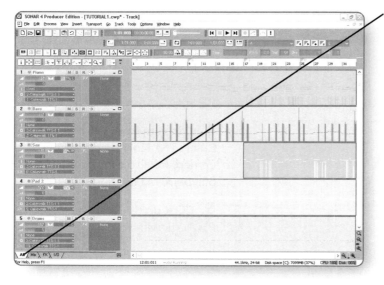

1. **Click** on the **All tab**. The All tab will come to the front.

2. **Press Ctrl+down arrow** a few times until the Bank and Patch fields are visible. The track height will increase with each key press.

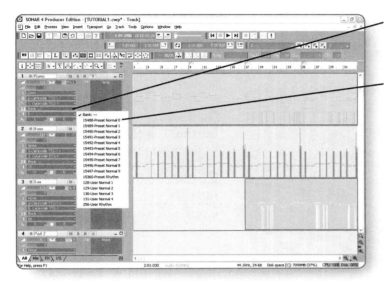

3. Click on the **down arrow** at the right of the Bank field. The Bank assignment menu will open.

4. Click on a **bank**. The menu will close, and the chosen bank will be displayed in the Bank field.

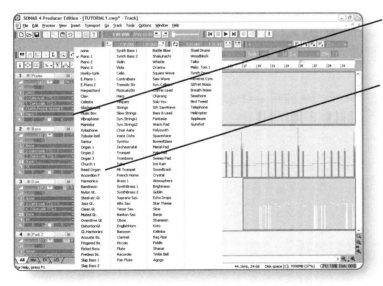

5. Click on the **down arrow** at the right of the Patch field. The Patch assignment menu will open.

6. Click on a **patch**. The menu will close, and the chosen patch will be displayed in the Patch field.

AUDITIONING PATCHES

Changing banks and patches on the fly during playback is a great way to hear the difference immediately. You may find it useful to use Loop playback (see Chapter 2, "Playing and Listening to SONAR Songs") so you can hear a section played in different sounds.

Inserting a Patch Change

SONAR even lets you change a track's assigned patch in the middle of a song. This is a convenient way to generate some sonic variety in an arrangement.

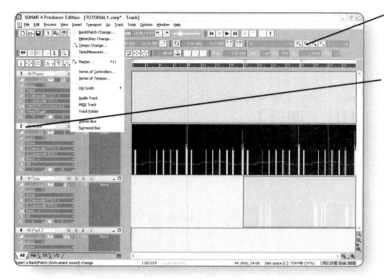

1. Click on the **Next Marker button**. The Now time will move to the next marker.

2. Click on the **track number** of the track into which you want to insert a patch change. The track will be highlighted.

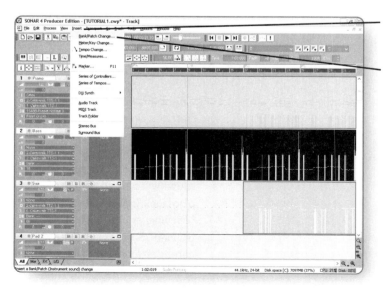

3. Click on **Insert**. The Insert menu will open.

4. Click on **Bank/Patch Change**. The Bank/Patch Change dialog box will appear.

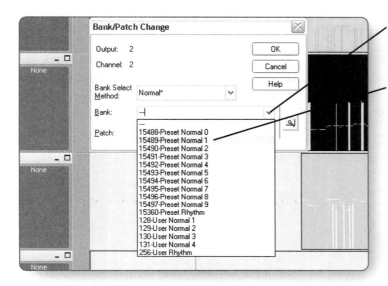

5. Click on the **down arrow** at the right of the Bank field. The Bank drop-down list will open.

6. Click on a **bank**. The list will close, and the chosen bank will be shown in the Bank field.

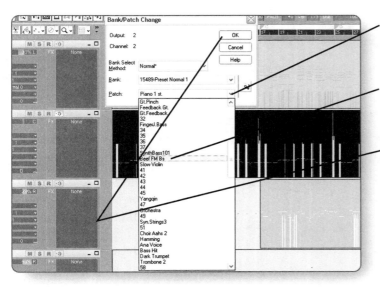

7. Click on the **down arrow** at the right of the Patch field. The Patch drop-down list will open.

8. Click on a **patch**. The list will close, and the chosen patch will be shown in the Patch field.

9. Click on **OK**. The dialog box will close, and the bank/patch change will be inserted into the track at the current Now time.

Changing Tempo Gradually

In Chapter 6, "Using Groove Clips," we covered setting and changing the project tempo, but what do you do if you want to accelerate or decelerate during a song? It's no problem—SONAR can do it.

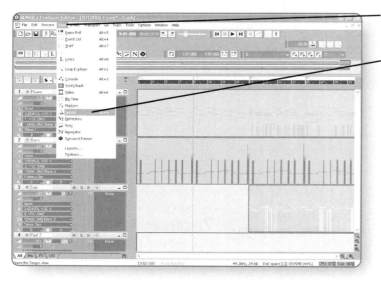

1. Click on **View**. The View menu will open.

2. Click on **Tempo**. The Tempo view will appear.

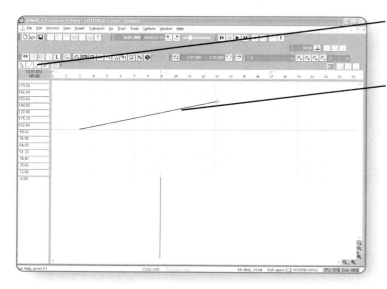

3. Click on the **Draw Line button**. The mouse pointer will appear as a plus sign (+).

4. Drag in the **tempo grid**. A line will appear connecting the point at which you clicked the mouse to the point at which you released the mouse.

5. Play the **project**. The tempo will change gradually according to the line you drew.

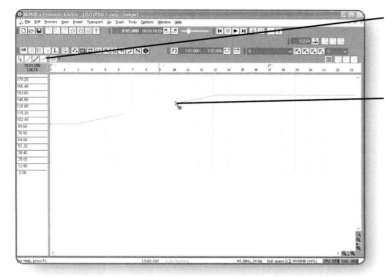

6. Click on the **Eraser button**. The mouse pointer will have a circle with a slash through it (the Eraser tool).

7. Drag in the **tempo grid**. Any existing tempo changes in the area in which you drag will be deleted.

TIMING IS EVERYTHING

To make very precise tempo changes, use the zoom controls in the lower-right corner of the Tempo view to zoom in close.

12

Editing MIDI

You can think of MIDI information in SONAR as a blueprint that your synthesizers will follow. You are the architect of your project, and you can change your mind whenever you wish. Each time your synthesizers "build the house," they will check the most recent blueprint and follow your instructions to the letter. In this chapter you will learn how to:

- Slip-edit and transpose MIDI clips
- Reverse and change the length of MIDI clips
- Edit notes in the Piano Roll view
- Add and delete notes
- Use the Controller pane to edit control data

Using MIDI Clips

SONAR 4 makes editing simple by using the same set of tools for both audio and MIDI data. That means that most of what you already know about editing audio clips applies equally well to editing MIDI clips. Because MIDI is a different sort of information from audio, though, there are a couple of differences, including the ability to transpose MIDI freely.

Slip-Editing MIDI Clips

Audio clips are made up of a series of samples, each of which is a miniscule fraction of a second long. It takes thousands of samples to make up an audio clip. MIDI clips, on the other hand, are primarily a series of messages telling a synthesizer to turn notes on and off. The highly technical terms for these two messages are *Note On* and *Note Off*. This means that when you slip-edit a MIDI clip so that you cut off a Note On message, the note will never be heard, even if the Note Off message is still present in the clip. If you slip-edit a MIDI clip so that you cut off a Note Off message, SONAR will simply slide the Note Off message along with the end of the clip, making the note shorter.

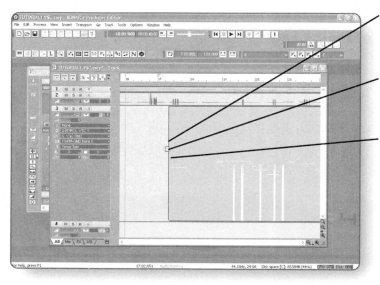

1. **Click** on **the left edge** of a **MIDI clip**. The mouse pointer will turn into the Trim tool.

2. **Drag** the **mouse pointer** to the right. The clip will become shorter.

3. **Drag** the **mouse pointer** past the beginning of a MIDI note. The note will disappear.

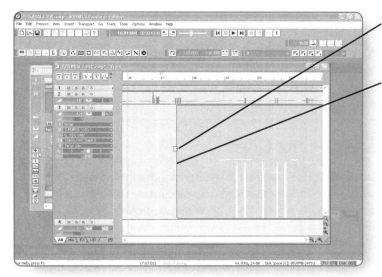

4. **Drag** the **mouse pointer** to the left. The clip will become longer.

5. **Drag** the **mouse pointer** past the beginning of the MIDI note that disappeared. The note will reappear.

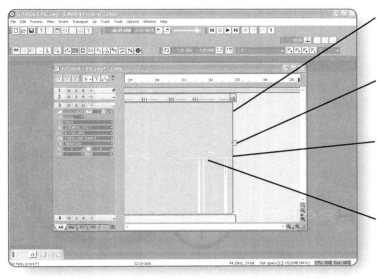

6. **Click** on the **right edge** of a **MIDI clip**. The mouse pointer will turn into the Trim tool.

7. **Drag** the **mouse pointer** to the left. The clip will become shorter.

8. **Drag** the **mouse pointer** past the end of a MIDI note. The note will become shorter along with the clip.

9. **Drag** the **mouse pointer** past the beginning of a MIDI note. The note will disappear.

GONE AND BACK AGAIN

When you drag the end of the clip back to the right, the note will reappear, eventually reaching its original length. The note will never end up being longer than it was originally, though.

Transposing Clips

Because MIDI clips are just instructions, changing their pitches is as easy as telling SONAR to add or subtract a few numbers from the original notes. You can transpose *chromatically*, meaning that a series of notes will retain their absolute pitch relationships, or *diatonically*, meaning that the intervals between notes will adapt to the scale tones of the project's key.

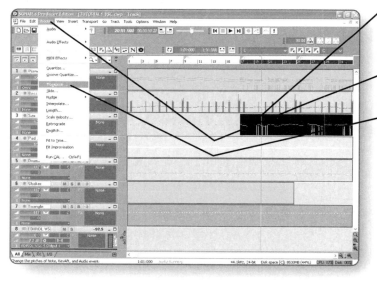

1. **Click** on a **MIDI clip** or **Ctrl+click** on **multiple MIDI clips**. The clip(s) will be selected.

2. **Click** on **Process**. The Process menu will open.

3. **Click** on **Transpose**. The Transpose dialog box will appear.

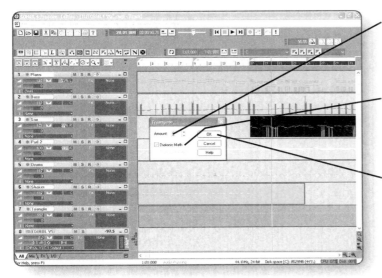

4. Type a **positive** or **negative number** in the **Amount field**. This is the number of semitones SONAR will transpose the clip(s).

5. Optionally, **click** in the **Diatonic Math check box**. A ✔ will appear to indicate that diatonic transposition is enabled.

6. **Click** on **OK**. The dialog box will close, and the clip(s) will be transposed accordingly.

TRANSPOSITION TIP

If you want something to sound as though it's in a completely different key, use chromatic transposition. Diatonic transposition is great for generating parallel harmony parts within the original key. Try cloning a melodic MIDI track and transposing the clone diatonically up or down by three (a diatonic third).

Reversing MIDI Clips

Reversing MIDI clips achieves a different effect than reversing audio clips. Instead of the unnatural backward-masking sound you get with reversed audio, reversed MIDI data just plays the notes in reverse order. The notes sound like normal notes because SONAR just turns the whole clip around, and then turns all Note Ons into Note Offs and vice versa. It can be a great tool for generating new ideas and jarring a creative block loose.

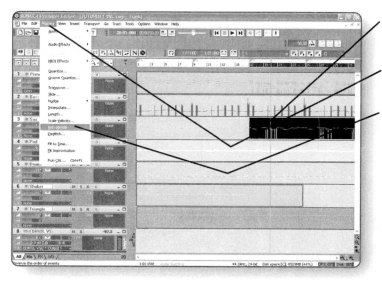

1. Select a **MIDI clip**. The clip will be highlighted.

2. Click on **Process**. The Process menu will open.

3. Click on **Retrograde**. The clip will be reversed.

ONE BY ONE

It's usually best to reverse MIDI clips one at a time. When you reverse multiple clips, the clip outlines don't move with the data, so you end up having to re-trim the clips.

Changing the Length of MIDI Notes

The duration of a MIDI note is simply the time elapsed between its Note On and its Note Off messages. That simple fact makes it easy to change the length of a note, a series of notes, or an entire clip.

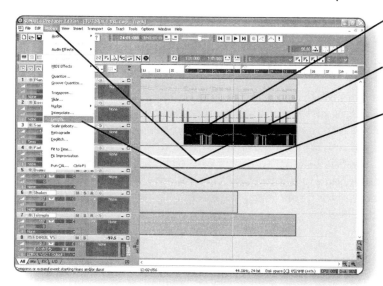

1. Select a **MIDI clip**. The clip will be highlighted.

2. Click on **Process**. The Process menu will open.

3. Click on **Length**. The Length dialog box will appear.

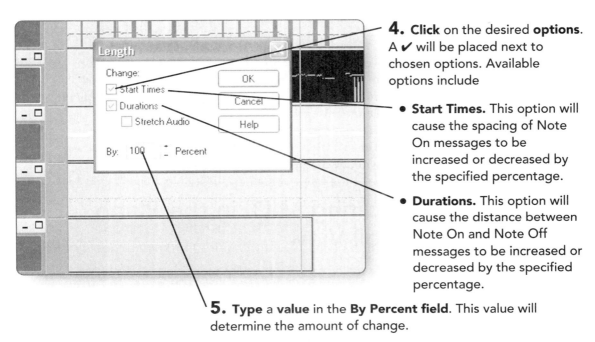

4. **Click** on the desired **options**. A ✔ will be placed next to chosen options. Available options include

- **Start Times.** This option will cause the spacing of Note On messages to be increased or decreased by the specified percentage.

- **Durations.** This option will cause the distance between Note On and Note Off messages to be increased or decreased by the specified percentage.

5. **Type** a **value** in the **By Percent field**. This value will determine the amount of change.

6. **Click** on **OK**. The dialog box will close, and the length of the selected MIDI data (and the clip, if necessary) will be changed by the specified percentage.

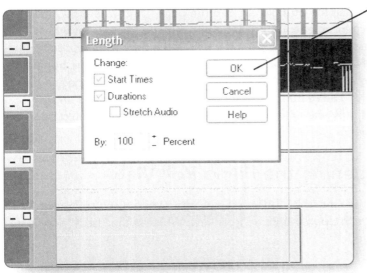

> ## THE FINER POINTS OF ARTICULATION
> To change the length of notes—in musical terms, to make the notes more *staccato* or *legato*—without changing the overall timing of the clip, choose only the Durations option. To speed up or slow down the clip without changing note length, choose only the Start Times option. To make the whole clip faster or slower without changing its internal feel, choose both.

Editing MIDI in the Piano Roll View

Clips are a convenient way of organizing blocks of MIDI events, but if you need to edit MIDI right down to the note level, the Piano Roll view is your tool of choice. One look and you'll know why it's called Piano Roll—it looks and acts just like the big paper rolls that made old-fashioned player pianos work. Each note had a rectangle cut into the paper, and when the piano's mechanism encountered the beginning of a cutout it would press a key, then release the key at the end of the cutout. SONAR's Piano Roll shows Note On messages as the beginning of a rectangular "cutout" and Note Off messages as the end of the rectangle. A grid shows you where notes are vertically and where beats are horizontally. What could be easier?

Opening the Piano Roll View

As with most SONAR functions, there are several different ways to open the Piano Roll view. Which is the "best" way is up to you.

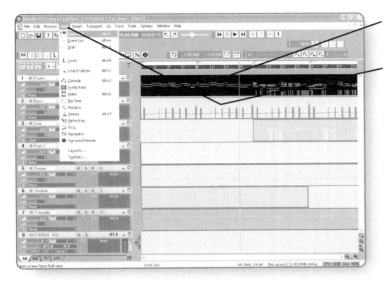

1. Click on a **MIDI clip**. The clip will be highlighted.

2a. Click on **View**. The View menu will open.

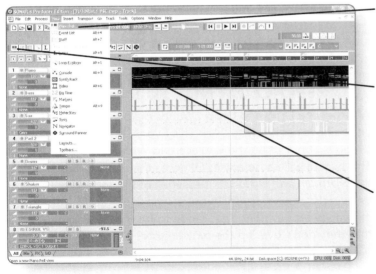

2b. Click on **Piano Roll**. The Piano Roll view will appear.

OR

2c. Click on the **Piano Roll view icon** on the Track view toolbar. The Piano Roll view will open.

OR

2d. Double-click on a **MIDI clip**. The Piano Roll view will open.

Moving and Copying Notes

The main window of the Piano Roll view is the Notes pane. Here you can move or copy any note earlier or later, and you can also change its pitch by dragging it up or down.

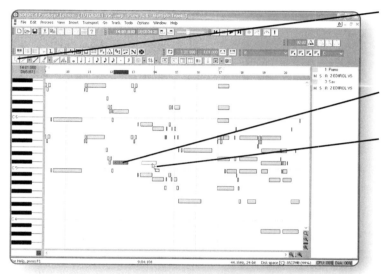

1. If necessary, **click** on the **Select tool button**. The mouse pointer will appear as a standard arrow.

2. **Click** on a **note**. The note will be highlighted.

3. **Drag** the **note** to the left or right. The note will move to the new location.

TO REPLACE OR NOT TO REPLACE?

Whether the Drag and Drop Options dialog box appears or you have set it not to "Ask This Every Time," be cautious about using the Replace Old With New option. This option will cause any MIDI notes that start between the Note On and Note Off messages of the moved note to be deleted and any MIDI notes whose Note Off messages occur during that range to be shortened so that they don't overlap the moved note.

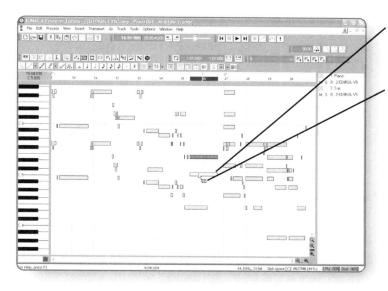

4. Drag a **note** up or down. The note will be assigned to a different pitch.

5. Ctrl+drag a **note**. The note will be copied, not moved.

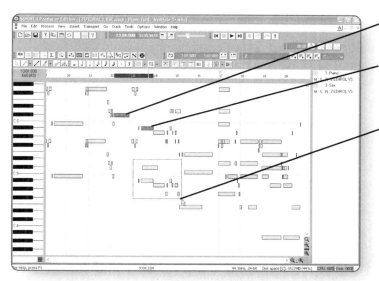

6. Click on a **note**. The note will be selected.

7. Ctrl+click on **another note**. The note will be added to the selection.

8. Ctrl+drag around **other notes**. The notes will be added to the selection.

LASSO THAT NOTE

When you lasso notes in this way, be sure to completely enclose all notes you want to include in the selection. Only notes that fall entirely within the lasso's outline will be selected.

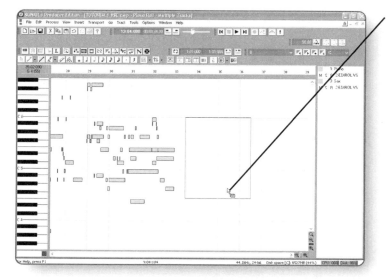

9. **Ctrl+drag any** of the **selected notes**. The entire selection will be copied.

THE SAME, ONLY DIFFERENT

Selecting only some of the notes in a phrase and copying them is a great way to build variety in your compositions. This is because our ears like the familiarity of repetition, but too precise a repetition causes us to lose interest.

Changing a Note's Length

Sometimes you've got a performance that's almost perfect—if only you'd held that note just a tiny bit longer! SONAR lets you tweak the length of individual notes in the Piano Roll view, naturally.

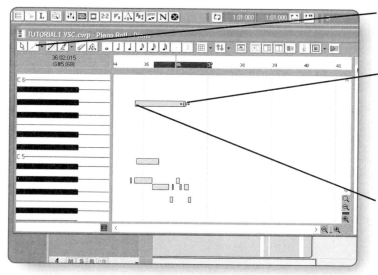

1. **Click** on the **Draw tool button**. The mouse pointer will appear as a pencil.

2. **Click** on the **end** of a **note**. The mouse pointer will appear as a two-headed horizontal arrow.

3. **Drag** the **end** of the **note** earlier or later. The note will grow longer or shorter.

4. **Drag** the **beginning** of a **note** earlier or later. The note's start time will change accordingly.

Adding and Deleting Notes

It will come as no surprise that within SONAR's graphical Piano Roll view, the tools to add and delete notes are drawing tools: a pencil and an eraser.

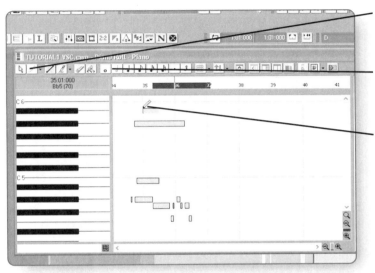

1. Click on the **Draw tool button**. The mouse pointer will appear as a pencil.

2. Click on a **note-duration button**. The button will be highlighted.

3. Click within the **grid**. A note of the specified duration will be created at that point.

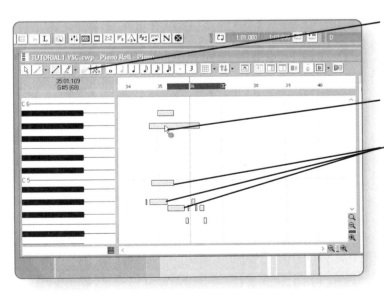

4. Click on the **Erase tool button**. The mouse pointer will appear as an arrow with a slashed circle attached.

5. Click on a **note**. The note will be deleted.

6. Drag across **multiple notes**. Each note will be deleted as the mouse pointer touches it.

Painting MIDI Note Patterns

Okay, so the idea of painting music takes the whole graphic-editing thing a bit far, but SONAR has a very cool Pattern Brush tool that can speed the process of building authentic drum tracks. Although the Pattern Brush will work on any MIDI track, it's designed for drum tracks, so to start with, try the following steps on a drum track.

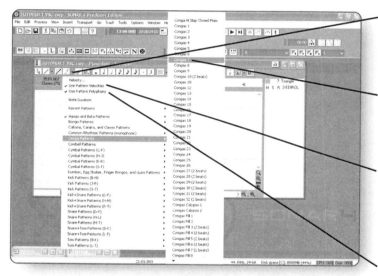

1. **Click** on the **down arrow** at the right of the **Pattern Brush button**. The Pattern Brush menu will open.

2. **Point** to a **pattern category** and then **click** on a **pattern**. A ✔ will appear next to the pattern, and the menu will close.

3. **Open** the **Pattern Brush menu** again and **click** on **Use Pattern Velocities**. A ✔ will appear next to that option, and the menu will close.

4. **Open** the **Pattern Brush menu** again and **click** on **Use Pattern Polyphony**. A ✔ will appear next to that option, and the menu will close.

BETTER BRUSHING

These two options tell SONAR to use the built-in pattern of accents and to use different notes when applicable, such as low and high agogo. You can overrule the built-in characteristics by choosing the Velocity and Note Duration options, which allow you to specify the default values.

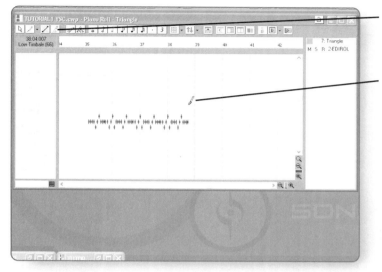

5. **Click** on the **Pattern Brush button**. The mouse pointer will appear as a paint brush.

6. **Drag** from **left** to **right** across the **grid**. The chosen pattern will appear in the grid.

PATTERN POLYPHONY

Because you've told SONAR to use the pattern polyphony, you don't even need to drag anywhere near the pattern's assigned notes! SONAR puts the notes in the right place no matter where you drag vertically.

Using the Controller Pane

MIDI needs more than Note On and Note Off messages to achieve expressive results, so the language includes a number of other parameters that let you control how hard a note is struck, how loud the synthesizer should play, and so forth. Most of these parameters are called *controllers*, and SONAR has a special window at the bottom of the Piano Roll view for editing them.

Showing and Hiding the Controller Pane

The Controller pane is not the sort of thing you'll work in all the time, so by default it's hidden. You can pop it up any time you need it, and then tuck it away to maximize the space to work in the Piano Roll view's Notes pane.

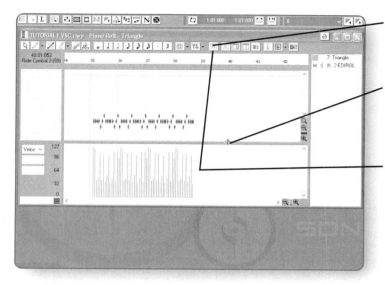

1. Click on the **Show/Hide Controller Pane button**. The Controller pane will appear.

2. Drag on the **upper border** of the **Controller pane**. The Controller pane will increase or decrease in height.

3. Click on the **Show/Hide Controller Pane button**. The Controller pane will disappear.

CONTROLLER PANE

Notice that no matter how tall you make the Controller pane, its vertical scale stays constant. There is no way to increase or decrease its vertical resolution.

Choosing Controllers

There are many different controllers from which to choose, so SONAR divides them up into categories for you. The most common ones are a single click away, while the more obscure ones take a couple more steps.

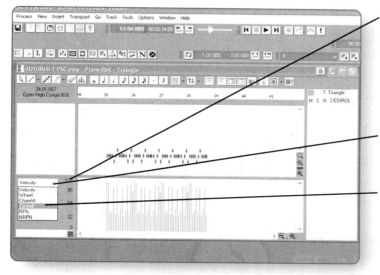

1. **Drag** the **vertical border** at the right of the **Controller pane** to the right. The controller selection area will expand so that you can actually read the text in the various fields.

2. **Click** on the **down arrow** at the right of the **top field**. The drop-down list will open.

3. **Click** on the desired **parameter** (in this example, Control). The list will close and display the name of the chosen parameter.

WHAT CONTROLLER NUMBER IS VELOCITY?

Readers who are already familiar with MIDI may observe that Velocity doesn't belong in this list because it's not a controller. For that matter, neither are pitch wheel (Wheel) and aftertouch (ChanAft). Don't worry— the folks at Cakewalk know this! It's just that this window is the perfect place to edit these parameters, and it just wouldn't sound right to call it the Controllers, Velocity, Pitch Wheel, and Aftertouch pane, would it?

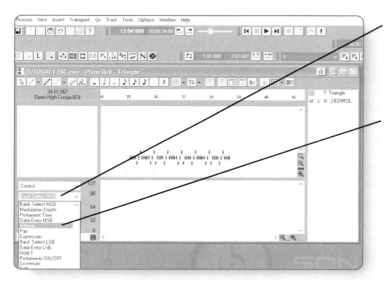

4. If you chose Control as your parameter, **click** on the **down arrow** at the right of the **middle field**. The drop-down list will open.

5. Click on the desired **controller**. The list will close and display the name of the chosen controller.

Editing Controllers

You can edit controllers using the same graphic tools you used to edit notes in the Notes pane.

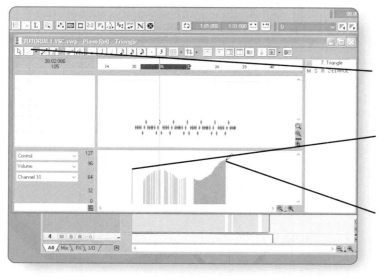

1. Choose a **controller** from the drop-down lists. The list will close and display your choice.

2. Click on the **Draw tool button**. The mouse pointer will appear as a pencil.

3. Click in the **Controller pane**. A vertical line will appear at the time and height at which you clicked.

4. Drag the **Draw tool** in the Controller pane. A solid shape will appear, reflecting the series of values you have drawn.

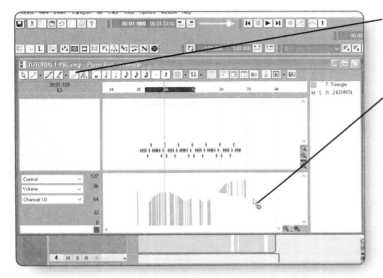

5. Click on the **Erase tool button**. The mouse pointer will appear as an arrow with a slashed circle attached.

6. Drag the **Erase tool** in the Controller pane. Any controller values in its path will be deleted.

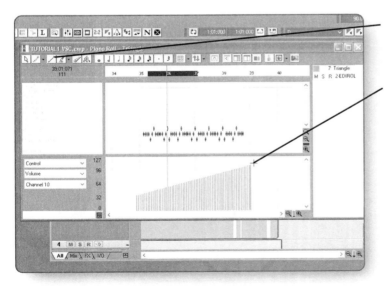

7. Click on the **Line tool button**. The mouse pointer will appear as a plus sign (+).

8. Drag the **Line tool** in the Controller pane. A linear series of values will appear.

13

Recording MIDI Tracks

Now that you've got a solid grasp of how SONAR displays and manages MIDI data, it's time to generate some of your own Note Ons and Note Offs. The process is quite similar to the process of recording audio, so most of what you learned in Chapter 8, "Recording Your Own Audio," will apply here as well. As you've seen, though, MIDI is more flexible than audio, so you have some additional options that can help you achieve great performances. Of course, you've still got the Undo option for those occasional less-than-great performances. In this chapter, you will learn how to:

- Choose your MIDI inputs and outputs
- Configure the metronome
- Set up a MIDI track for recording
- Record, punch-record, and loop-record MIDI

Choosing MIDI Inputs and Outputs

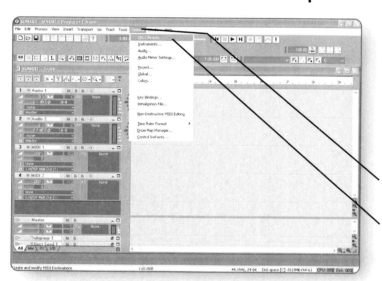

So far, you've dealt only with internal MIDI connections by using the Cakewalk TTS-1. To record MIDI you'll need at least one MIDI Input port enabled, and if you're going to trigger hardware synthesizers you'll need at least one MIDI Output port enabled.

1. **Click** on **Options**. The Options menu will open.

2. **Click** on **MIDI Devices**. The MIDI Devices dialog box will appear.

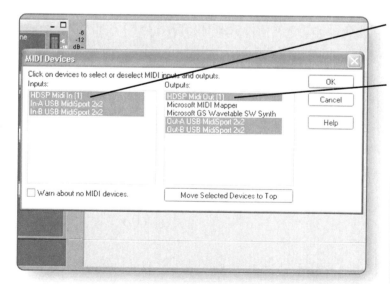

3. **Click** on one or more **MIDI inputs**. The inputs will be highlighted.

4. **Click** on one or more **MIDI outputs**. The outputs will be highlighted.

HIGHLIGHTING MIDI I/O

It's not necessary to Ctrl+click or Shift+click to select multiple MIDI inputs or outputs in this window. They stay highlighted until you click on them again to deselect them.

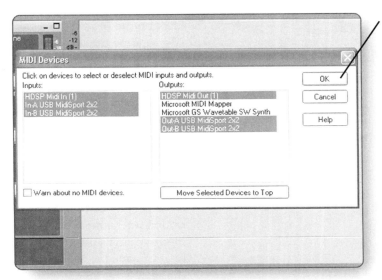

5. Click on **OK**. The dialog box will close, and the selected MIDI ports will be enabled.

Configuring the Metronome

If you want to use SONAR's Time Ruler and grid to edit your performance, you need to know where SONAR's beats are. That's what the metronome does for you. Some musicians refer to the metronome as a *click track*, a series of audible clicks that help them keep track of the tempo. The metronome will follow any tempo changes you have in your session, too.

1. Click on **Options**. The Options menu will open.

2. Click on **Project**. The Project Options dialog box will appear.

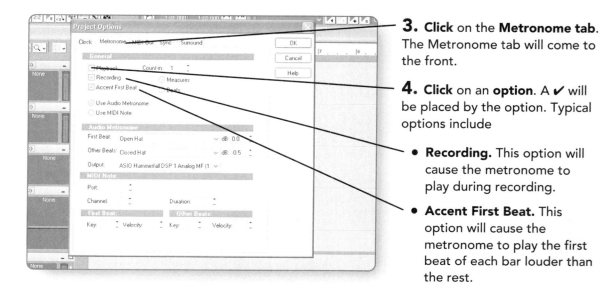

3. Click on the **Metronome tab**. The Metronome tab will come to the front.

4. Click on an **option**. A ✔ will be placed by the option. Typical options include

- **Recording.** This option will cause the metronome to play during recording.

- **Accent First Beat.** This option will cause the metronome to play the first beat of each bar louder than the rest.

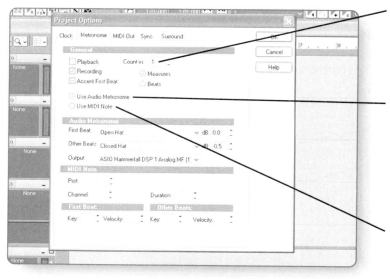

- **Count-in.** This option tells the metronome to click a specified number of measures or beats prior to the Now time.

- **Use Audio Metronome.** New to SONAR 4, this option utilizes a dedicated software metronome whose parameters are specified in the Audio Metronome section.

- **Use MIDI Note.** This option causes the metronome to play the click through a hardware synthesizer connected to the port and channel specified in the MIDI Note section.

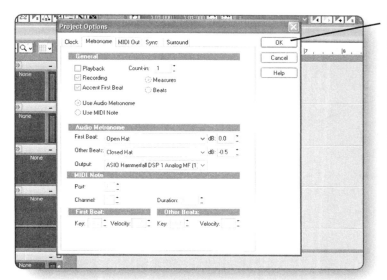

5. Click on **OK**. The dialog box will close, and the metronome will be set up.

PRECIOUS POLYPHONY

Using the audio metronome saves you from wasting polyphony on a hardware synthesizer.

Setting Up for Recording

There are just a few things you need to do to be sure you're ready to make your first MIDI recording. After you do this a couple of times, it will become second nature.

Assigning the MIDI Track Input and Output

By default, MIDI tracks are set up with no input so you don't get any surprises. Just as you assigned audio inputs, MIDI, and audio outputs, you simply have to choose your source from a menu.

YOUR CHOICE

You can use either the TTS-1 or a hardware synthesizer for the following steps. If you want to use the TTS-1, open the Synth Rack and start the TTS-1 as you did in Chapter 11, "Using the Cakewalk TTS-1," before continuing.

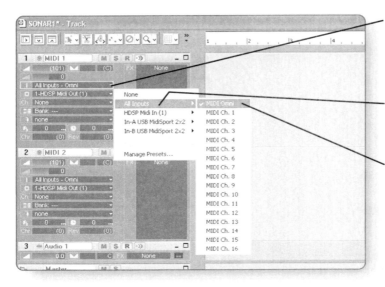

1. **Click** on the **down arrow** at the right of a MIDI track's **Input** field. The MIDI Input menu will open.

2. **Point** to **All Inputs** or to a specific **MIDI input**. The Channels submenu will open.

3. **Click** on **MIDI Omni** or on a specific **MIDI channel**. The menu will close, and the track's Input field will display your choice.

ALL INPUTS OR NOT?

Most of the time, you can choose All Inputs, MIDI Omni for all of your MIDI tracks. This setting lets any incoming MIDI data from any connected MIDI device be recognized by the track. If you want to take advantage of SONAR 4's multi-channel MIDI input recording (we'll get to that in Chapter 15, "Mastering MIDI's Ins and Outs"), you'll want to set each track's input to a specific MIDI input and channel.

4. **Click** on the **down arrow** at the right of the **MIDI Output field**. The MIDI Output menu will open.

5. **Click** on **Cakewalk TTS-1** or the physical MIDI output to which your hardware synthesizer is connected. The menu will close, and the MIDI Output field will reflect your choice.

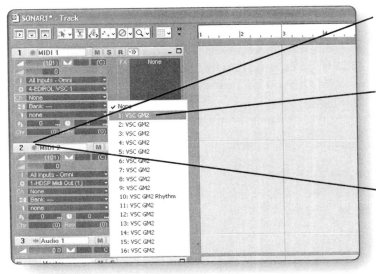

6. Click on the **down arrow** at the right of the **MIDI Channel field**. The MIDI Channel menu will open.

7. Click on the **MIDI channel** you want this track to trigger. The menu will close, and the MIDI Channel field will reflect your choice.

8. Choose the **bank** and **patch** you want this track to use, following the procedure used in Chapter 11. The Bank and Patch fields will reflect your choices.

BY THE NUMBERS

If you are using a hardware synthesizer, your Bank and Patch menus will show only numbers, not names. Chapter 15 will cover using SONAR's instrument definitions to fix this. For now, you can either set Bank and Patch to None and set them from your synthesizer's front panel, or check your synthesizer's documentation for the bank and patch numbers to use.

Getting Ready to Record

Your track is now wired correctly to accept MIDI coming in from your keyboard and pass it on to a hardware or software synthesizer. Now all you need to do is tell the track to capture that data and spit it back out, and you're ready to record.

LOCAL CONTROL

If your controller keyboard has its own synthesizer sounds, you should turn its Local setting to Off. If Local is set to On, you will hear every note you play being doubled.

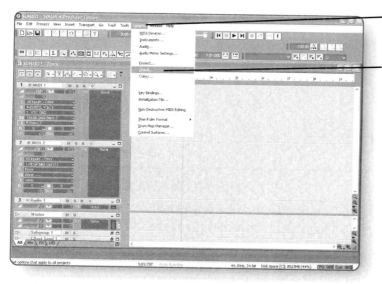

1. Click on **Options**. The Options menu will open.

2. Click on **Global**. The Global Options dialog box will appear.

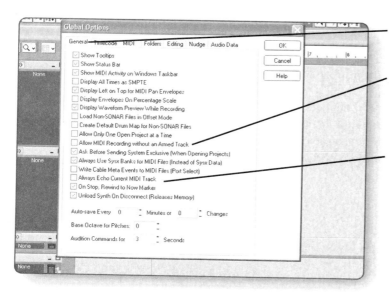

3. Click on the **General tab**. The tab will come to the front.

4. Deselect the **Allow MIDI Recording without an Armed Track option**. The option's check box will be empty.

5. Deselect the **Always Echo Current MIDI Track option**. The option's check box will be empty.

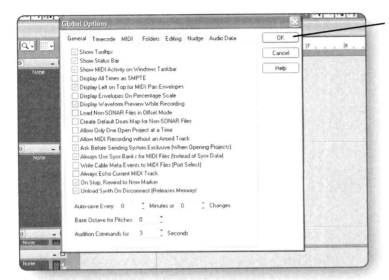

6. Click on **OK**. The dialog box will close.

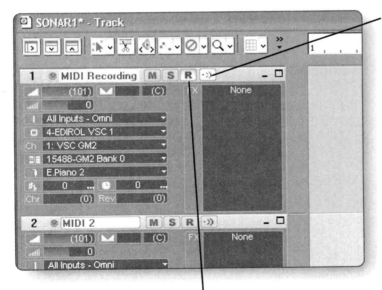

7. Click on the **Input Echo button** of a MIDI track. The button will be highlighted, and any MIDI notes you play on your keyboard will be played through the track's MIDI output.

LATENCY

If you hear a time lag between pressing a key and hearing the TTS-1, refer to Appendix A, "Setup and Troubleshooting," for suggestions on reducing latency.

8. Click on the **Record Arm button** of the MIDI track. The button will turn red.

Recording Your First MIDI Part

You've got your MIDI inputs and outputs enabled and assigned, you've got the metronome set to give you a steady click, and you've got your MIDI track set up both to record and to echo your performance. Now pick a tempo (and a key if you want) and go for it!

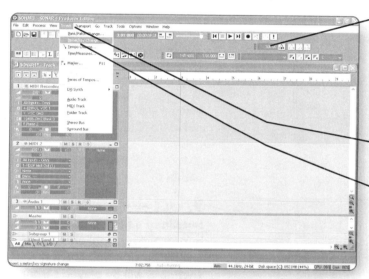

1. **Click** on the **Tempo** display. The current tempo will be highlighted.

2. **Type** in a **tempo** and **press Enter**. The new tempo will be displayed.

3. Optionally, **click** on **Insert**. The Insert menu will open.

4. **Click** on **Meter/Key Change**. The Meter/Key Signature dialog box will appear.

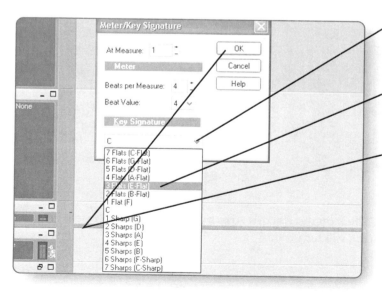

5. **Click** on the **down arrow** at the **Key Signature drop-down list box**. The list will open.

6. **Click** on a **key signature**. The list will close, and your choice will be displayed.

7. **Click** on **OK**. The dialog box will close, and the new key signature will be enabled.

KEY SIGNATURE

The key signature has no effect on recording or on most editing functions, but it defines the way notes are displayed in the Staff view and how diatonic transposition is calculated.

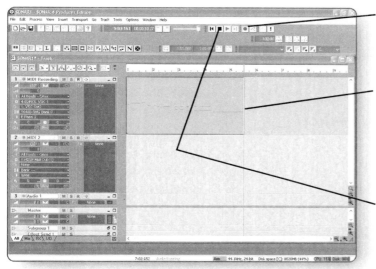

8. Click on **Record**. The metronome will click the count-off you specified, and then recording will begin.

9. Play on your **MIDI instrument**. SONAR will draw a new MIDI clip starting wherever you played your first note, and each new note will be displayed within that clip.

10. Click on **Stop**. Recording will cease, and the new MIDI clip will appear in the track, beginning at the first note you played and ending at the release of the last note you played.

11. In the unlikely event that your performance was less than perfect, **press Ctrl+Z** to undo the recording. The MIDI clip will be deleted.

Punch-Recording MIDI

Just as you were able to punch in and replace portions of audio recordings, you can do the same with MIDI recordings. Once you get the hang of this technique, you'll find it's far more efficient than re-recording an entire section.

Using Auto Punch

Auto Punch lets you specify exactly where you want to punch in and out, right down to the split second. This is more convenient and far more accurate than punching in and out manually, but it only lets you do one punch selection at a time.

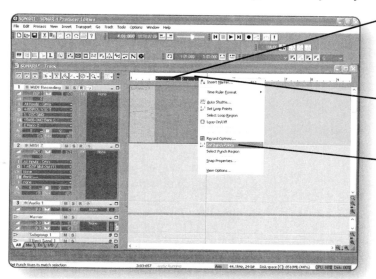

1. Drag in the **Time Ruler** from the beginning to the end of the phrase you want to replace. The selection will be highlighted.

2. Right-click on the **Time Ruler**. The context menu will appear.

3. Click on **Set Punch Points**. The context menu will close, and red punch markers will bracket your time selection.

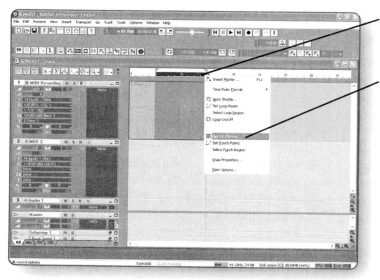

4. Right-click on the **Time Ruler**. The context menu will appear.

5. Click on **Record Options**. The Record Options dialog box will appear.

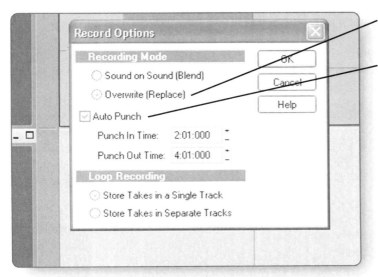

6. Click on **Overwrite (Replace)**.

7. Click on **Auto Punch**.

8. Optionally, **change** or **fine-tune** the **Punch In** and **Punch Out Time settings**.

REPLACE OR BLEND?

By choosing Sound on Sound (Blend), you would cause SONAR to combine your new performance with the old. You could use that technique to add a harmony part.

9. **Click** in the **Time Ruler** to set the Now time to some convenient point prior to the punch region. The Now time will reflect the point you chose.

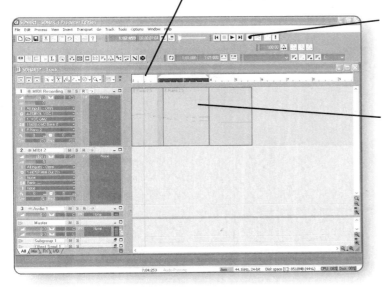

10. **Click** on the **Record button**. Playback will begin at the Now time, and recording will begin at the punch-in marker and end at the punch-out marker.

11. **Play** the **replacement phrase**. The new MIDI notes will appear as you play.

12. **Click** on the **Stop button**. Playback will stop, and a new clip will appear between the punch markers.

Manual Punch

If you need to punch in multiple times in a single pass, you can punch in and out manually. This is not quite as precise as Auto Punch, but it's the only way to do multiple punches.

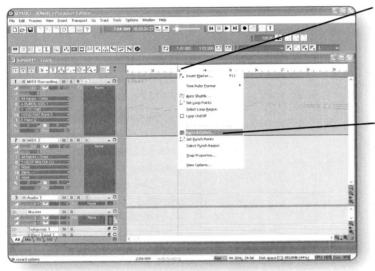

1. With a MIDI track prepared for recording as described in the section "Setting Up for Recording," **right-click** in the **Time Ruler**. The context menu will open.

2. Click on **Record Options**. The Record Options dialog box will appear.

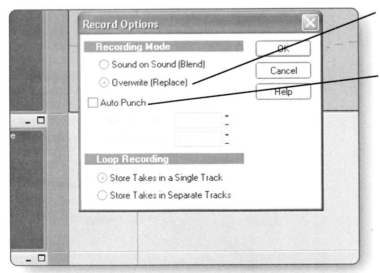

3. Click on **Overwrite (Replace)**. The option will be selected.

4. If necessary, **click** on **Auto Punch** to deselect that option.

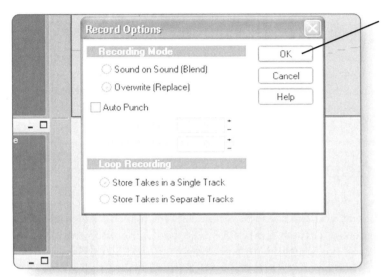

5. Click on **OK**. The dialog box will close.

6. Set the **Now time** to a few bars before the first phrase you want to replace.

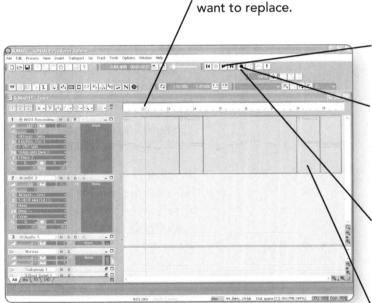

7. Click on **Play**. Playback will begin, and you will hear the existing MIDI part.

8. At the point in the phrase you wish to replace, **click** on **Record** and play the new part. The track will begin to record your MIDI input, replacing the existing MIDI data.

9. At the end of the replacement part, **click** on **Record**. Playback will continue, and you will once again hear the existing MIDI part.

10. At the point of each phrase you wish to replace, **punch in** by **clicking Record**, then **punch out** by **clicking Record** again. Each time you punch in and out, a new MIDI clip will appear at that point, replacing the previous MIDI performance.

> ## PLAY AND RECORD SHORTCUTS
>
> You may find it much easier to press the R key on your keyboard instead of clicking Record each time you punch in and out. For that matter, you will probably find it easier to use the spacebar instead of clicking Play and Stop (it does both).

Loop Recording

Loop recording MIDI is a time-honored tradition—at least, as close as you can come to time-honored in such a new field. In particular, virtually every R&B beat you've heard in the last decade has started with a producer laying down a kick drum, and then layering first a snare and then a hi-hat as the kick track looped. This is slightly different from the way we loop-recorded audio in Chapter 8, "Recording Your Own Audio." Note that this is just a convention, and you can use either type of loop record with MIDI or audio.

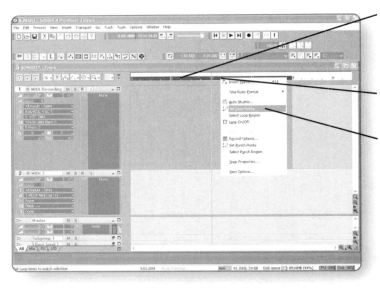

1. **Drag** in the **Time Ruler** from the start of the loop to the end of the loop. The selection will be highlighted.

2. **Right-click** in the **Time Ruler**. The context menu will appear.

3. **Click** on **Set Loop Points**. The selection will be bracketed by yellow loop markers, and the Loop On/Off button will be turned on.

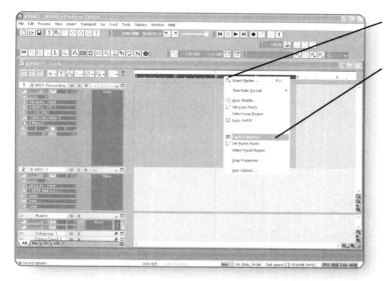

4. Right-click in the **Time Ruler**. The context menu will open.

5. Click on **Record Options**. The Record Options dialog box will appear.

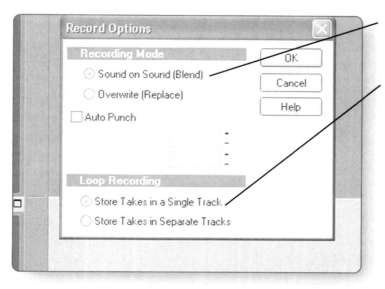

6. Click on **Sound on Sound (Blend)**. The option will be highlighted.

7. Click on **Store Takes in a Single Track**. The option will be highlighted.

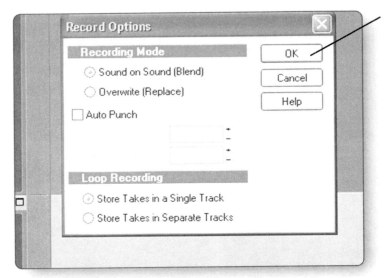

8. Click on **OK**. The dialog box will close.

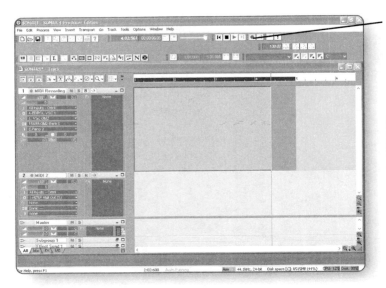

9. Click the **Record button** and play the first part. Recording will begin, looping from the end back to the beginning until you stop it.

TAKE YOUR TIME

When the loop starts over, you will hear whatever you played on the first pass. You can either start the second part immediately, or you can listen to the first part until inspiration strikes. SONAR will continue to loop, waiting for your next note, until you're ready.

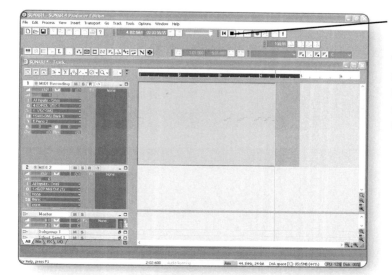

10. **Click** the **Stop button**. Recording will stop, and the various takes will appear side by side in the track, which has automatically been made into a multi-lane track (as discussed in Chapter 9, "Editing Audio").

MERGING TAKES

If you're happy with the way the part turned out, you can merge the different layers into a single clip by dragging around them to select them all and choosing Bounce to Clip(s) from the Edit menu. This will make it easier to copy, paste, trim, and otherwise edit and manipulate the part.

14

Cleaning Up Your MIDI Act

One of the things that makes MIDI and computers such a good match is that they're both mathematical in nature. MIDI expresses every aspect of a performance as a number—note numbers, channel numbers, patch numbers—and a computer is fundamentally an overgrown calculator. This makes manipulating, fixing, and modifying MIDI an absolute cakewalk for a computer (pun intended). In this chapter, you will learn some of these techniques, including how to:

- Fix timings with Quantize
- Improve timings with Groove Quantize
- Use logical processes to modify MIDI data
- Use track parameters to alter a performance

Fixing Timing with Quantize

Because SONAR knows the tempo, generates the metronome, and records the timing of every note you record, it can easily compare what you played with its own timing grid and, at your request, fix the timing. This is called *quantization*, and it's not only a convenient tool for correcting a performance but also a major stylistic component of modern dance music. Strictly quantized drum beats are fundamental for generating that driving dance floor groove. Here's how to make it happen.

1. Click on a **MIDI clip**. The clip will be selected.

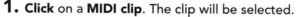

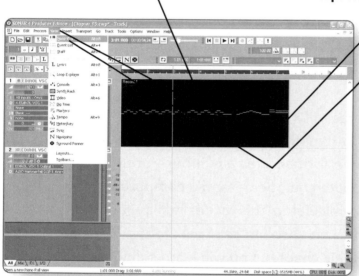

2. Click on **View**. The View menu will open.

3. Click on **Piano Roll**. The Piano Roll view will appear.

JUST FOR APPEARANCES

You don't have to be in Piano Roll view to quantize, but it will help you see the notes snap to the grid as you quantize them.

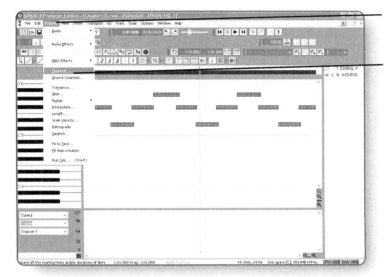

4. Click on **Process**. The Process menu will open.

5. Click on **Quantize**. The Quantize dialog box will appear.

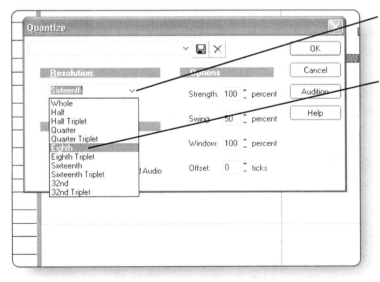

6. Click on the **down arrow** at the right of the **Resolution drop-down list box**. The list will open.

7. Click on the desired **resolution**. The list will close and display your choice.

LOWEST COMMON DENOMINATOR

For best results, always choose the smallest rhythmic subdivision of the passage you're quantizing.

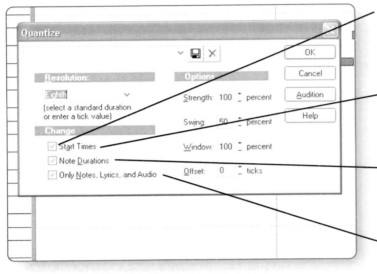

8. Click on the desired **Change parameters**. A ✔ will appear next to chosen parameters, which include

- **Start Times.** This option will cause the beginnings of notes (the Note On messages) to be quantized.

- **Note Durations.** This option will cause the ends of notes (the Note Off messages) to be quantized.

- **Only Notes, Lyrics, and Audio.** This option will exempt all other MIDI data from being quantized.

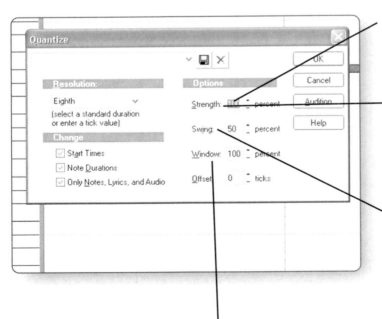

9. Click in an **Options number box** and **type** a **new value**. The number box will display your new value. Options include

- **Strength.** This option controls how perfectly timed the results will be. A value of 100 snaps change-enabled parameters exactly to the grid.

- **Swing.** This option allows the eighth or sixteenth subdivisions to be asymmetrical, as in swing or shuffle rhythms. A value of 50 is "even eighths," and a value of 66 is "textbook swing."

- **Window.** Values of less than 100 allow notes that are way off the grid to go unchanged.

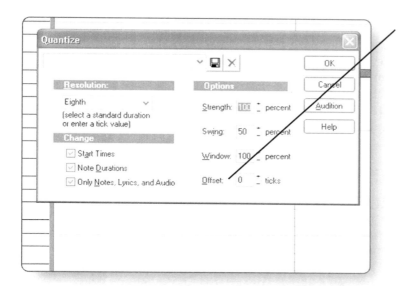

- **Offset.** This option shifts the quantization grid slightly earlier or later. Positive values move the grid later, negative values earlier.

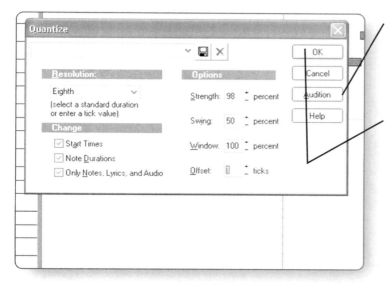

10. Optionally, **click** on **Audition** to preview the results. A few seconds of the selected clip will be quantized and played for your approval.

11. Click on **OK**. The dialog box will close, and the selected MIDI data will be quantized.

CRITICAL QUANTIZATION

To tighten up the timing of a performance without making it sound too mechanical, quantize start times but not durations, and use a Strength value of less than 100. To eliminate gaps between notes—to make them more *legato*—quantize both start times and durations.

Better Timing with Groove Quantize

Being perfect isn't all it's cracked up to be—trust me on this! There are subtle rhythmic variations that skilled musicians do that transcend mechanical accuracy. Performers *push* a beat to unsettle you and *pull* a beat to relieve the tension, and Quantize doesn't understand that stuff. Fortunately, SONAR also provides Groove Quantize, a more intelligent and flexible way of defining a quantization grid that "breathes" like a human.

1. **Click** on a **MIDI clip**. The clip will be highlighted.

2. **Click** on **Process**. The Process menu will open.

3. **Click** on **Groove Quantize**. The Groove Quantize dialog box will appear.

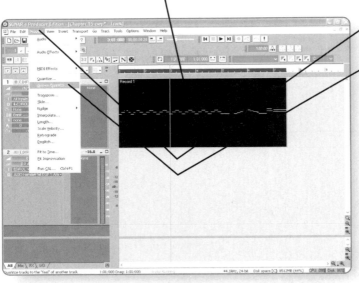

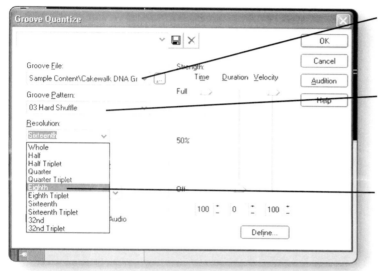

4. **Choose** a **groove file** from the **Groove File drop-down list**. This file contains the groove patterns.

5. **Choose** a **groove pattern** from the **Groove Pattern drop-down list**. Each pattern represents a different style or variation.

6. **Choose** a **resolution** from the **Resolution drop-down box**. As with the regular Quantize feature, your choice should reflect the smallest rhythmic subdivision of the selected clip.

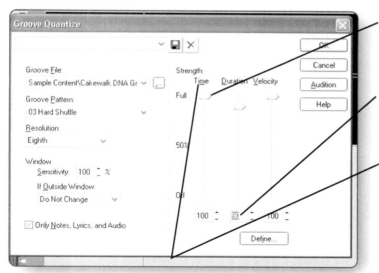

7a. **Drag** the **Strength sliders** to appropriate values.

OR

7b. **Type** appropriate **values** in the **Strength number boxes**. The Strength options include

- **Time.** This affects how closely Note On messages will be moved to the Groove Quantize grid. A value of 100% moves all Note On messages precisely to the grid.

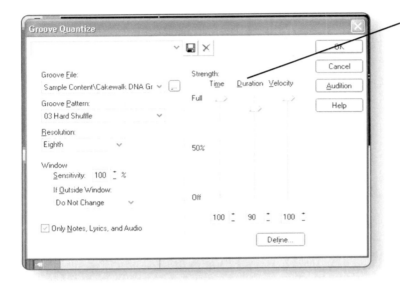

- **Duration.** This affects how closely Note Off messages will be moved to the Groove Quantize grid.

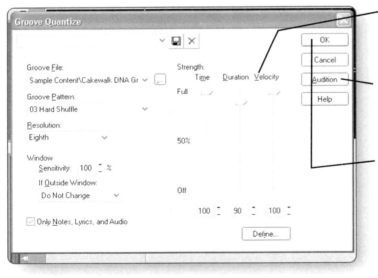

- **Velocity.** This affects how closely note velocities will be changed to the Groove Quantize velocity template.

8. Optionally, **click** on **Audition** to preview the results. SONAR will play a short part of the clip groove quantized.

9. Click on **OK**. The clip will be quantized to the groove pattern.

KEEPING THE GROOVE

Groove patterns have a separate grid for Note Off messages, so although it was more natural not to quantize durations with the standard Quantize feature, you should at least audition Groove Quantize with Duration Strength set at or near 100 percent, and then adjust to taste. Note also that Groove Quantize takes velocity into consideration, comparing the clip to its own pattern of accents.

Using Logical MIDI Processes

A *logical process* is any function that performs some kind of numerical evaluation of MIDI data, and then makes changes according to what it finds. Quantize and Groove Quantize are two special types of logical processes, but SONAR has several more. Let's explore a few of them.

Scaling Velocity

MIDI *velocity* is a measure of how hard you struck the controller keyboard when you first played the note. Most synthesizers map velocity to the intensity of a note, and some map it also to timbre, making notes brighter at higher velocities. SONAR lets you scale the velocities of a selection from low to high, creating a *crescendo*, or from high to low, creating a *decrescendo*.

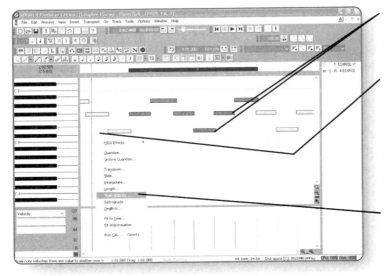

1. **Select** a **MIDI clip** or a **group of notes**. The selection will be highlighted.

2a. **Right-click** in the **Piano Roll view**. The context menu will open.

OR

2b. **Click** on **Process**. The Process menu will open.

3. **Click** on **Scale Velocity**. The Scale Velocity dialog box will appear.

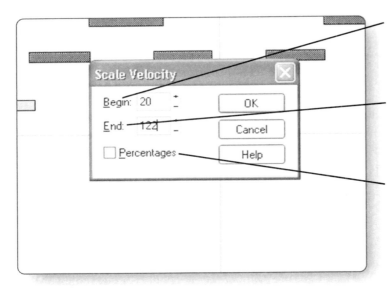

4. **Enter** a **value** in the **Begin number box**. This is the velocity that will be assigned to the first note in the selection.

5. **Enter** a **value** in the **End number box**. This is the velocity that will be assigned to the last note in the selection.

6. Optionally, **click** on the **Percentages check box.** A ✔ will appear in the box, and the velocities of the selected notes will be scaled by a percentage of their current values, rather than adjusted absolutely.

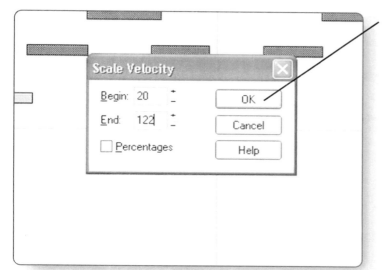

7. Click on **OK**. The dialog box will close, and the velocities of the selected notes will be scaled accordingly.

IT'S ALL RELATIVE

Scaling by percentage retains some of the "feel" of the original perform-ance. In fact, if you like a performance but it's just too soft, try scaling by percentage with Begin and End values of 125 or so. This will increase every velocity in the selection by 25% while maintaining their relative values.

Sliding MIDI Data

SONAR gives you a lot of different ways to move notes and clips around. You can drag them, quantize them, copy and paste them, and you can also *slide* them. Sliding data is just another way of moving it earlier or later. Its advantage is that it's more precise than dragging and less mechanical than quantizing. Like the way you played a phrase, except that you dragged a bit? Slide it earlier. Want to write a new two-measure turnaround before the bridge? Slide the bridge two bars later.

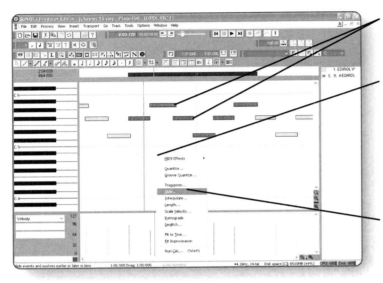

1. Select a **MIDI clip** or a **group of MIDI notes**. The selection will be highlighted.

2a. Right-click in the **Piano Roll view**. The context menu will open.

OR

2b. Click on **Process**. The Process menu will open.

3. Click on **Slide**. The Slide dialog box will appear.

RIGHT-CLICKING POWER

The Piano Roll view's context menu is almost identical to the Process menu, so if you're in the Piano Roll view already, it's easier to right-click if you want to get at these functions.

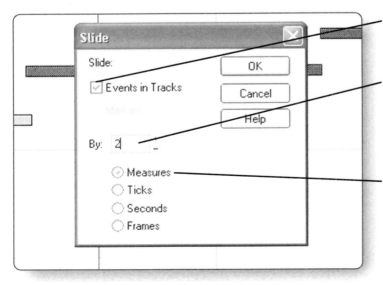

4. If necessary, **click** on **Events in Tracks**. A ✔ will appear next to the option.

5. Enter a **number** in the **By number box**. Positive numbers will move the selection later, and negative numbers will move the selection earlier.

6. Click on the desired **unit of movement**. The chosen unit's option button will be highlighted.

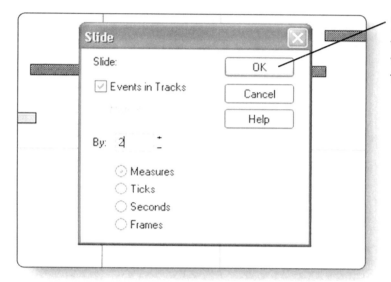

7. Click on **OK**. The dialog box will close, and the selected data will be moved earlier or later by the specified distance.

Deglitching MIDI

Deglitching is SONAR's way of helping you eliminate minor mistakes in your MIDI performances. The Deglitch function lets you identify notes as errors (glitches) if they are too high, too soft, or too short to be taken seriously. Because most minor slip-ups fit this description, Deglitch can be a useful tool in cleaning things up.

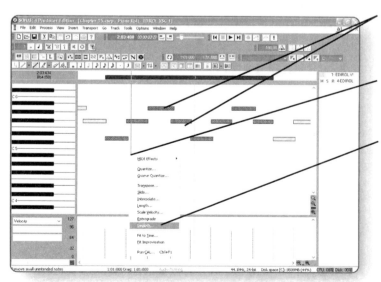

1. Select a **MIDI clip** or **multiple MIDI notes**. The selected data will be highlighted.

2. Right-click in the **Notes pane**. The context menu will open.

3. Click on **Deglitch**. The Deglitch dialog box will appear.

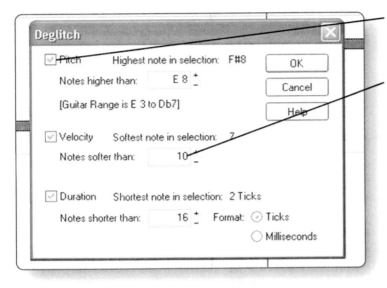

4. Click on the desired **parameters**. A ✔ will appear next to each chosen parameter.

5. Enter appropriate **values** in the **number boxes**. The Deglitch filter will use these values to define what is to be removed.

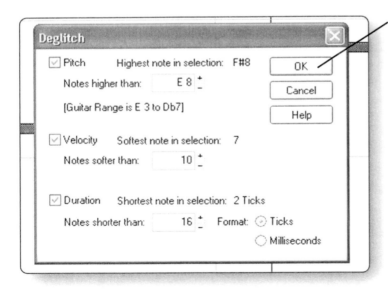

6. Click on **OK**. The dialog box will close, and notes matching the specified description will be deleted.

Using Track Parameters

Each MIDI track in SONAR has a set of MIDI parameters that are used to adjust playback of that track. These parameters don't change the MIDI notes themselves, but simply alter the way they are played. These parameters are found in the All tab of the Track view.

Using Velocity Trim (Vel+)

Velocity Trim adds or subtracts a specified value from the velocity of every note in the track. This preserves the relative velocities of a performance while boosting or cutting the overall intensity. Positive values will increase intensity, and negative values will decrease the track's intensity.

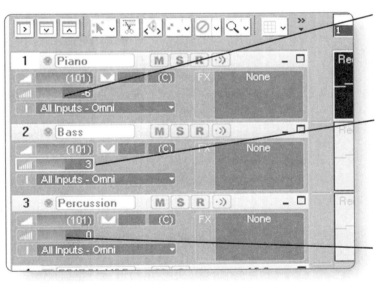

1a. **Drag** the **Velocity Trim slider**. The Velocity Trim value will increase or decrease accordingly.

OR

1b. **Click** on the **Velocity Trim field**. The field will be outlined in gold.

1c. **Press** the **plus (+)** or **minus (−) keys**. The value will increase or decrease accordingly.

2. **Double-click** on the **Velocity Trim field**. The Velocity Trim value will be reset to zero.

Using Time Offset (Time+)

Time Offset adds or subtracts a specified value from the time position of every note in a track. One way you might use this is if you had quantized a synth pad, but its slow attack made it sound late. By "cheating" the track a bit earlier with Time Offset, you could make the pad sound on time. Positive Time+ values will delay a track, and negative values will cause it to play earlier.

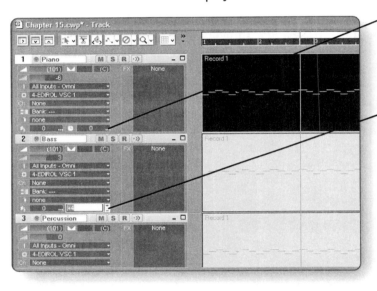

1. Click on the **ellipsis (...)** at the right of the **Time+ field**. The current value will be highlighted, and plus (+) and minus (−) buttons will appear.

2a. Click on the **plus (+)** or **minus (−) buttons**. The Time+ value will be adjusted accordingly.

OR

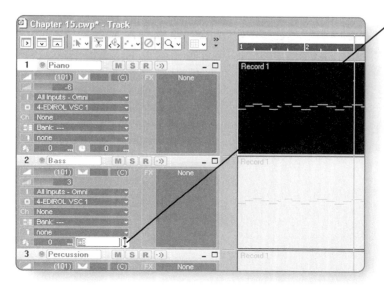

2b. **Point** the mouse pointer at the small **space between the buttons.** The mouse pointer will appear as a double-headed vertical arrow.

2c. **Drag** the mouse pointer **up** or **down.** The Time+ value will be adjusted up or down quickly.

3. **Press Enter** or **Tab.** The Time+ field will return to normal and display the value you entered.

DIFFERENT STROKES

You can use either of these techniques for Key+, and you can use the technique described below for Key+ to adjust Time+. You can also use the plus and minus keys for either, as described previously in the section "Using Velocity Trim (Vel+)." Find the technique that makes you comfortable, and stick with it!

Using Key Offset (Key+)

In a manner similar to Velocity Trim and Time Offset, Key Offset applies a non-destructive adjustment to the pitches of all *notes* in a track. The most common use for this is to drop a bass line down an octave. In fact, if you have a MIDI keyboard with limited range, you can use this adjustment during recording. Every note that you play from your keyboard will be echoed back to the assigned synth an octave lower (or whatever you set it to) than you play it. You never have to play in a difficult key again! Positive values will transpose a track up by semitones, and negative values will transpose it down by semitones. A value of 12, for example, will cause the track to play back one octave higher.

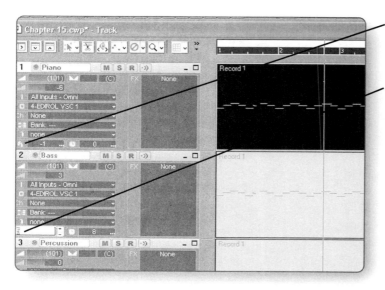

1. **Double-click** on the **Key Offset** field's icon or value. The value will be highlighted.

2. **Type** a new **value** and press **Enter** or **Tab**. The Key+ field will return to normal and display the value you entered.

MENU ITEMS

There's another way to adjust these three parameters. Under Track, Properties, you can open a dialog box for each of them. If you select multiple tracks, and then open the parameter dialog box, your adjustment will be applied to all of the selected tracks.

USING MIDI EFFECTS

For information about using SONAR MIDI effects, including real-time Quantize, real-time Transpose, Cakewalk velocity FX, and the Arpeggiator, in addition to the steps to take to create echoes and delays, see this book's companion Web site.

15

Mastering MIDI's Ins and Outs

MIDI was designed to be a universal language, allowing you to control synthesizers and other devices with a standard set of instructions regardless of brand or model. This universality makes a comprehensive sequencing environment like SONAR powerful enough to control many instruments at once, but it can also make managing your MIDI inputs and outputs seem quite complex. SONAR gives you tools to manage this complexity, and with a little advance work you can set things up so you won't have to stop in the middle of a creative thought to decipher your MIDI setup. In this chapter, you will learn how to:

- Import and use SONAR's instrument definitions
- Record from multiple MIDI instruments simultaneously
- Filter out unwanted MIDI input messages

Using Instrument Definitions

MIDI labels everything with numbers—channel 10, bank 0, patch 117—so it can be adapted to any manufacturer's devices. Unfortunately, this sometimes makes dealing with MIDI a little too much like balancing your checkbook. SONAR's instrument definitions allow you to give meaningful names to the various channels and patches of the hardware synthesizers you have connected to your system.

Assigning Instruments

Instruments are defined at each channel of each MIDI output. Before you can define instruments on a MIDI output, the output must be enabled under Options, MIDI Devices as discussed in Chapter 13, "Recording MIDI Tracks." To assign an instrument definition, follow these steps.

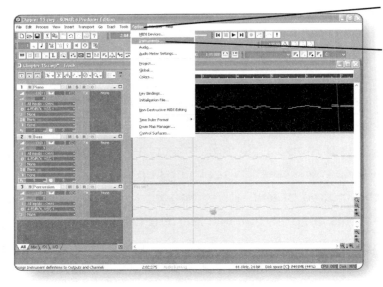

1. Click on **Options**. The Options menu will open.

2. Click on **Instruments**. The Assign Instruments dialog box will appear.

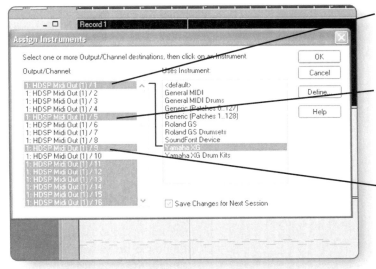

3. Click on a specific **channel** of a particular output in the **Output/Channel pane**. The channel will be highlighted.

4a. Optionally, **Ctrl+click** on another **channel**. The channel will be added to the selection.

OR

4b. Shift+click on another **channel**. A contiguous block of channels will be selected between the first channel selected and the channel on which you click.

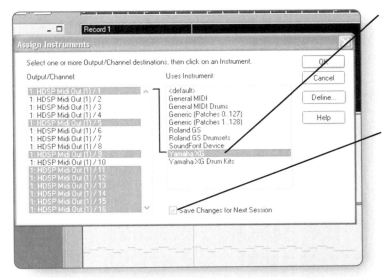

5. Click on an **instrument** in the **Uses Instrument pane**. The instrument will be highlighted, and a black line will connect the selected channel(s) and the instrument.

6. Optionally, **click** on **Save Changes for Next Session**. A ✔ will appear next to the option, and the assignment of instruments will be recalled for subsequent sessions.

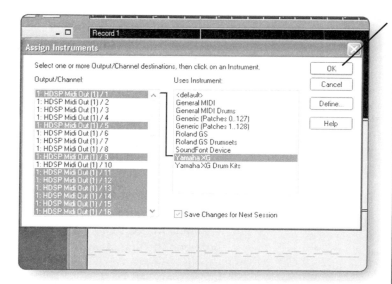

7. **Click** on **OK**. The dialog box will close, and your choices will be remembered.

GM DRUMS

It's customary to use channel 10 for all drum sounds on a General MIDI instrument. For GM instruments, assign channel 10 to General MIDI drums. Do the same for GS and XG instruments, choosing Roland GS drum sets and Yamaha XG drum kits, respectively.

8. **Click** on the **MIDI Output field** of a MIDI track. The MIDI Output menu will open, showing all enabled MIDI outputs.

9. **Click** on the **MIDI output** to which you just assigned an instrument. The menu will close, and the field will display your choice.

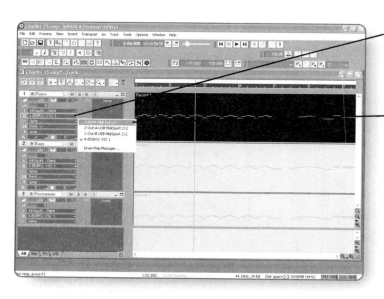

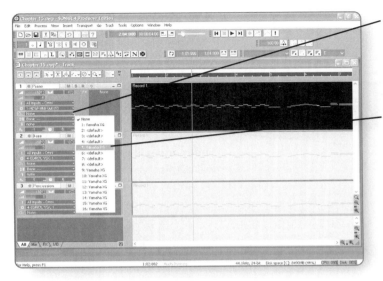

10. Click on the **Channel field** of the MIDI track. The Channel menu will open, showing the name of the instrument you assigned.

11. Click on the desired **channel**. The menu will close, and the field will display your choice.

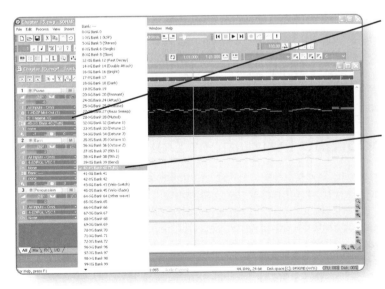

12. Click on the **Bank field** of the MIDI track. The Bank menu will open, showing the specific bank names of the instrument you assigned to that MIDI output.

13. Click on the desired **bank**. The menu will close, and the field will display your choice.

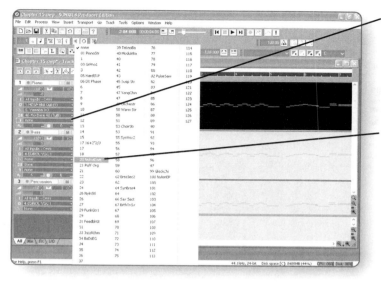

14. **Click** on the **Patch field** of the MIDI track. The Patch menu will open, showing the names of all patches available in the chosen bank of the instrument you assigned.

15. **Click** on the desired **patch**. The menu will close, and the field will display your choice.

THAT'S MORE LIKE IT!

You can see that assigning a specific instrument definition to that MIDI output made choosing banks, channels, and patches a lot friendlier. Once you've got your whole studio set up this way, you'll be more efficient than ever before!

Importing Instrument Definitions

By default, SONAR gets its list of available instrument definitions from a master file that contains a few common instrument definitions. For many instruments, especially newer or less-common instruments, you will have to add information about your instrument by importing an instrument-definition (INS) file (characterized by the .ins file extension). Such files are available on the SONAR installation discs and online at www.cakewalk.com. Here's how to import the required information about your instrument.

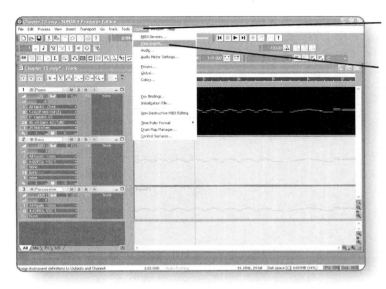

1. Click on **Options**. The Options menu will open.

2. Click on **Instruments**. The Assign Instruments dialog box will appear.

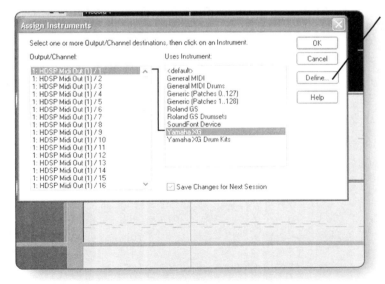

3. Click on **Define**. The Define Instruments and Names dialog box will appear.

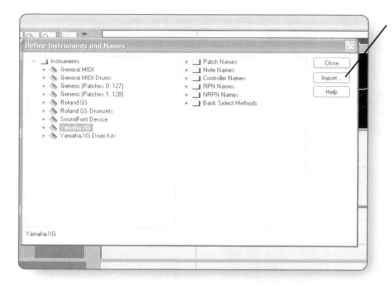

4. Click on **Import**. The Import Instrument Definitions dialog box will appear.

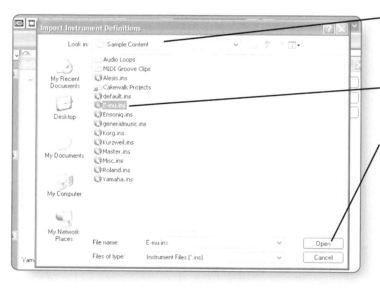

5. If necessary, **navigate** to the **location** of the desired instrument-definition file.

6. Click on an **instrument-definition file**. The file will be highlighted.

7. Click on **Open**. The dialog box will show a list of available instruments.

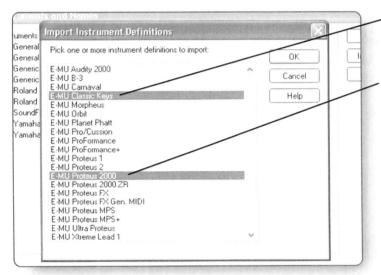

8. Click on the **name** of the desired **instrument**. The instrument will be highlighted.

9. Optionally, **Ctrl+click** on **additional instruments**. The additional instruments will be added to the selection.

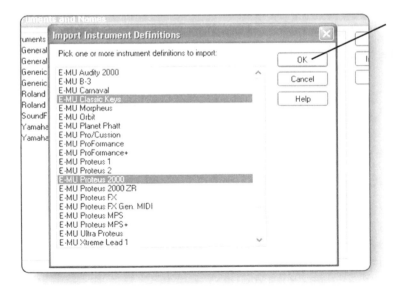

10. Click on **OK**. The Import Instrument Definitions dialog box will close, and the Define Instruments and Names dialog box will be updated to list the imported instruments.

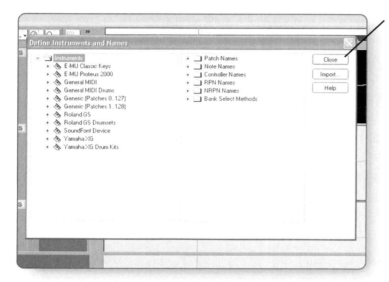

11. Click on **Close**. The Define Instruments and Names dialog box will close, and the imported instruments will now be listed in the Uses Instrument pane of the Assign Instruments dialog box.

12. Assign the **imported instruments** to the desired **channels** as described previously in the section "Assigning Instruments." SONAR will use the new instrument definitions.

INS FILES

As you've seen, SONAR's instrument definitions reside in files with the extension .ins, many of which are quite small. These files can reside anywhere on your hard drive, or even on a CD or other removable drive. The files that ship with SONAR 4 are grouped by manufacturer, and each file contains definitions for a number of different models. In the event your model is not listed, you might find it at Cakewalk's Web site.

Recording Multiple Inputs

By default, SONAR accepts MIDI input from any enabled input port. In fact, if it receives input from more than one input at a time, it combines all the input into one stream of data, and echoes and records it as though it were from a single input. There are times when you don't want this to happen, such as when you are playing a bass line with your left hand on one synthesizer and a lead line with your right hand on another. In this case, you would want SONAR to distinguish between the two inputs and allow you to direct what your right hand plays to one track and what your left hand plays to another. SONAR makes this easy to set up.

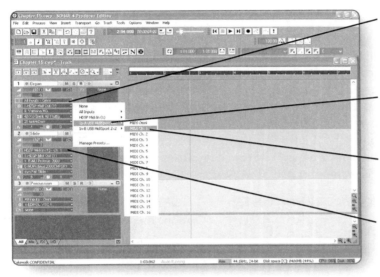

1. Click on the **down arrow** at the right of the **MIDI Input field** of a track. The MIDI Input menu will open.

2. Point to the desired **MIDI input** for that track. The Channels submenu will open.

3. Click on the desired **channel**. The menu will close, and the field will reflect your choice.

4. Repeat Steps 1–3 for any additional tracks. SONAR will direct MIDI input from each input/channel combination to the specified track.

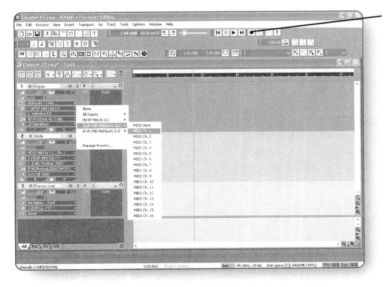

5. Click on **Record** and record as usual. MIDI input will be recorded into separate tracks.

ALL INPUTS

To return to SONAR's default behavior of merging all MIDI inputs, simply choose All Inputs, Omni as the track's MIDI input.

Filtering MIDI Input

MIDI instruments are capable of sending a wide variety of messages. Sometimes these messages aren't entirely necessary, but even so they take up space in the MIDI pipeline. In extreme cases, these extraneous messages can clog things up and disrupt playback. Although you can always select and delete the data after it has been recorded, it's often more efficient to prevent it from being recorded in the first place. This is the purpose of SONAR's MIDI Input filter.

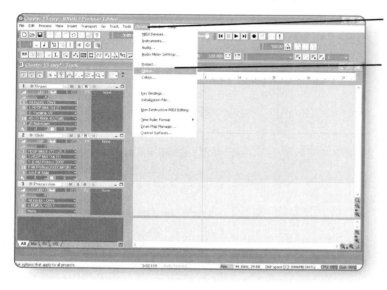

1. **Click** on **Options**. The Options menu will open.

2. **Click** on **Global**. The Global Options dialog box will appear.

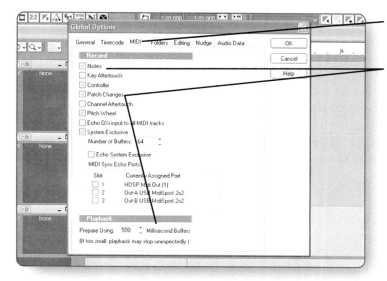

3. Click on the **MIDI tab**. The tab will come to the front.

4. Click on the **messages** you want to record. A ✔ will appear next to messages you choose to record, and everything else will be filtered.

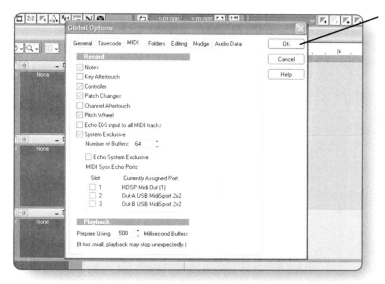

5. Click on **OK**. The dialog box will close, and the chosen messages will be neither recorded nor echoed.

FILTER WHAT?

SONAR's default setting is to record everything but Key (mono) Aftertouch and Channel (poly) Aftertouch messages, because few synthesizers use them. Filtering Controller messages can be useful as a troubleshooting technique, and on some instruments it's helpful to filter Pitch Wheel messages.

PART V

Effects and Mixing

16

Using Audio Effects

Except for the most purist classical projects, much of the sound of modern recordings is shaped by the judicious use of audio effects. Reverberation, delay, equalization, and compression—these are primary tools for the mix engineer. A traditional studio has racks full of hardware boxes that accomplish these effects, but SONAR includes numerous plug-in effects that let you process the sound without ever leaving the computer. In this chapter, you will learn how to:

- Use real-time audio effects
- Use and create plug-in presets
- Bypass and change the order of effects
- Apply audio effects offline

Using Real-Time Audio Effects

If you've ever used a stomp-box with your guitar, run your vocals through a reverb—heck, if you've even used the tone controls on your stereo—you've used real-time audio effects. Like SONAR's MIDI effects, audio effects work their magic during playback, but unlike MIDI effects they operate directly on the sound of the audio.

SONAR's real-time audio effects operate as *plug-ins*, separate programs that only run within a host program such as SONAR. This plug-in architecture allows you to buy third-party effects to expand your sonic palette, although SONAR includes plenty of high-quality effects to begin with. There are, in fact, far more plug-ins in SONAR than we can cover, so let's take a look at some representative real-time effects. The following examples cover the techniques you need to know to explore and experiment with the whole collection. Some of the windows may look slightly different depending on whether you use them on a mono or stereo track.

Using Cakewalk FxChorus

A *chorus* effect makes a sound seem thicker or more dense by layering it with slightly altered copies of itself. This is similar to the sound of someone singing the same thing several times and then blending the various takes together (think Enya). Cakewalk's FxChorus is one of several effects in the DSP-FX series, designed for high quality and efficient use of CPU resources.

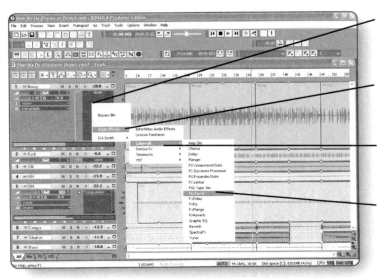

1. Right-click in the **FX Bin** of an audio track. The FX menu will open.

2. Point to **Audio Effects**. The Audio Effects submenu will open.

3. Point to **Cakewalk**. The Cakewalk effects submenu will open.

4. Click on **FxChorus**. The FxChorus window will appear.

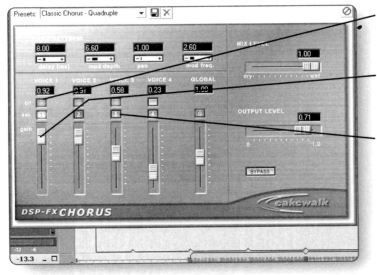

5. Click on a **voice's On button**. The voice will toggle on and off with successive clicks.

6. Drag a **voice's Gain slider**. The voice's volume will increase or decrease.

7. Click on a **voice's Select (Sel.) button**. The voice's parameters will be displayed in the Voice Settings displays at the top of the window.

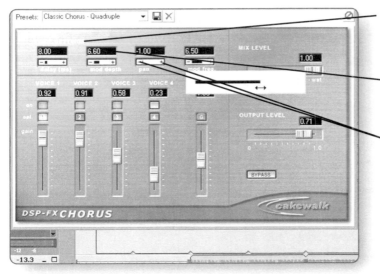

8. Adjust the various **Voice Settings** using the following techniques:

- **Double-click** in a **field** and **type** a **value**. The field will reflect the value you type.

- **Click** on a **field's plus (+)** or **minus (−) buttons**. The values will increase or decrease, respectively.

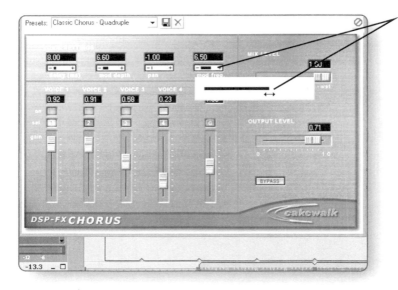

- **Click** and **drag** on a **value slider**. An expanded value slider will appear, and the value will update as you drag the expanded slider.

9. **Drag** the various **global parameter sliders**. The global parameters include

- **Global.** This slider adjusts the gain of the four voices while maintaining their relative values.

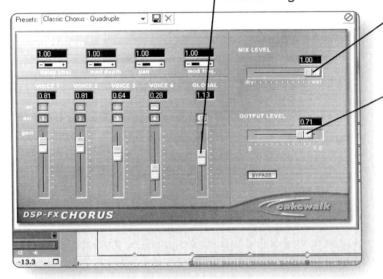

- **Mix Level.** This slider controls the relative level of the original (dry) signal and the processed (wet) signal.

- **Output Level.** This slider allows you to lower the final volume of the effect's output in case the addition of the four voices adds too much volume or causes clipping.

CLOSE THE WINDOW

Once you've adjusted the parameters of a plug-in, you can either minimize or close the plug-in window. Neither will stop the plug-in from processing the audio. To re-open a plug-in window, simply double-click on the plug-in's name in the FX Bin.

Using Sonitus:fx Equalizer

EQ stands for *equalization*, which is a way of shaping the frequency content of a signal. The bass and treble controls on your stereo are an elementary form of EQ. The Sonitus:fx Equalizer is one of the exceptional Ultrafunk plug-ins included with SONAR 4 Producer Edition. This plug-in not only shows you a graphic display of the effect, it lets you edit parameters directly from the graphic display. (Users of SONAR 4 Studio Edition can substitute the Cakewalk FXeq, although it does not support dragging directly on the graphic display.)

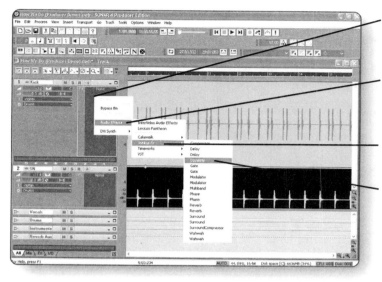

1. **Right-click** in the **FX Bin** of an audio track. The FX menu will open.

2. **Point** to **Audio Effects**. The Audio Effects submenu will open.

3. **Point** to **Sonitus:fx**. The Sonitus:fx submenu will open.

4. **Click** on **Equalizer**. The Sonitus:fx Equalizer window will appear.

MORE THAN ONE WAY

You can use the same techniques to adjust the Sonitus:fx Equalizer's settings that you used in FxChorus: dragging sliders, toggling buttons, and typing values. The following steps explore additional techniques.

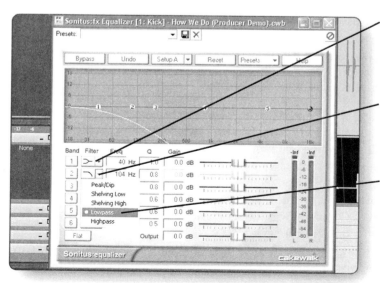

5. **Click** on a band's **Filter Type button**. The filter type will change, cycling through the five filter types with each click.

6. **Click** on the **down arrow** to the right of the **Filter Type button**. The Filter Type drop-down list box will open.

7. **Click** on the desired **filter type**. The list will close, and the filter type will change.

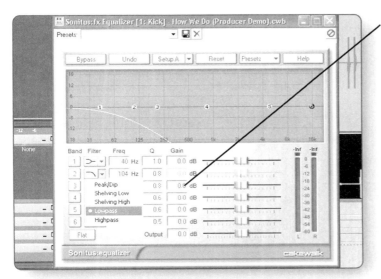

8. Click and **drag** in a **value field**. Dragging up or to the right will increase the value, and dragging down or to the left will decrease the value.

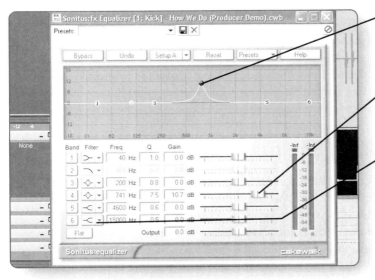

9. Drag a **yellow filter marker**. The gain and frequency of the band will be adjusted accordingly.

10. Double-click on a **slider**. The band's gain will be reset to 0.

11. Click on the **Flat button**. All bands' gain will be reset to 0.

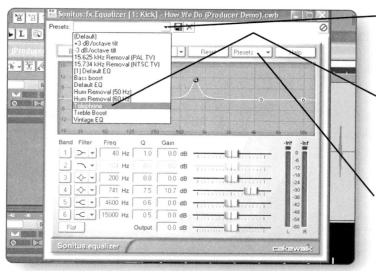

12. **Click** on the **down arrow** at the right of the **Presets drop-down list box.** The Presets drop-down list will open.

13. **Click** on the desired **preset.** The list will close, and the parameters will be updated with the values stored in the preset.

The Sonitus:fx plug-ins have a separate Presets drop-down list box. It gives you the same list of presets as the default SONAR drop-down list box.

USE YOUR EARS

You can (and should) adjust effects parameters while you are playing the audio. This allows you to hear exactly what the changes are doing to the sound. Remember: The numbers are useful for reference, but the only thing that really matters is what it sounds like!

Using Sonitus:fx Compressor

A *compressor* is used to control the dynamics of audio. In essence, it narrows the gap between loud sounds and soft sounds by turning down any sounds that exceed a certain volume. You could theoretically accomplish the same thing by keeping your hand on the volume control and turning the volume down whenever it got loud and back up whenever it got soft, but you wouldn't be able to react as quickly or as precisely as a compressor. Sonitus:fx Compressor operates in much the same way as Sonitus:fx Equalizer. Here are the pertinent functions for controlling dynamics with this plug-in.

• **Threshold.** This is the volume above which the signal will be attenuated (turned down).

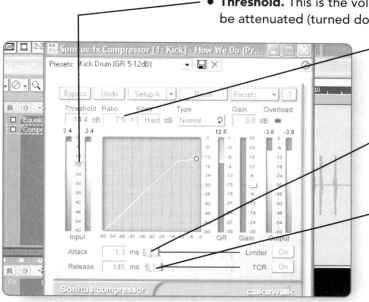

• **Ratio.** This is how aggressively the signal will be attenuated. Higher ratios attenuate the signal more severely.

• **Attack.** This is how quickly the compressor will kick in once a signal exceeds the threshold.

• **Release.** This is how quickly the compressor will let go once a signal drops below the threshold.

Creating Effects Presets

As you've seen, it's very helpful to be able to recall all parameters of a plug-in by choosing a preset. A *preset* is just a snapshot of all the settings, and you can save presets of your own to use along with all of the included presets.

1. Adjust the **parameters** of a plug-in as desired.

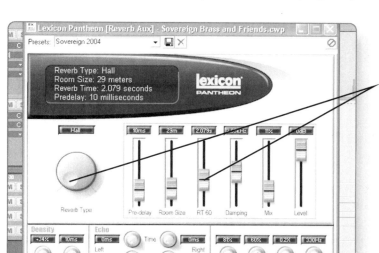

2. Click in the **Presets field** and type a name for your preset.

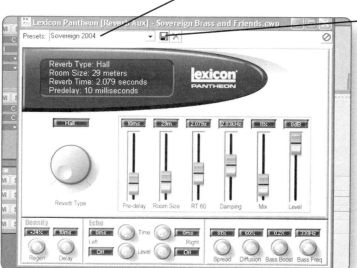

3. Click on the **Save button** next to the Presets field. The parameters will be saved under the preset name you typed.

SAVE CAREFULLY

If you click the Save button while the name of an existing preset is displayed, you will write the current parameters to that preset, replacing whatever values were originally stored under that name.

Bypassing an Effect

It's often useful to be able to hear the original, unprocessed sound of a track or a mix. When you *bypass* an effect, you effectively re-route audio past the effect so it does nothing to the sound. There are two ways to do this in SONAR.

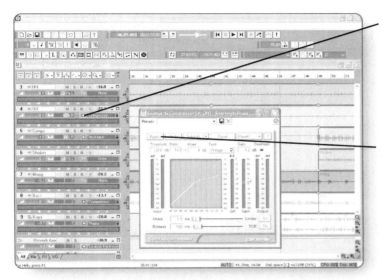

1a. **Click** on the **green button** to the left of a plug-in's name in the FX Bin. The button will turn grey, indicating that the effect is bypassed.

OR

1b. **Click** on the **Bypass button** in the plug-in's edit window. The button will turn yellow, indicating that the effect is bypassed.

2. **Click either button** again. The button will return to its normal color, indicating that the effect is in effect.

DOUBLE BYPASS

These two bypass buttons work independently of each other, so if either one is in bypass mode, the effect will not be heard. Both must be in normal mode for the effect to be heard.

Changing the Order of Effects

Ask any guitarist: The order in which effects processing is applied can change the results completely. Do you want to compress the EQ or EQ the compressor? The answer is different depending on the situation, and experimentation is the key to finding the right order. SONAR makes it easy to change the order of effects without changing anything else about them, so you can switch, listen, and switch back as often as you like.

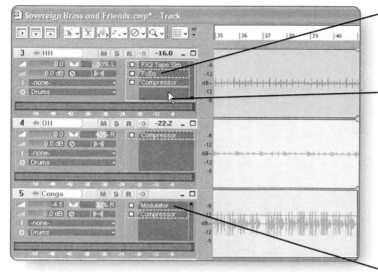

1. **Click** and **hold** on a **plug-in's name** in the FX Bin. The plug-in name will be outlined, and a red line will appear just above it.

2. **Drag** the **plug-in up** or **down** in the FX Bin. The red line will indicate the plug-in's new position.

3. **Release** the **mouse button**. The plug-in will appear in its new position, and the order of processing will reflect the new sequence of plug-ins.

4. **Drag** a **plug-in** to the **FX Bin** of a different track. The plug-in will be moved to the new track.

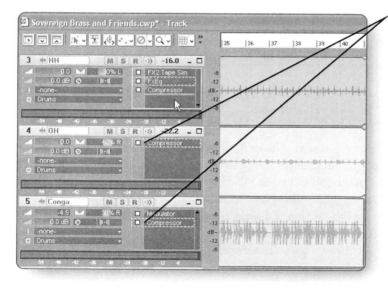

5. **Ctrl+drag** a **plug-in** to the **FX Bin** of a different track. The plug-in will be copied to the new track.

Using File-Based Audio Effects

File-based effects are processes that operate directly on audio clips, changing them more or less permanently. You can undo a file-based effect if you change your mind, but once you have saved your project, the file is forever changed. For this reason it's common to operate on copies of audio clips so you always have the original to use.

SAFE FX

Before using file-based effects, clone and archive the tracks you'll be working on, following the procedures outlined in Chapter 10, "Managing Audio." Archived tracks use no resources, and if you later change your mind about the effects you applied, you can go back to the original tracks.

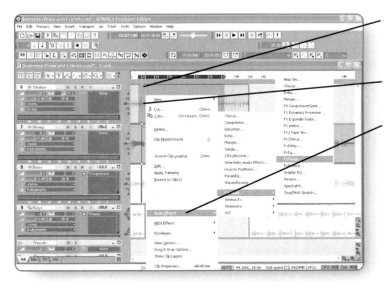

1. Select one or more **clips** or a **partial clip**. The selected clips will be highlighted.

2. Right-click on a **selected clip**. The context menu will open.

3. Point to **Audio Effects**. The Audio Effects submenu will open.

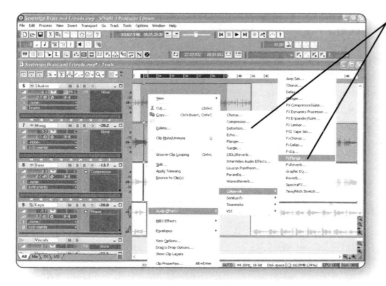

4. Click on an **effect** or **choose** an **effect** from a submenu. The effect's edit window will appear.

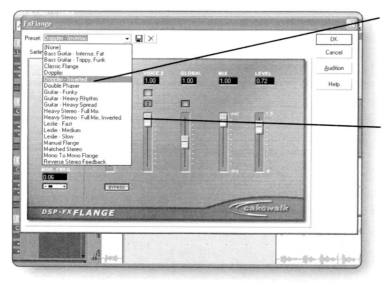

5a. Choose a **preset** as discussed previously. The parameters will update to the values stored in the preset.

OR

5b. Adjust **parameters** as desired.

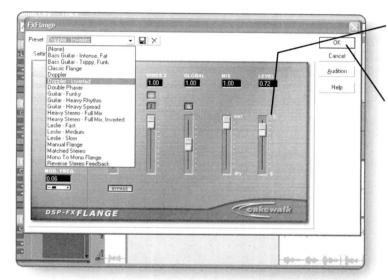

6. Optionally, **click** on **Audition**. SONAR will play a short segment of the clip with the effect applied.

7. Click on **OK**. The effect will be applied to the selected audio.

AUDITION TIME

You can change the amount of time SONAR uses to audition a file-based effect. The Audition commands for ___ seconds setting is found under Options, Global, General.

Freezing Audio Tracks

In a host-based system like SONAR, where all audio processing is handled by the computer's CPU, it's almost inevitable that you will want to add more effects than your system can handle in real time. When this happens, SONAR 4's Freeze function can be used to apply any real-time effects you have on a track to the clips as though they were file-based processes. After SONAR has applied the effects, it bypasses the effects bin, thereby freeing up some of your CPU's attention for those additional effects you wanted to add.

1. **Select** an **audio track**. The track will be highlighted.

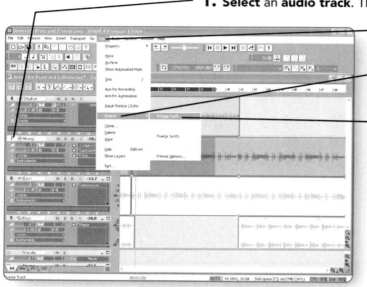

2. **Click** on **Track**. The Track menu will open.

3. **Point** to **Freeze**. The Freeze submenu will open.

4. **Click** on **Freeze Track**. All clips on the track will be processed with effects to new clips, and the track's effects bin will be bypassed, freeing up CPU resources.

UNFREEZING

If you want to change something in a frozen track, simply select the track and choose Unfreeze Track from the Track, Freeze menu. The original clips will be restored, and the effects bin will be enabled. You can edit the audio or tweak the plug-ins and then re-freeze the track.

17

Mastering Audio's Ins and Outs

You've already seen how SONAR lets you communicate with the outside world—recording from inputs on your audio interface and playing back through outputs on your audio interface. Now it's time to explore the inner world of SONAR audio. Version 4.0 finally brings the world of surround sound to SONAR users! In this chapter, you'll learn how to:

- Work with buses
- Create a headphone mix and add effects to it
- Use sends to control reverb effects
- Create subgroups, submixes, and stems
- Use SONAR's new surround features

Using the Bus Pane

A *bus* can be thought of as an internal audio pathway, kind of like a virtual audio cable that you can use to connect from some internal source to some internal destination. It's a powerful way to be able to group signals together for efficient processing or to recombine them in a way that is different from the main output. In this first section you'll create a few buses that you'll then use through the rest of the chapter. Let's make a clean start by creating a blank project.

MULTI-CHANNEL OR STEREO

Some of the procedures in this chapter assume that you have a multi-channel audio interface. If you have a stereo (two-channel) interface, your capabilities will be somewhat reduced—obviously surround mixing is out of the question—but the same principles apply.

---

1. **Click** on **File**. The File menu will open.

2. **Click** on **New**. The New Project File dialog box will appear.

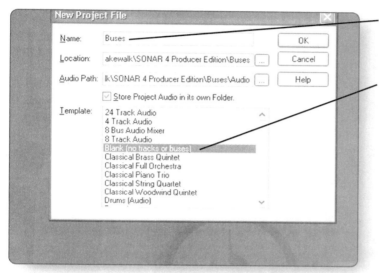

3. **Click** in the **Name field** and **type** a **name** for the project. The name will be displayed.

4. **Click** on the **Blank (no tracks or buses) template**. The template will be highlighted.

PER-PROJECT AUDIO FOLDERS

You will not be offered the option to name the project at this point if you do not have Per-Project Audio Folders enabled. See Chapter 10, "Managing Audio," for details on this option.

---

5. **Click** on **OK**. The dialog box will close, and a project with no tracks of any kind will appear.

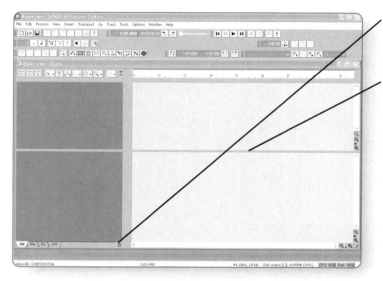

6. If necessary, **click** on the **Show/Hide Bus Pane button**. The Bus pane will open.

7. Drag the **splitter bar** upward to enlarge the Bus pane. The Bus pane will now give you more room to work.

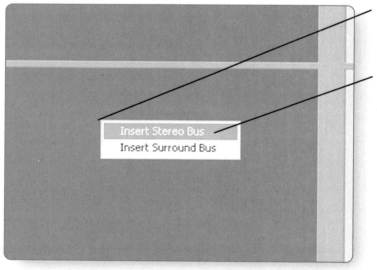

8. Right-click in the **left side** of the **Bus pane**. The Bus pane context menu will appear.

9. Click on **Insert Stereo Bus**. A new stereo bus will be created in the Bus pane.

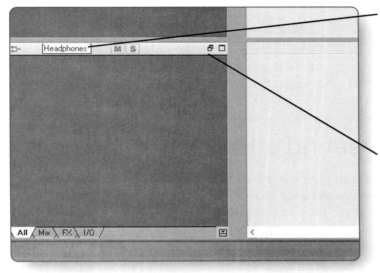

10. Double-click on the **bus name** and **type** a new **name**, such as **Headphones**. The new name will appear in the name field.

11. Press Enter. The new name will be confirmed.

12a. If necessary, **click** on the **Restore Strip Size button**. The track will expand vertically.

OR

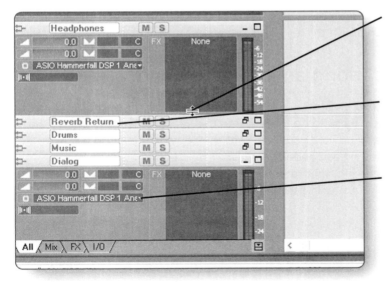

12b. If necessary, **drag** the **bottom border** of the **track down**. The track will expand vertically.

13. Create four new stereo buses using the preceding steps, and **name** them **Reverb Return**, **Drums**, **Music**, and **Dialog**.

14. If the Bus Output field does not already list the name of your primary stereo output, **click** on the **down arrow** at the right of the **Bus Output field** of each bus and **click** on the **name** of your **main stereo output**. The output of the bus will be assigned to the main stereo output.

> ### BUSES FOR THE FUTURE
> You will be using these buses throughout the rest of this chapter to illustrate some common procedures that take advantage of SONAR 4's sophisticated bus architecture.

Creating a Headphone Mix

Unless you are doing live classical recording, you will almost always need to set up a *cue mix*, which is routed to the headphones so the performers can hear themselves along with any existing tracks. Although it's sometimes sufficient to have them listen to exactly what is coming through your monitors, it's a good idea to have a separate headphone mix. Two of the many reasons you might choose to do this are that it allows you to change the balance of parts the performers are hearing without affecting your mix and it allows you to change the volume of their mix independently of yours. You ordinarily accomplish this by using a send.

Creating an Interface Send

A *send* creates an exact copy of the audio running through a track. By sending this copy to the headphones, you create the cue mix. Once you have sent the copy, you can use a bus to modify it as needed. We'll start by creating a simple headphone mix that redirects the signal straight out your interface without passing through a bus.

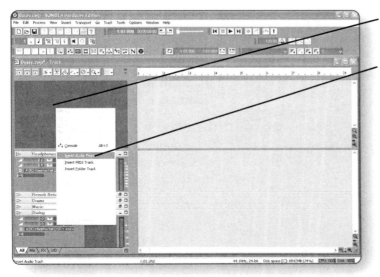

1. Right-click in the **Track pane**. The context menu will open.

2. Click on **Insert Audio Track**. The menu will close, and a new audio track will be created.

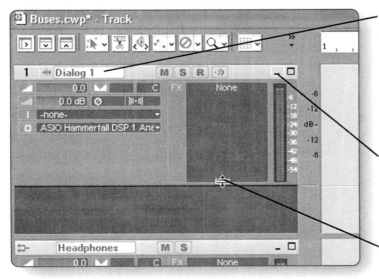

3. Double-click in the **track name field** and **type** a new **name**, such as **Dialog 1**. The new name will appear in the Name field.

4. Press Enter. The new name will be confirmed.

5a. If necessary, **click** on the **Restore Strip Size button**. The track will expand vertically.

OR

5b. If necessary, **drag** the **bottom border** of the **track down**. The track will expand vertically.

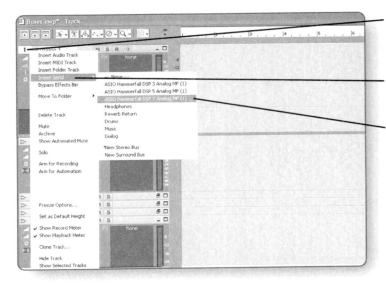

6. **Right-click** on the **track number**. The context menu will open.

7. **Point** to **Insert Send**. The Insert Send submenu will open.

8. **Click** on an **interface output**. The submenu will close, and a new send will be created on the track.

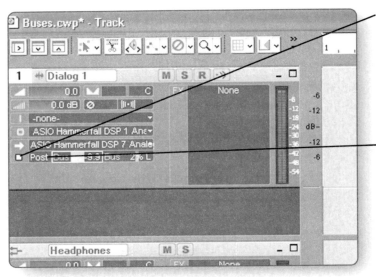

9. **Click** on the **enable button**. The button will turn green, and the send will be active.

10. **Adjust** the **send controls** as necessary. The controls include

- **Post/Pre.** This button toggles between pre-fader and post-fader operation, which determines whether the track's volume fader has any effect on the send's level.

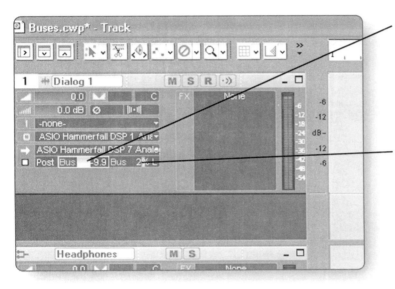

- **Send Level.** This control determines the volume of the signal being sent to the output, so you can adjust the balance of the headphone mix. Double-click this control to reset it to 0.0.

- **Send Pan.** This control determines the pan position of the signal being sent to the output, so you can adjust the pan of elements in the headphone mix. Double-click this control to reset it to center.

Creating a Bus Send

Let's put one of those buses to good use. By running the headphone mix through a bus first, you can control the level of the headphone mix and add effects to it if you want.

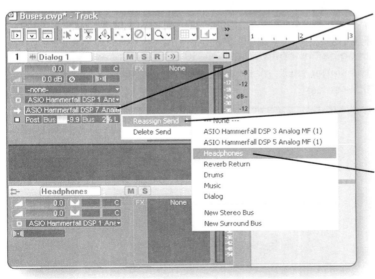

1. Click on the **down arrow** at the right of the **Send Output drop-down list** box on the Dialog 1 track. The drop-down list will open.

2. Point to **Reassign Send**. The Reassign Send submenu will open.

3. Click on **Headphones**. The submenu will close, and the send output will be reassigned to the Headphones bus.

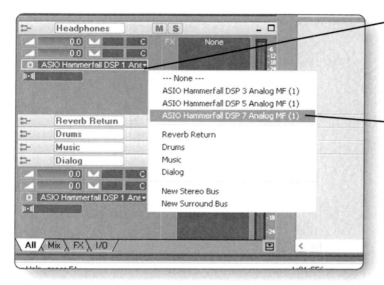

4. **Click** on the **down arrow** at the right of the **Bus Output drop-down list box** on the Headphones bus. The drop-down list box will open.

5. **Click** on the **name** of the **interface output** to which the send had been assigned. The drop-down list will close, and the bus output will be reassigned to that interface output.

A DIFFERENT ROUTE

The signal from the send is still going to the output where your headphone system is connected, but it passes through the Headphones bus first. With one source track, this doesn't seem like a big deal, but if you've got 20 or 30 tracks being mixed to the head-phones, you'll be glad to have the bus to control them. Imagine having to adjust 20–30 send faders every time the singer says "make it a little louder," then "make it a little softer!"

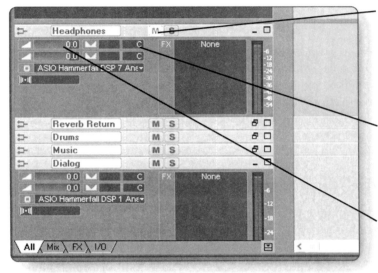

6. Click on the **Mute button** on the Headphone bus. The button will turn yellow, and all sound to the headphone mix will be muted. **Click** again to hear the headphone mix again.

7. Click and **drag** the **Output Pan slider** on the Headphone bus. The sound of the headphone mix will shift to the left or right without affecting your main mix.

8. Click and **drag** the **Output Volume slider** on the Head-phones bus. The volume of the entire headphone mix will increase or decrease while maintaining its internal balance.

VOLUME VERSUS BALANCE

Control the overall volume of the headphone mix from the bus, and control the balance of the headphone mix from the send levels of the various tracks.

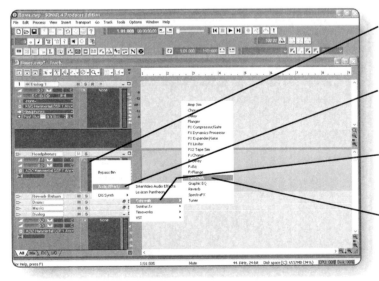

9. Right-click in the **FX Bin** of the Headphones bus. The FX Bin context menu will open.

10. Point to **Audio Effects**. The Audio Effects submenu will open.

11. Point to an **effects category**. The category's submenu will open.

12. Click on the desired **effect**. The effect's edit window will appear.

> ### ONE-CLICK CONTROL
> As you can see, routing the headphone mix through a bus gives you one-click control over muting and volume, and it allows you to sweeten the mix to make the performers more comfortable. Keep in mind that you can do all this without affecting your control-room mix in the least.

Using a Send to Apply Reverb

The technique you learned in Chapter 16, "Using Audio Effects"—inserting an effect directly on the audio track—is generally considered standard procedure for effects such as compression and equalization where you want to change the signal completely. However, when engineers use time-based effects such as reverb, it's common to mix the original (dry) signal with the processed (wet) signal. There are historical, practical, and aesthetic reasons behind this practice, and although in music no rule is absolute, it's always a good idea to learn the standard way before breaking the rules.

This technique, then, can be considered the standard routing for adding reverb effects to your tracks. It involves using a send from each track to split off a copy of its audio; all of these copies are then sent to a single bus. A reverb is inserted on the bus and set to 100 percent wet. This gives you complete, independent control over the balance of dry (the audio tracks) and wet (the bus), so you can make the simulated reverb chamber as big or as small as you want without having to edit a setting on every single audio track. If you're familiar with mixing consoles, you'll recognize this as a typical aux send/aux return scenario.

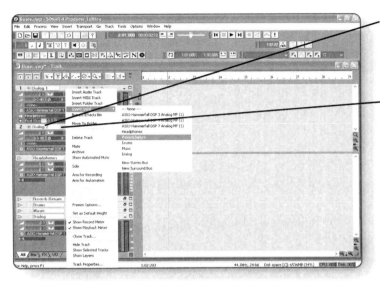

1. Create a **new audio track** and **name** it **Dialog 2** using techniques you know well by now.

2. Right-click on the track's **title bar**. The context menu will open.

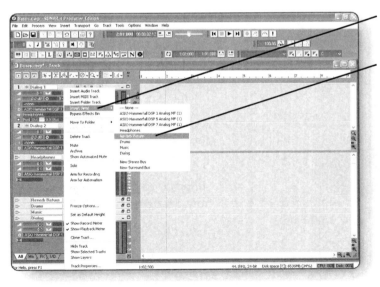

3. Point to **Insert Send**. The Insert Send submenu will open.

4. Click on **Reverb Return**. The submenu will close, and a new send will be created on the track.

5. Repeat the process for Dialog 1. A new send will be created on that track.

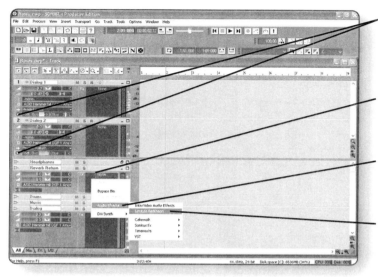

6. Click on the **Send enable button** of each audio track. The buttons will turn green, and the sends will be active.

7. Right-click in the **FX Bin** of the Reverb Return bus. The FX Bin menu will open.

8. Point to **Audio Effects**. The Audio Effects submenu will open.

9. Point to **Lexicon Pantheon**. The Lexicon Pantheon reverb's edit window will appear.

STUDIO EDITION

If you have SONAR 4 Studio Edition, you have Lexicon Pantheon LE, which lacks some of the bells and whistles of the full version. It may look slightly different, but it will work the same way for the purpose of this exercise.

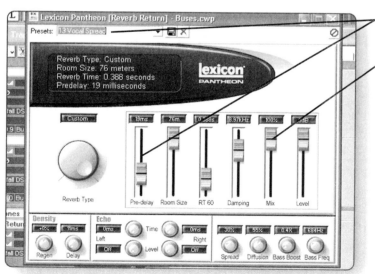

10. Adjust parameters or choose a preset as desired.

11. If necessary, **drag** the **Mix slider up** to **100%**. Pantheon will now pass nothing but wet signal.

12. Click on the **Close button**. The Pantheon edit window will close.

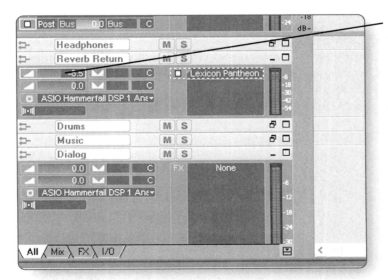

13. **Click** and **drag** the **Output Volume slider** on the Reverb Return bus. The volume of the wet mix will increase or decrease, while the volume of the dry mix stays constant.

WET VERSUS DRY

Change the dry mix—the balance of the audio tracks—by adjusting the volume faders on the audio tracks. Change the wet mix—the balance of the audio tracks passing through the reverb—by adjusting the sends on the audio tracks. Change the wet/dry balance by adjusting the volume fader of the Reverb Return bus. This arrangement gives you complete and independent control over all aspects of your reverb processing.

Creating Subgroups, Submixes, and Stems

Subgroups, submixes, and stems are three different mix scenarios that use essentially the same technique. The real difference is how each is used. All three involve using a bus or buses to create a partial mix prior to the final output. Unlike the send/return scenarios discussed previously, this technique routes the *outputs* of audio tracks to buses.

Creating a Subgroup

A subgroup allows you to treat several audio tracks as a single unit. In this example, you will use a subgroup to combine all of your drum tracks to a single bus so you can apply a compressor plug-in to the entire kit at once.

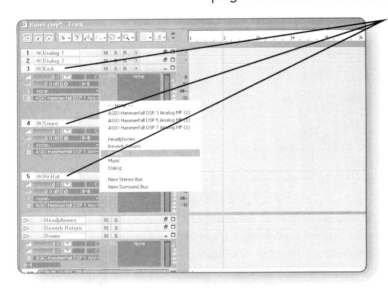

1. Create three audio tracks and name them **Kick**, **Snare**, and **Hi-Hat**. These tracks will represent your drum kit.

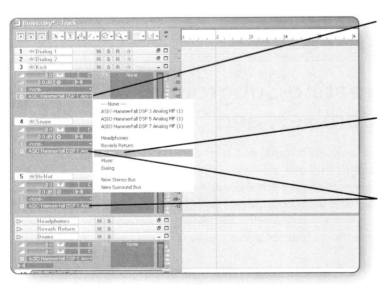

2. Click on the **down arrow** at the right of the **Track Output field** of one of the drum tracks. The Track Output drop-down list will open.

3. Click on **Drums**. The list will close, and the output of the track will be reassigned to the Drums bus.

4. Repeat this process for the other two drum tracks. All of the drum kits will now be heard only through the Drums bus.

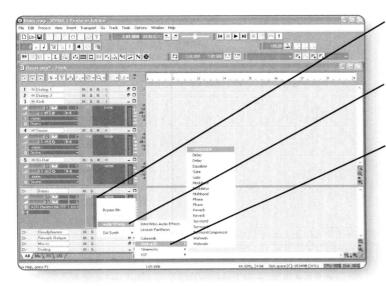

5. Right-click in the **FX Bin** of the Drums bus. The FX Bin context menu will open.

6. Point to **Audio Effects**. The Audio Effects submenu will open.

7. Point to **Sonitus:fx**. The Sonitus:fx effects submenu will open.

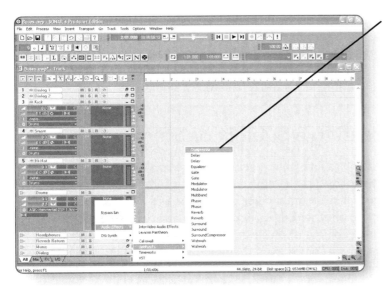

8. Click on **Compressor**. The Sonitus:fx Compressor edit window will appear.

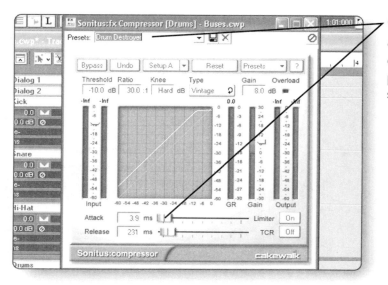

9. Adjust parameters or choose a preset as desired. The entire drum kit will be compressed according to your specifications.

ONE WAY OR ANOTHER

Although you could certainly apply a separate compressor to each audio track of the drum kit, that would eat up system resources and would have a different sound from this technique, which compresses the entire kit as though it were a single instrument.

Creating a Submix or Stem

A *submix* is just what it sounds like: a small part of a larger mix. In the following example, you will use submixes to combine all of your instrumental parts to one bus and all of your dialog parts to another bus, giving you the ability to change the relative volume of music and dialog with only two faders. The term *stems* comes from the field of audio for film, and it refers to the many submixes that make balancing complex film mixes manageable.

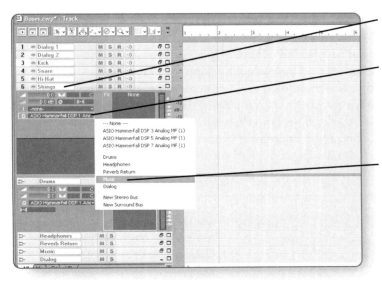

1. **Create** an **audio track** and name it **Strings**.

2. **Click** on the **down arrow** at the right of the **Track Output field** of the Strings track. The Track Output drop-down list will open.

3. **Click** on **Music**. The list will close, and the output of the track will be reassigned to the Music bus.

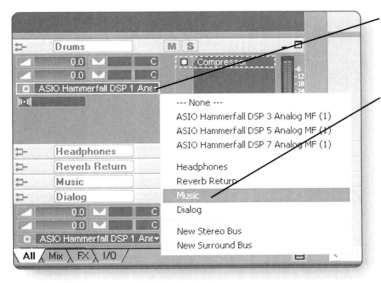

4. **Click** on the **down arrow** at the right of the **Track Output field** of the Drums bus. The Track Output drop-down list will open.

5. **Click** on **Music**. The list will close, and the output of the bus will be reassigned to the Music bus.

BUS TO BUS

That's right, the output of a bus can be routed to another bus! Because it all happens in the digital domain, there's no additional noise or sonic compromise to doing this. Why do it? The Drums bus is used for compressing the drum kit, and then you're combining the compressed drum kit with the strings to create a submix of all of the instrumental parts at the Music bus.

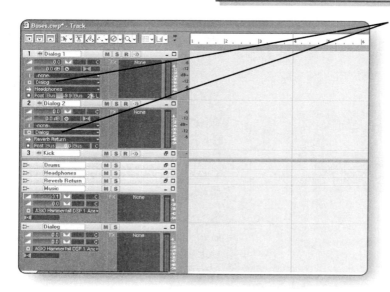

6. Using the same technique, **assign** the **track outputs** of the **Dialog tracks** to the **Dialog bus**. All of the dialog audio will be heard only through the Dialog bus.

7. Adjust volume, **pan**, and **other parameters** of the Music and Dialog buses to balance and blend the two submixes.

KEEPING IT SIMPLE

Use this technique any time you have a complex mix to simplify the process of balancing different sections of the mix. In a typical rock/pop mix, you might have separate submixes for the keyboards, guitars, drums, and vocals. If the drums are too loud, you move one fader and fix it! You always have the ability to change the internal balance of the members of a submix by adjusting their track volume faders.

Surround Mixing

SONAR 4 brings the world of surround sound to your desktop. Almost any imaginable surround format up to 8.1—meaning eight surround channels plus a Low Frequency Effects (LFE) channel—can be used. Of course, you need to have enough output channels on your sound card to be able to take advantage of this, and you also need corresponding speakers to experience the effect. Many home-theater systems have multi-channel analog inputs that you could connect to your sound card's outputs.

Surround sound raises the level of your project's complexity substantially, and the topic of surround could fill an entire book by itself. Our discussion here will give you the tools you need to get SONAR ready for surround and to get started creating your own surround mixes.

Setting SONAR's Surround Format

Stereo mixing is a snap compared to surround mixing—you've got two channels, so you have a 50/50 chance of getting left and right routed to the correct outputs. For that matter, if you get them backwards, you may never notice! With more channels comes more possibility for error, so there are two things you must establish before you start. First, you need to decide how many channels you're going to use and how they are to be arranged. Second, you need to ensure that each channel is mapped to the correct physical output so you hear it coming from the correct speaker.

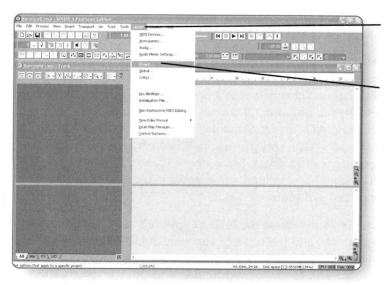

1. Starting with a new blank project, **click** on **Options**. The Options menu will open.

2. Click on **Project**. The Project Options dialog will appear.

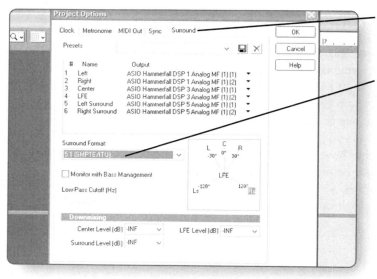

3. Click on the **Surround tab**. The Surround tab will come to the front.

4. Click on the **Surround Format drop-down list** and choose a surround format.

SURROUND FORMATS

The most common surround format is called *5.1*, meaning five channels surrounding the listener and one LFE channel. Most DVDs feature 5.1 soundtracks, and most home-theater systems use this format. I highly recommend that you start your surround experience by choosing 5.1 (SMPTE/ITU) from the Surround Format drop-down list.

The surround channels—Left, Right, Center, Left Surround, and Right Surround—should be arranged in a circle around the listening position. The subwoofer, which carries the LFE channel (as well as the bass content of the surround channels in most home-theater systems) can be placed almost anywhere.

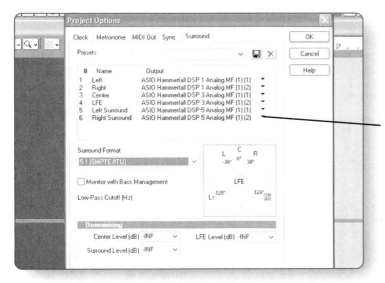

5a. Ensure that **your six speakers are connected** to the proper outputs, as shown in the Output window.

OR

5b. Use the **Output window's drop-down lists** to change the output channel assignments so they match your speaker connections.

Using Surround Tracks and Buses

Surround tracks and buses use the same basic concepts and controls as stereo tracks and buses. The biggest difference is of course in panning, which now covers a lot more ground. In order to deal with the increased possibilities, SONAR provides a dedicated Surround Panner window. That's where the real fun begins.

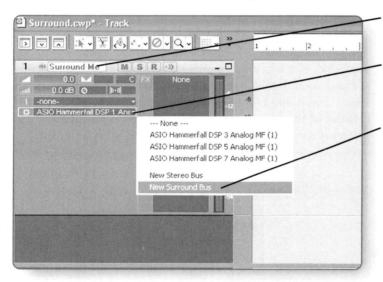

1. Create a **new audio track** and **name** it appropriately.

2. Click on the track's **Output field**. The Track Output drop-down list will open.

3. Click on **New Surround Bus**. The list will close, a new Surround bus will be created, and the track's output will be assigned to that bus.

4. Note the following differences from what you've seen previously:

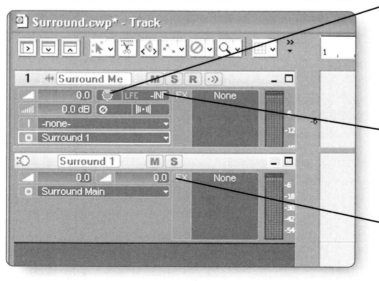

- The Pan control on the audio track is a small circle, representing the surrounding speakers. Although this control is functional, *it's tiny!* That's why there's a dedicated Surround Panner window.

- The audio track has a slider for LFE level so you can determine how much of its bass content should be included in the LFE channel.

- The Surround bus has no panner at all. All surround panning happens at the track level.

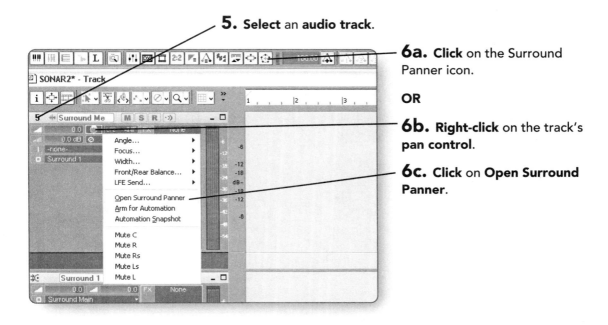

5. **Select** an **audio track**.

6a. **Click** on the Surround Panner icon.

OR

6b. **Right-click** on the track's **pan control**.

6c. **Click** on **Open Surround Panner**.

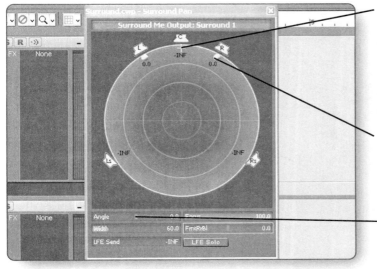

7. **Click** on the **plus sign (+)** and **drag** the **sound** wherever you want it to go. This is the angle and focus marker, and it represents the position of the track's sound in the Surround field.

8. **Drag** either of the **width markers** to change the apparent size of the track's signal. Other controls include

- **Angle.** This controls whether the sound is in front of you, behind you, or to your side. Zero degrees is directly in front, −90 is to your left, and so on.

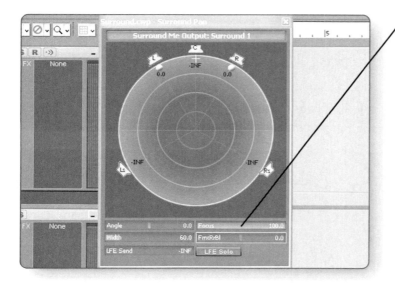

- **Focus.** This controls the distance from the listener. A setting of 100 is far away, and a setting of 0 is in your lap. You can also think of this as the size of the surround circle.

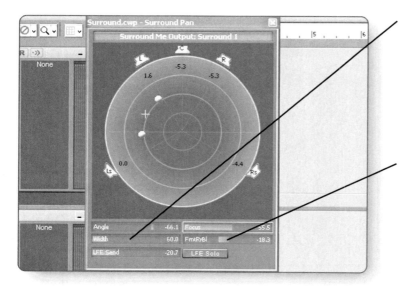

- **Width.** This is the same as the width markers. A setting of 0 makes the sound seem to come from a single speaker. Larger settings spread the sound across more speakers, making it seem wider.

- **Front/Rear Balance (FrntRrBl).** This controls whether the sound comes from the front speakers or the rear speakers. Zero is equally balanced, positive numbers move the sound forward, and negative numbers move the sound backward.

GOING IN CIRCLES

Hold down the Alt key while panning to lock the Focus value. This lets you pan in a perfect circle. Just don't do it too much, or you'll get motion sickness!

Using Surround Effects

Using plug-ins for audio effects in a surround mix isn't that different from using stereo effects. There are two ways you can accomplish this. The first is by using dedicated multi-channel plug-ins, such as the Sonitus:fx Compressor 8.1. This is ideal, because such plug-ins are smart enough to consider all six (or more) channels as a unit. The second way is to utilize your existing effects through SONAR's SurroundBridge, but you can only use the SurroundBridge on buses.

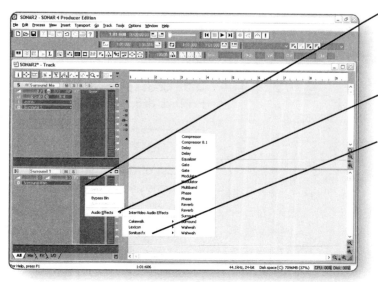

1. Right-click in the **FX Bin** of a surround track or Surround bus. The FX Bin context menu will appear.

2. Point to **Audio Effects**. The Audio Effects submenu will open.

3. Point to **Sonitus:fx**. The Sonitus:fx submenu will open.

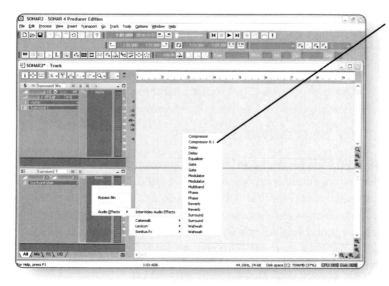

4. **Click** on **Compressor 8.1.** The menu will close, and the Sonitus:fx Compressor 8.1 edit window will appear.

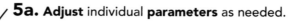

5a. **Adjust** individual **parameters** as needed.

OR

5b. **Choose** a **preset** from the **Presets drop-down list**.

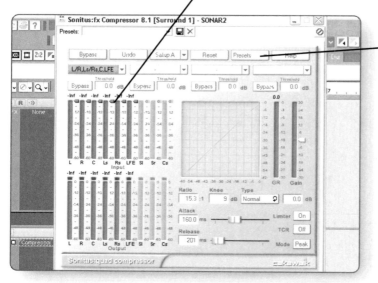

SONITUS PRESETS

Most of the Sonitus:fx plug-ins allow you to choose from the same set of presets, whether you use the SONAR Presets drop-down list or the plug-in's Presets drop-down list. The Compressor 8.1, however, keeps its own list separate from SONAR presets.

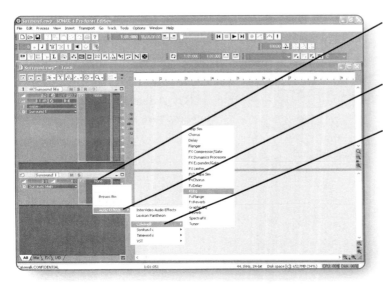

6. **Right-click** in the **FX Bin** of a Surround bus. The FX Bin context menu will appear.

7. **Point** to **Audio Effects**. The Audio Effects submenu will open.

8. **Point** to a **plug-in category**. That submenu will open.

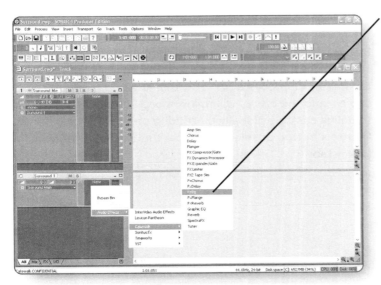

9. **Click** on a **non-surround plug-in**. The submenu will close, and the plug-in's edit window will appear.

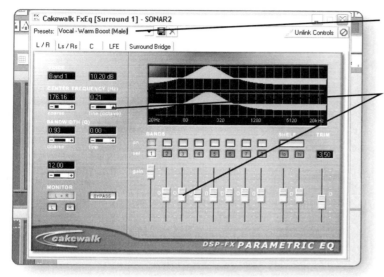

10a. Choose a **preset** from the **Presets drop-down list**.

OR

10b. Adjust individual **parameters** as needed.

LINKING PLUG-INS WITH SURROUNDBRIDGE

By default, SONAR's SurroundBridge creates multiple linked copies of stereo or mono plug-ins. Adjust a parameter or choose a preset within any of the linked copies, and the others will follow along. You can choose to unlink controls globally by clicking on the Unlink Controls button or selectively from the SurroundBridge Linker tab.

18

Using the Console View

SONAR's Console view is modeled after a traditional mixer, with big faders and meters and individual vertical channel strips for each track. It really doesn't offer any functions that aren't available in the Track view, but it lays out the controls you need to mix your project in a very efficient, manageable, and—for anyone used to physical mixers—familiar way. To take advantage of this view, you simply need to understand its layout, control its display, and learn how to accomplish tasks you already know from the Track view. In this chapter, you will learn how use the Console view to:

- Show and hide Console view controls
- Assign inputs and outputs
- Adjust level and pan
- Create audio and MIDI tracks, buses, and sends
- Use the channel EQ (Producer Edition only)
- Configure the appearance of the Console view

Assigning Inputs and Outputs

The Console view is laid out in three sections: tracks, buses, and main outs. The main outs are the actual physical outputs of your audio interface, and the only control you have over them is volume and mute. On the audio and MIDI tracks, however, you can also assign inputs and outputs just as you did in the Track view, and you can assign outputs to buses as well. Instead of being right next to each other, though, in the Console view the inputs are all the way at the top of the channel strip and the outputs are all the way at the bottom.

1. **Click** on **View**. The View menu will open.

2. **Click** on **Console**. The Console view will appear.

3. Optionally, **drag** the **lower-right corner** of the **Console view** to resize the window. The window will be resized.

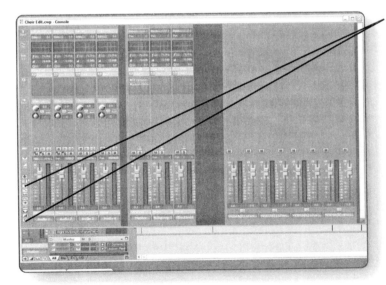

4. If necessary, **Shift+click** on the **Show/Hide Input** and **Show/Hide Output buttons**. The Input and/or Output controls will be shown.

SHOW/HIDE

The Show/Hide buttons toggle display of various controls on and off. Simply Shift+click the button again to toggle the control's display status. You could just click, but holding Shift while you click prevents the Console view from resizing itself every time you show or hide a control.

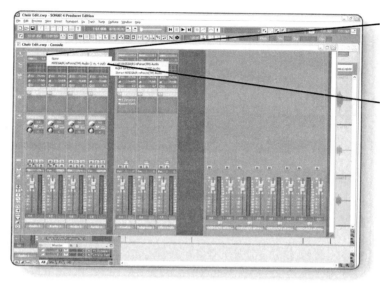

5. Click on the **lower-right corner** of the **Input field** of an audio track. The Input menu will open.

6. Point to the **name** of the desired **audio interface**. The interface submenu will open.

7. Click on the **name** of the desired **input**. The menu will close and the Input field will reflect your choice.

A DIFFERENT VIEW

Your Input menu and any submenus may look quite different from the menu shown in this book, depending on your audio interface's options.

8. **Click** on the **Output field** of an audio track or bus. The Output menu will open and display all available outputs and buses.

9. **Click** on the desired **output** or **bus** or on **New Stereo Bus** (or **New Surround Bus**). The menu will close, and the Output field will reflect your choice. If you choose New Stereo Bus or New Surround Bus, a new bus will be created, and the output will be assigned to it.

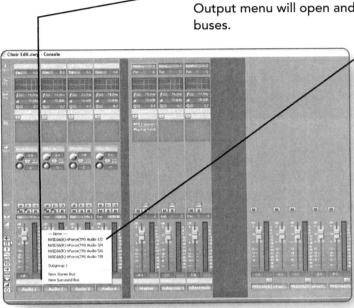

Adjusting Level and Pan

The Console view is not just a distillation of mixing controls from the Track view—its controls are truly optimized for their functions. For example, the volume fader on a track is several times larger in the Console view, allowing for more precise control.

1. If necessary, **Shift+click** on the **Show/Hide Volume** or **Show/Hide Pan button**. The controls will be displayed.

2. Drag the **volume fader** of an audio or MIDI track, bus, or main out up or down. The track's level will increase or decrease, respectively.

3. Double-click a **volume fader**. The fader will snap to its default position.

4. **Drag** the **Pan slider** of an audio or MIDI track, bus, or main out left or right. The track's sound will move left or right, accordingly.

5. **Double-click** a **Pan slider**. The slider will snap to its default position.

SNAP-TO

The default snap-to position for volume on an audio track is 0.0 dB. For MIDI volume, it's 101. Pan will snap to center.

Creating Tracks, Sends, and Buses

There's no need to return to the Track view in order to add audio or MIDI tracks, buses, or sends to your project. All of these functions are available from the context menu in the Console view.

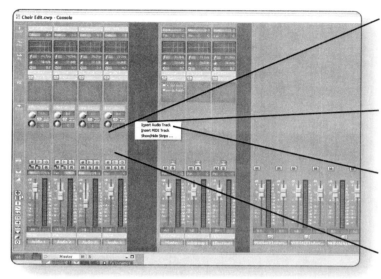

1a. **Right-click** in a **blank area** within a **track**. The context menu will open.

OR

1b. **Right-click** in any **blank area** within the **Track pane**. The context menu will open.

2. **Click** on **Insert Audio Track** or **Insert MIDI Track**. The menu will close, and the appropriate track will be created.

3. Optionally, **click** and **hold** in any **blank area** within a **track** and **drag** the **track left** or **right**. The track order will change accordingly in both the Console and Track views.

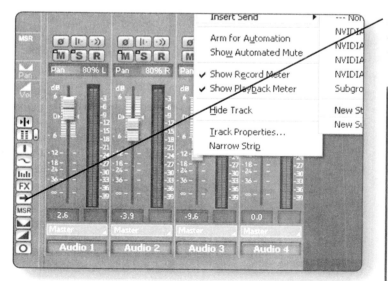

4. If necessary, **Shift+click** on the **Show/Hide Sends button**. The Sends area will be displayed.

SENDS VIEWS

The Sends area has three display modes: hidden, two sends, and four sends. If there are more sends on a track than the current mode can show, a scroll arrow appears at the top or bottom of the Sends area.

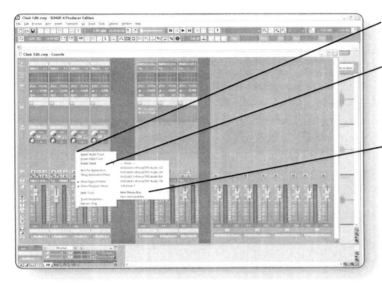

5. **Right-click** in the **Sends area**. The context menu will open.

6. **Point** to **Insert Send**. The Insert Send submenu will open, showing all available outputs and buses.

7. **Click** on the desired **output** or **bus** or on **New Stereo Bus** (or **New Surround Bus**). The menu will close, and the send will be assigned to the chosen bus or output. If you choose New Stereo Bus or New Surround Bus, a new bus will be created, and the send will be assigned to it.

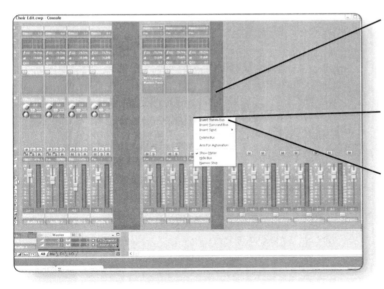

8a. **Right-click** in any **blank area** within the **Bus pane**. The context menu will open.

OR

8b. **Right-click** in any **blank area** within a **bus**. The context menu will open.

9. **Click** on **Insert Stereo Bus** or **Insert Surround Bus**. A new bus will be created.

Using the Channel EQ (Producer Edition)

In a typical contemporary music mix, equalization is used to help parts fit together within a dense arrangement. As a result, most big-ticket consoles include EQ on every channel. SONAR 4 Producer Edition follows this tradition, but if you have the Studio Edition, never fear—you can still insert an EQ plug-in on as many channels as your CPU will allow. You haven't sacrificed sound, you only lack some conveniences.

1. If necessary, **Shift+click** on the **Show/Hide EQ** and **Show/Hide Plot buttons**. The controls will be displayed.

EQ VIES

Like the Sends area, the EQ display has three modes: hidden, one band, and four bands. Unlike the Sends area, though, you can't scroll to see the fifth and sixth bands. To see all six bands, you must open the EQ edit window by double-clicking on the *plot*—the graphic display of the frequency curve.

2. **Click** on the **EQ Enable button**. The button will turn green to indicate that the EQ is enabled.

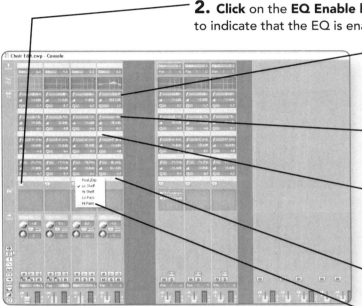

3. **Drag** a **parameter slider** to adjust its value. The parameter value will be displayed numerically next to the slider.

4. **Double-click** a **parameter slider**. The parameter will be reset to its snap-to value.

5. **Click** on the **Band Enable button**. The button will be highlighted to indicate that the band is enabled.

6. **Click** on a **Band Type field**. The Band Type menu will open.

7. **Click** on the desired **band type**. The menu will close, and the new band type will be displayed in the field.

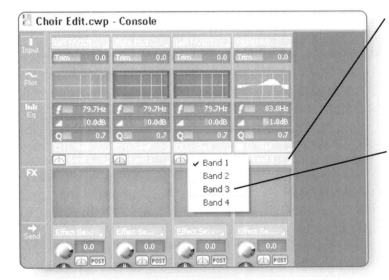

8. If only one band is visible, **click** on the **Band # field**. The Band # menu will open.

9. **Click** on the desired **band**. The menu will close, and the chosen band's parameters will be displayed.

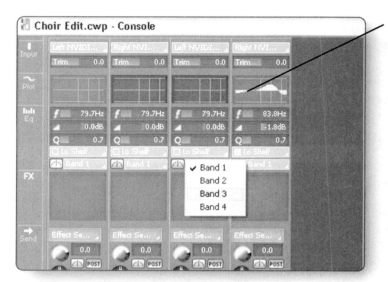

10. **Double-click** on the **plot**. The full FX:Equalizer edit window will open.

Configuring the Console View's Appearance

As you've seen, the Console view can expand to include quite a few different controls. When you display all its controls across a large number of tracks, it can become cumbersome. SONAR lets you configure the Console's display so you can deal with a manageable number of tracks and controls. In addition to the Show/Hide buttons you've already used, you can make tracks narrow or wide, change the width of the three panes, and hide meters and even tracks.

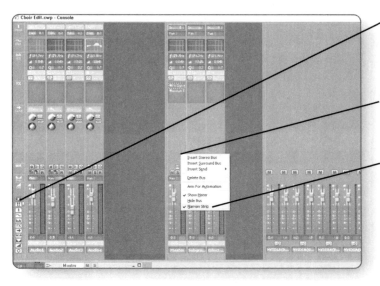

1. **Click** on the **Narrow/Widen All Strips button**. All tracks, buses, and main outs will be made narrower.

2. **Right-click** on a **track**, **bus**, or **main out**. The context menu will open.

3. **Click** on **Narrow Strip**. The track will be widened.

TOGGLING TRACK WIDTH

Clicking on the Narrow/Widen button or the Narrow Track command toggles the status of the track or tracks between narrow and wide display with each successive click.

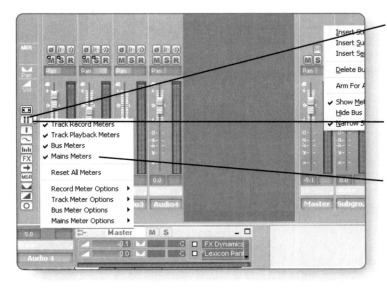

4. **Click** on the **Show/Hide All Meters button**. The display status of all meters in the Console view will be toggled on or off.

5. **Click** on the **Meter Options button**. The Meter Options menu will open.

6. **Click** on a **meter type**. The menu will close, and the display status of that meter type will be toggled on or off.

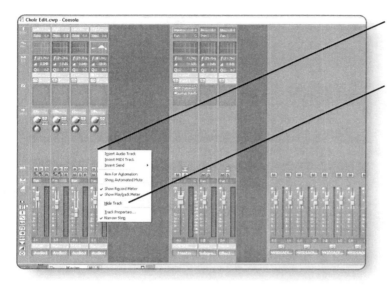

7. Right-click on a **channel strip**. The context menu will appear.

8. Click on **Hide Track**. The track will be hidden from view.

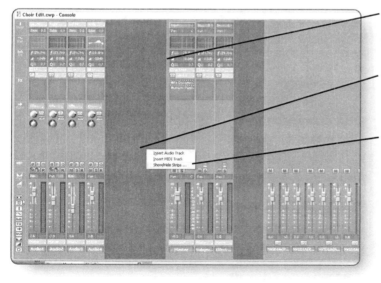

9. Drag the **divider bar** between two panes. The panes will be resized accordingly.

10. Right-click in the **blank space** of a **pane**. The context menu will open.

11. Click on **Show/Hide Strips**. The Track Manager dialog box will appear.

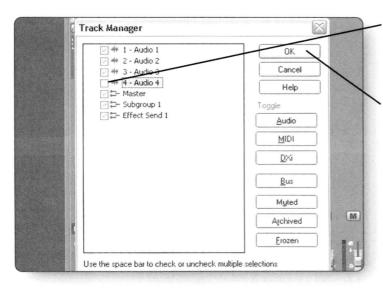

12. **Click** on a **track's check box**. The ✔ next to the track will toggle on or off, depending on its previous status.

13. **Click** on **OK**. The dialog box will close, and the tracks' display status will be updated as you specified.

19

Capturing Your Mix for CD and the Internet

Sooner or later, your music will be ready to share with your adoring fans. When that time arrives, you will most likely produce a CD, streaming audio files such as MP3s, or both. It's increasingly common for musicians to post portions of their songs on their Web sites as MP3s to whet their fans' appetites for buying the CD, so SONAR gives you the tools to create several types of output files. SONAR can't burn the actual CD for you, but it will enable you to prepare files that are ready to be burned from your CD application. In this chapter, you will learn how to:

- Record external synthesizer parts to audio tracks
- Export a mix ready for a CD
- Export a mix ready for the Internet

Recording External Synth Parts

If you don't have any MIDI tracks, you can go straight to the next section. If you do have MIDI parts, though, this is an extremely important step—and one that in many people's minds is shrouded in far more mystery than it deserves. It's quite simple, really: If you have any MIDI parts that are routed to hardware (external) synthesizers, you must record those synthesizers to audio tracks before you export your mix.

Like most host-based digital audio workstations, SONAR creates output files as quickly as your CPU can manage. A relatively simple mix can be turned into a stereo WAV file in a few seconds, and a complex mix with lots of effects can actually take longer than it would take to play the song through. This wreaks havoc on MIDI parts that are triggering external synthesizers, though, so SONAR doesn't even play them while it exports files. If you are using only DXi synthesizers such as the Cakewalk TTS-1, SONAR will include those MIDI parts with no problem, but if you are using any external synthesizers, connect their outputs to inputs on your audio interface and follow these steps.

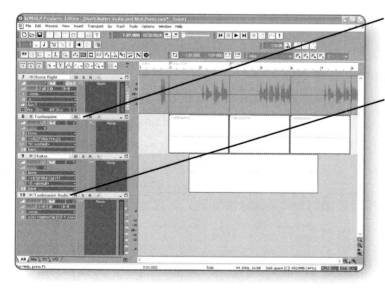

1. **Click** on the **Solo button** of a MIDI track that is triggering a hardware synthesizer. The track will be the only thing that plays.

2. **Create** a **new audio track** and **name it** after the MIDI track you're recording.

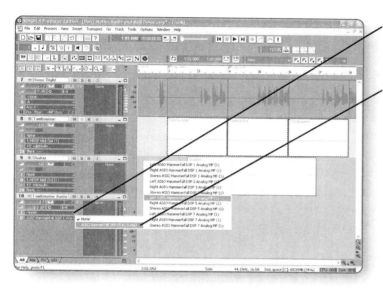

3. Click on the new track's **Input field**. The Input menu will open.

4. Point to the **name** of your audio interface. The interface submenu will open.

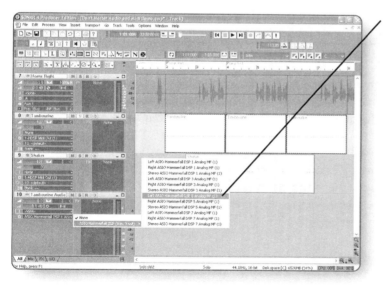

5. Click on the **input** to which your hardware synthesizer is connected. The menu will close, and the track will receive audio from that input.

6. **Click** on the track's **Record Arm button**. The button will turn red, and the track will be ready to record.

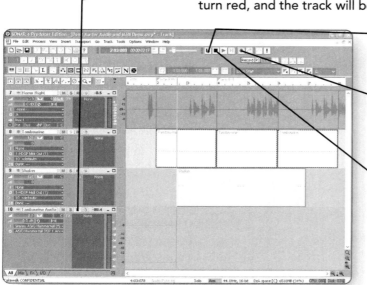

7. **Click** on the **Rewind button**. The Now time will be reset to the beginning of the project.

8. **Click** on the **Record button**. SONAR will record the synthesizer's output to the audio track.

9. When you reach the end of the MIDI track, **click** on the **Stop button**. Recording will stop, and a new clip will appear in the audio track.

INPUT ECHO

If you want to hear the synthesizer track as it is being recorded, turn Input Echo on for the audio track. Don't forget the guidelines discussed in Chapter 8, "Recording Your Own Audio," under "Preparing an Audio Track for Recording" about getting the right input volume for recording. (Hint: It depends on the volume of the synthesizer!)

10. **Click** the **Solo button** of the MIDI track. The button will turn gray.

11. **Click** the **Mute button** of the MIDI track. The button will be highlighted, and the MIDI track will no longer play.

12. **Click** on the **Record Arm button** of the audio track. The button will turn gray.

13. **Click** on **Play**. The project will play back, with the new audio track substituting for the sound of the synthesizer being triggered by the MIDI track. If you are satisfied with the recorded track, repeat Steps 1–12 for any other MIDI tracks that trigger hardware synthesizers.

ARCHIVE IT

It's a good idea to archive each MIDI track as you commit it to an audio track. That way, you preserve its data for reference, but it will not play back.

DON'T SAY THAT!

This process is often mistakenly called "converting MIDI to audio." Even SONAR's documentation uses this misnomer! You can't "convert" MIDI messages to audio, but you can (and just did) record the results of those MIDI messages as they trigger a synthesizer.

Exporting Audio

Now that you've got your MIDI tracks in shape, it's time to export your mix as a single file that can be burned to CD or posted to your Web site. The first part of this process is the same no matter what format you're exporting, so I'll cover it in detail for a WAV file and then discuss the differences for each of the other formats.

Exporting as a WAV File

All Windows computers and most Macintosh applications recognize a WAV file as a standard digital audio file. It has the advantage of being an uncompressed *linear PCM* file, so it doesn't suffer any degradation from the extreme data reduction used in streaming formats. The other side of that coin is that WAV files are quite large, requiring 10MB for each minute of CD-quality audio. This combination makes them ideal for creating audio CDs and impossible for Internet streaming.

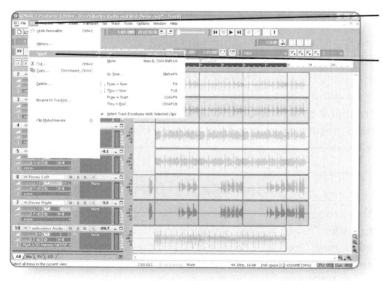

1. Click on **Edit**. The Edit menu will open.

2. Point to **Select**. The Select submenu will open.

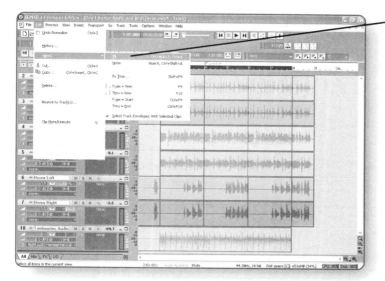

3. Click on **All**. The menu will close, and all clips in all tracks will be selected.

KEEP THE TAIL

If you have any effects such as reverb that have long decays, you will want to lengthen the selection so that you don't cut off the effect "tail." Shift+click in the Time Ruler about 2–3 seconds after the end of the project, and SONAR will continue exporting long enough to catch the effect.

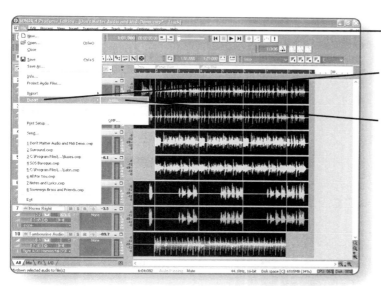

4. Click on **File**. The File menu will open.

5. Point to **Export**. The Export submenu will open.

6. Click on **Audio**. The Export Audio dialog box will appear.

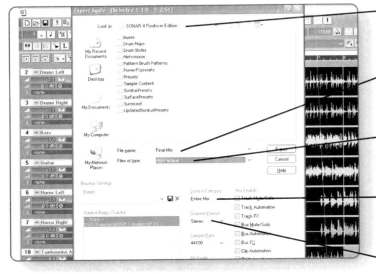

7. Navigate to the desired **folder**. The mix will be exported to this location.

8. Type a **name** for the exported file in the File name field.

9. Choose RIFF Wave from the **Files of type drop-down list box**.

10. Choose Entire Mix from the **Source Category drop-down list box**.

11. Choose Stereo from the **Channel Format drop-down list box**.

EXPORTING STEMS

If you have split your mix out into stems as discussed in Chapter 17, "Mastering Audio's Ins and Outs," you can export each stem to a separate file by choosing Buses from the Source Category drop-down list box.

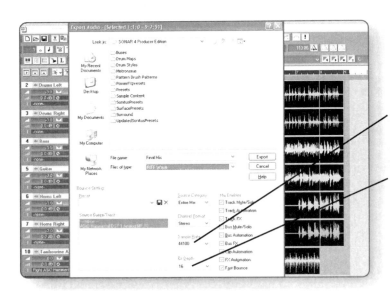

12. Choose 44100 from the **Sample Rate drop-down list box**.

13. Choose 16 from the **Bit Depth drop-down list box**.

WHAT RESOLUTION?

If you are planning to burn this song to CD, 16 bits and 44,100 samples per second is the proper resolution. If, however, you are planning either to send the file to a mastering engineer or to work on it in a mastering program, you should instead export a 24-bit file at the sample rate of your session.

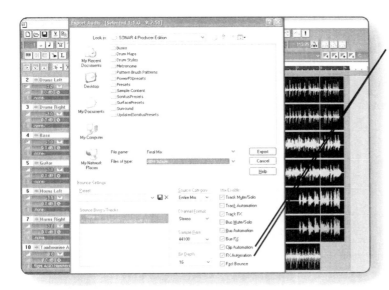

14. If necessary, **click** on the **check box** of any **Mix Enables item** that isn't already checked. A ✔ will appear next to the item.

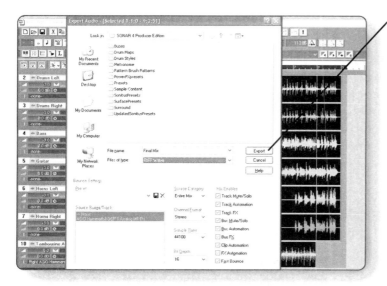

15. **Click** on **Export**. The dialog box will close, and the file (or files) will be created.

THAT'S PROGRESS

As the mix is being exported, a progress bar will appear at the bottom of the SONAR application window. You can click Cancel on the progress bar if you wish to stop the export. When the progress bar is complete, the file is done. This may take anywhere from a few seconds to quite a few minutes, depending on the length of the song, the complexity of the mix, and the speed of your computer.

BOUNCE PRESETS

SONAR 4 allows you to save your bounce settings as a preset. Before you click Export, type a name for these settings in the Preset text box in the Bounce Settings area of the Export Audio dialog box, and click the floppy disk icon. The next time you export audio, you can recall these settings from the Preset drop-down list box.

Exporting an MP3 File

The term *MP3* is one of those rare cases of a truly nerdy word becoming a household name. It refers to an industry-standard type of lossy data reduction for audio files. By applying psychoacoustic principles, scientists came up with a way of removing most of the data from an audio file while maintaining much of the original sound. The sound quality of an MP3 file ranges from recognizable at very low bit rates to almost indistinguishable from the original at higher bit rates. At higher bit rates, the file size can be reduced by 80–90 percent compared to the original WAV file, and at the lowest bit rates the file is only 1–2 percent of its original size!

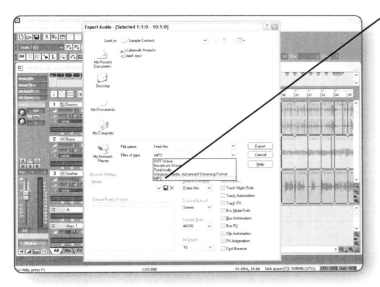

1. Follow the entire procedure above for exporting a WAV file, except at Step 9, **choose MP3 from the Files of type drop-down list box**. When you click on Export, the MP3 Export Options dialog box will appear.

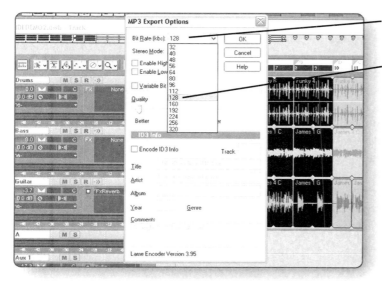

2. Click on the **Bit Rate drop-down list box.** The list will open.

3. Click on the desired **bit rate**. The list will close, and the field will reflect your choice.

WHAT RATE?

If you intend to stream this file over the Internet, a bit rate of 32 kilobits per second (Kbps) will allow users with dial-up connections to receive the stream in real time. If you plan only to play the file locally or if your intended audience has broadband Internet connections, choosing a bit rate of 128 Kbps or higher will yield a much better-sounding result.

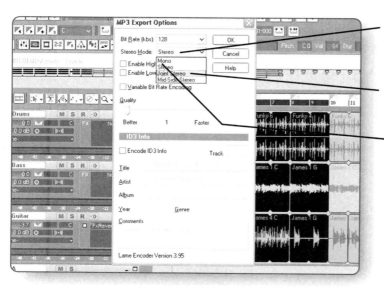

4. Click on the **Stereo Mode drop-down list box.** The list will open.

5. Click on the desired **stereo mode.** The choices include

- **Mono.** This mode will combine your left and right channels, resulting in the loss of all panning and stereo effects from your mix. If the stereo image of your mix is not critical, mono mode allows the file to retain better fidelity at the expense of stereo.

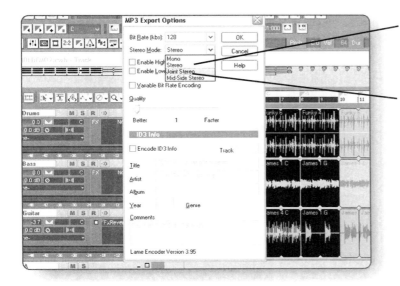

- **Stereo.** This mode will retain the stereo information of your mix. Use it if the stereo image of your mix is critical.

- **Joint Stereo.** This mode saves space by representing stereo information in a useful but less-precise way. Use it as a compromise between mono and stereo.

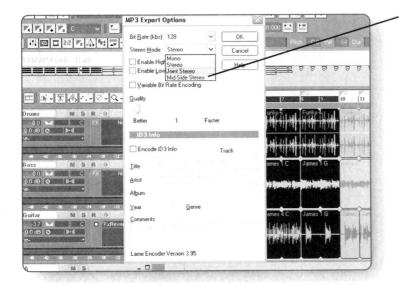

- **Mid-Side Stereo.** This mode is similar to Joint Stereo, but it is especially useful when the mix has a lot of elements panned to the center.

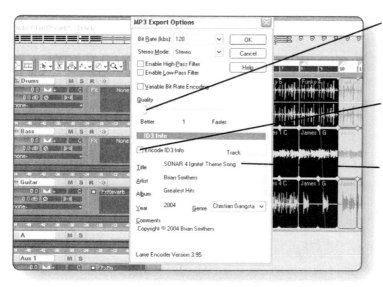

6. **Drag** the **Quality slider** to **Better**. This causes the encoder to take longer and do a better job.

7. Optionally, **click** on **Encode ID3 Info**. A ✔ will appear next to the option.

8. Optionally, **enter** the desired **information** in the **ID3 Info fields**. This information will be displayed when the file is played in an ID3-compatible player.

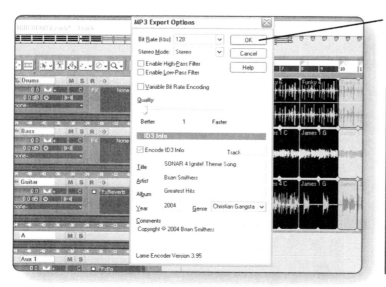

9. **Click** on **OK**. A progress bar will appear, and when it completes the file will be ready.

EXPORTING REALAUDIO AND WINDOWS MEDIA FILES

For information about exporting RealAudio and Windows Media files, see this book's companion Web site.

PART VI

Hidden Magic

20

Working with Notes and Lyrics

SONAR 4 includes two views that many musicians and songwriters will find essential—the Staff view and the Lyrics view. If you already read music, you may find the Staff view to be the most efficient way to get your ideas down, and if you don't read traditional music notation you'll find it helpful in communicating with musicians who do. Although SONAR won't actually sing your lyrics, it allows you to assign lyrics to notes in the Staff view and display them in a separate Lyrics view as well. To top it all off, you can print out scores, parts, and lead sheets, complete with chord symbols. In this chapter, you will learn how to:

- ◯ Enter and edit notes in the Staff view
- ◯ Add expression marks
- ◯ Work with lyrics in the Staff and Lyrics views
- ◯ Print parts and scores

Using the Staff View

As a classically trained musician, I went straight for SONAR's Staff view when I first started sequencing. (To be completely honest, it was Cakewalk 3.0, 11 versions ago!) It just made sense to use the language I knew so well as a starting point when everything else about the program was so new to me. In the long run I have found that I use it less, because the Piano Roll view is more efficient and represents MIDI data more precisely than the Staff view. This is because Piano Roll makes clear all the things that musicians take for granted when they see traditional notation, such as the different meanings of a staccato marking from one tempo to another. Still, SONAR's notation capabilities have many uses, as you'll see.

Configuring the Staff View

The Staff view can display a single track or multiple tracks, so you can print parts or a score. It offers several common clefs, including grand staff, and can even show you a fretboard layout so you can see your MIDI parts from a guitarist's perspective. Here's how to see just what you want to see in the Staff view.

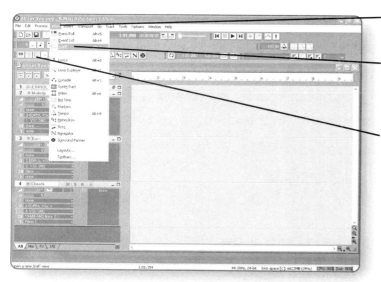

1a. **Click** on **View**. The View menu will open.

1b. **Click** on **Staff**. The Staff view will appear.

OR

1c. **Click** on the **Staff View button**. The Staff view will appear.

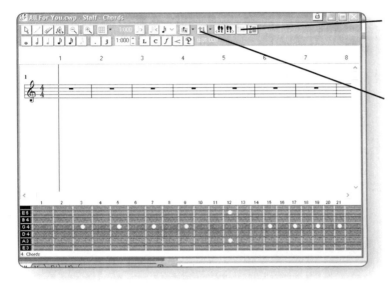

2. Optionally, **click** the **Fret View button**. The Fret view will toggle open or closed, depending on its current state.

3. Click the **Pick Tracks button**. The Pick Tracks dialog box will appear.

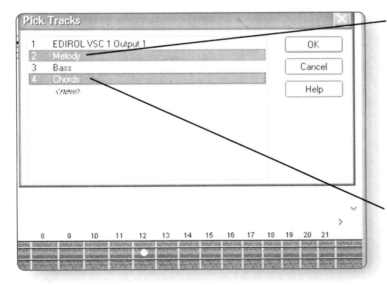

4a. Click on the **name** of the track you want displayed. The track name will be highlighted.

OR

4b. Press the **down arrow** key or **up arrow** key on your computer keyboard. The track highlight will move up or down one track at a time.

5. Optionally, **Shift+click** or **Ctrl+click** to **select additional tracks**. The tracks will be added to the selection.

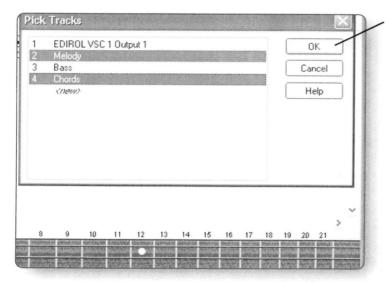

6. **Click** on **OK**. The dialog box will close, and the track(s) you chose will be displayed.

7a. **Click** on the **Zoom In** or **Zoom Out buttons**. The staves will be displayed larger or smaller, respectively.

OR

7b. **Click** and **hold** on the **Zoom slider** and **drag up** or **down**. The staves will be displayed larger or smaller, respectively.

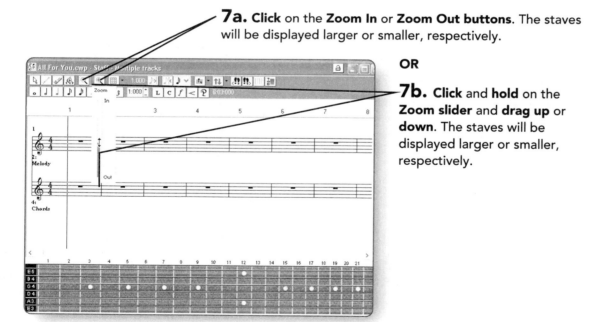

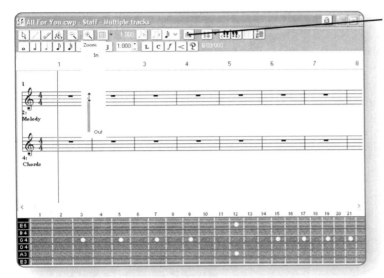

8. Click on the **Layout button**. The Staff View Layout dialog box will appear.

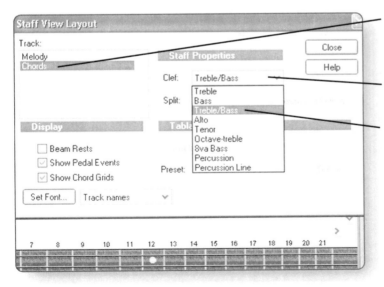

9. Click on a **track name** in the Track list. The track name will be highlighted.

10. Click in the **Clef field**. The Clef drop-down list will open.

11. Click on the desired **clef**. The list will close, and display your choice.

12. Click on **Close**. The dialog box will close, and the Staff view will be updated with your changes.

Working with Notes

Working with notes in SONAR's Staff view uses the same basic principles as adding and editing notes in the Piano Roll view. You enter notes with a pencil, remove them with an eraser, and drag them around with the mouse until you've got the right sound.

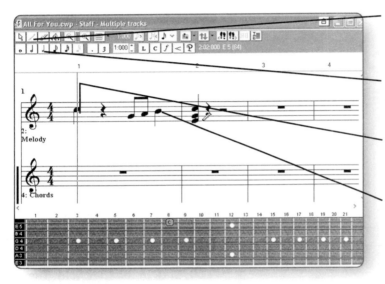

1. Click on the **Draw Tool button**. The mouse pointer appears as a pencil.

2. Click on the desired **note-duration button**. The button will be highlighted.

3. Click on the **staff**. A note of the chosen duration will be placed where you click.

4. Click elsewhere on the **staff**. A new note will be placed where you click, and appropriate rests will fill the space between the two notes you have drawn.

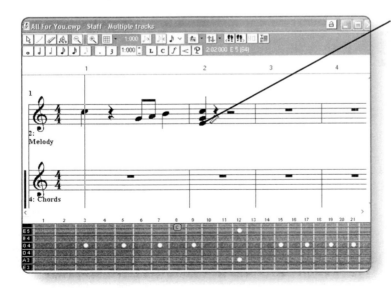

5. Click directly **above** or **below** one of the **notes** you just drew. The notes will be joined as a chord.

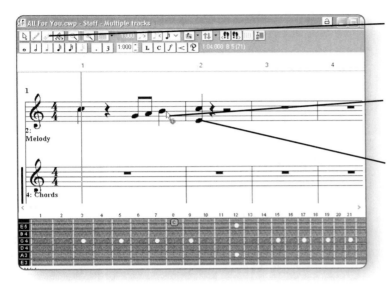

6. Click on the **Erase Tool button**. The mouse pointer appears as an arrow with a slashed circle.

7. Click on a **note**. The note is erased, and rests appear to fill the space it occupied.

8. Click on a **chord note**. The clicked note is erased, but the other notes remain unaffected.

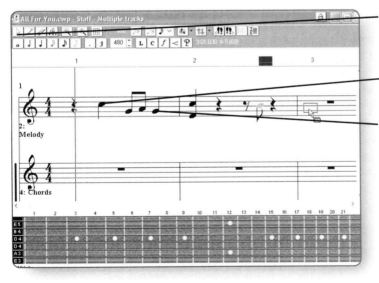

9. Click on the **Select Tool button**. The mouse pointer returns to its default arrow.

10. Drag a **note left** or **right**. The note is repositioned in time.

11. Drag a **note up** or **down**. The note is transposed.

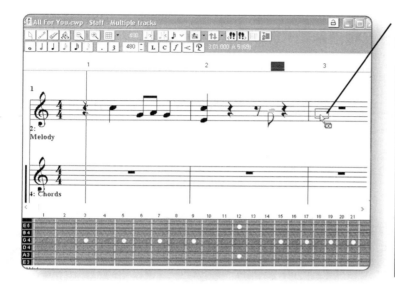

12. Ctrl+drag a **note**. The note is copied.

BLEND OR REPLACE

Depending on how your Drag and Drop Options are set, you may be prompted to choose how the edit is performed when you drag notes. If you choose Blend Old and New, you can actually build chords by dragging notes on top of each other.

Changing How Notes Are Displayed

When you work with notes in SONAR's Staff view, it's essential to understand the difference between what's being displayed and what's being played. In general, the notes you see in the Staff view are being played as you would expect, but the timing resolution of the notation and the actual MIDI notes is very different. Imagine a series of eighth notes played staccato (short)—if you wrote the figure literally, it would be something like a series of 32nd notes with rests between them, but that would be too difficult to read. Because the MIDI data must perform the phrase accurately, it retains such fine detail, but the Staff view can optionally round up the notes to eighth notes for a more appropriate appearance.

1. **Click** on the **Fill Durations button**. The button will be deselected.

2. **Use** the **Draw tool** to **enter** a series of **sixteenth notes**.

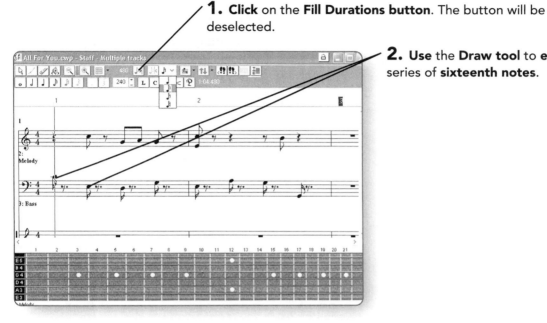

3. **Click** on the **Display Resolution drop-down list box**. The list will open.

4. **Click** on the **eighth note**. The list will close, and the appearance of the notes will change.

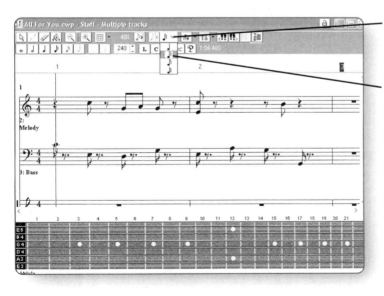

LOOKING BETTER

The Display Resolution setting allows you to minimize the number of rests shown in the Staff view. This changes only the display of the notes without changing the actual MIDI data.

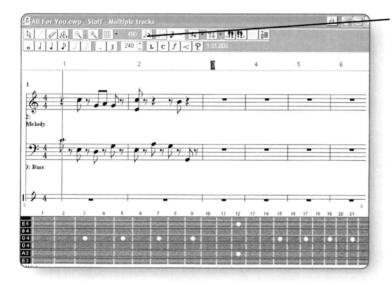

5. Click on the **Fill Durations button**. The appearance of the notes will change.

FEWER RESTS

The Fill Durations setting rounds up the value of notes (in this case to quarter notes) to minimize extraneous rests even further. The big difference between the Fill Durations and Display Resolution settings is that you can't enter rhythmic values smaller than the display resolution, while Fill Durations doesn't restrict your choice of rhythms.

Using the Fret View

The Fret view shows you exactly what's happening when a guitarist plays your music. Each note appears as a note name icon placed on the correct fret. It even supports alternate tunings.

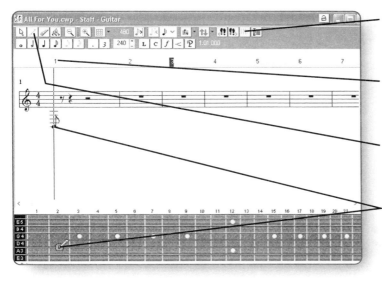

1. If necessary, **click** on the **Fret View button**. The Fret view will appear.

2. Click in the **Time Ruler**. The Now time will snap to where you click.

3. Click on the **Draw Tool button**. The mouse pointer will appear as a pencil.

4. Click on a **string** in the Fret view. A note will appear both on the string and in the staff.

5. Click on the **Erase Tool button**. The mouse pointer will appear as an arrow with a slashed circle.

6. Click on a **note icon** in the Fret view. The note will be deleted.

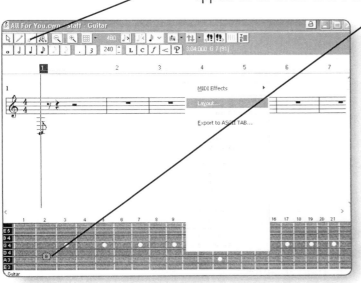

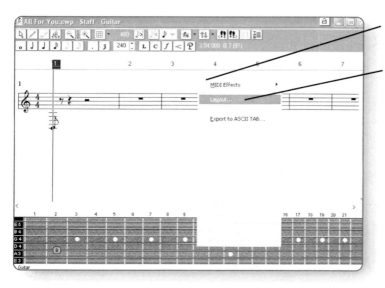

7. Right-click on the **Fretboard**. The context menu will open.

8. Click on **Layout**. The Staff View Layout dialog box will appear.

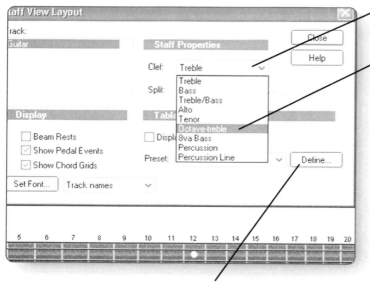

9. Click on the **Clef field**. The Clef drop-down list will open.

10. Click on **Octave-treble**. The list will close and display your choice.

GUITAR CLEF

Octave-treble is the standard clef for guitar notation. This causes all pitches to be written one octave higher than they actually sound, which keeps guitarists from having to switch between bass and treble clefs all the time.

---

11. Click on the **Define button**. The Tablature Settings dialog box will appear.

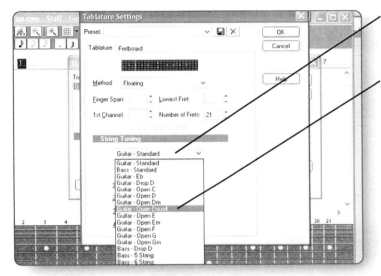

12. **Click** on the **String Tuning drop-down list box**. The String Tuning drop-down list will open.

13. **Click** on the desired **tuning**. The list will close and display your choice.

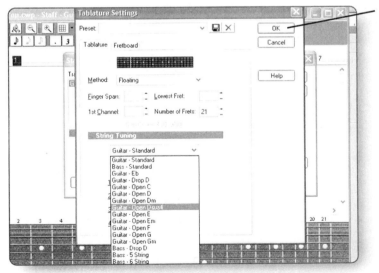

14. **Click** on **OK**. The dialog box will close.

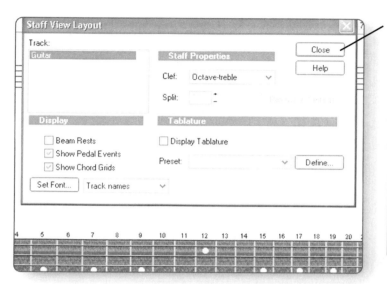

15. Click on **Close**. The dialog box will close, and the clef and string tuning will be changed to reflect your choices.

TUNING

The notes on the staff will not change as a result of the new string tuning, but the position of the note icons on the frets will change accordingly.

Adding Expression Marks

SONAR lets you add certain types of expression marks, such as dynamics and hairpins, which are displayed and printed but have no audible effect. Pedal markings can also be added, and they do transmit MIDI events that emulate the behavior of a piano's sustain pedal.

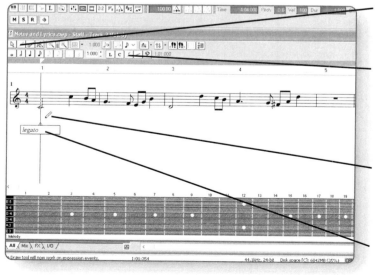

1. Click on the **Draw Tool button**. The mouse pointer will appear as a pencil.

2. Click on the **Expression Tool button**. The mouse pointer will be a pencil only when you position it about two leger lines below the staff.

3. Click below the **note** or **rest** at which you want the expression mark to appear. A text box will appear.

4. Type in the **text box**. The text will appear as you type it.

5. **Press Enter**. The text box will close, and the expression mark will appear.

TEXT AND DYNAMICS

SONAR will display whatever you type as a text marking unless it is a standard dynamic marking such as *mp* or *f*, in which case the corresponding dynamic symbol will be used.

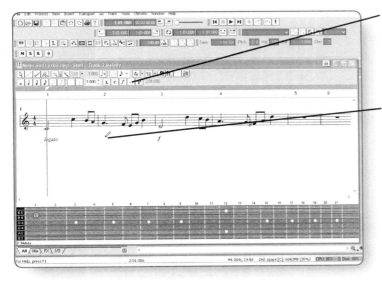

6. **Click** on the **Hairpin Tool button**. The mouse pointer will change to a pencil only when you position it about two leger lines below the staff.

7. **Click below** the **note** or **rest** at which you want the hairpin to begin. A hairpin symbol will appear.

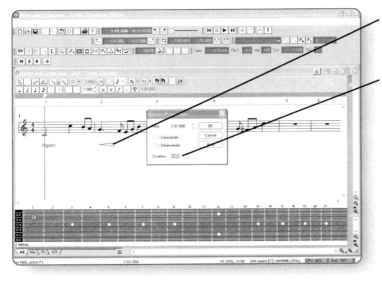

8. Right-click on the **hairpin**. The Hairpin Properties dialog box will appear.

9. Click on the desired **options** or **type values** in number boxes to set the hairpin's parameters.

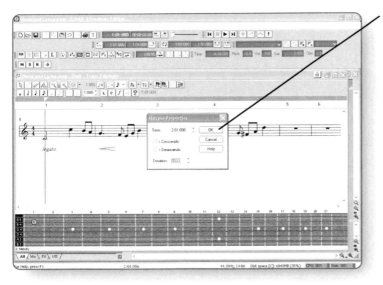

10. Click on **OK**. The dialog box will close, and the hairpin will be updated according to your specifications.

HAIRPIN MEMORY

The next time you click to create a hairpin, it will use the most-recently specified parameters.

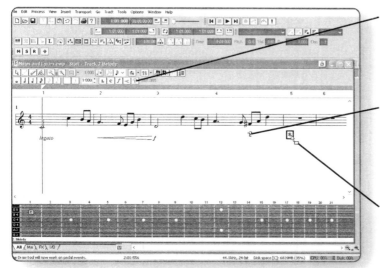

11. **Click** on the **Pedal Tool button.** The mouse pointer will change to a pencil only when you position it about two leger lines below the staff.

12. **Click below** the **note** or **rest** at which you want the pedal marking to begin. A pair of symbols (down and up) will appear.

13. Optionally, **drag one** or **both** of the **pedal markings** to a new location. The pedal events will be relocated.

PEDALS IN ORDER

Because the pedal markings have meaning as MIDI events, it's important to keep them in order. The *P* must always be followed by the * or you will not get the desired effect.

Using Lyrics

Lyrics will make absolutely no difference to the sound of your song, but SONAR gives songwriters the power to keep track of their lyrics, print them, and use them as a guide when recording vocals.

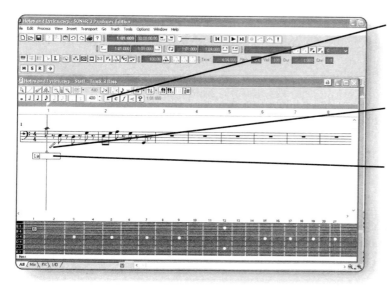

1. **Click** on the **Lyrics Tool button**. The mouse pointer will change to a pencil only when you position it directly below a note.

2. **Click below** the **note** at which you want the lyrics to begin. A text box will appear.

3. **Type** your **lyrics** in the text box.

4. **Press Enter**. The box will close, and your lyrics will appear below the notes.

TYPING TIPS

The text box will advance to the next note whenever you type a space or a hyphen, so you can type as many lyrics as you have notes. You can type multiple hyphens for syllables that last over several notes.

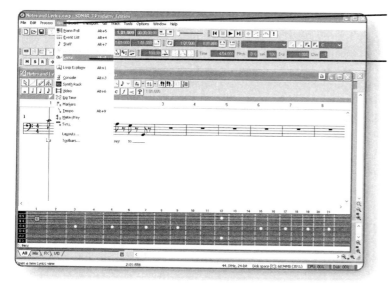

5. **Click** on **View**. The View menu will open.

6. **Click** on **Lyrics**. The Lyrics view will appear.

7. If necessary, **click** on the **Pick Tracks button** and use the dialog box that appears to choose the correct track.

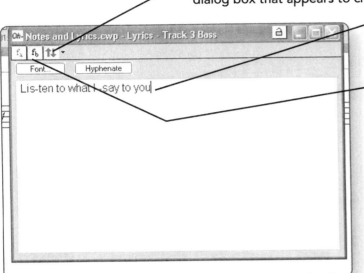

8. Type lyrics in the text box. The lyrics will be updated in the Staff view as you type them.

9. Optionally, **click** the **Select font B button**. The lyrics will be displayed in a much larger font designed to be visible from a distance (as when recording the vocal part).

Printing Parts and Scores

By Cakewalk's own admission, SONAR's Staff view is not intended to replace high-end music notation programs. It does, however, let you make decent reference parts and lead sheets for getting your ideas across quickly and clearly to your fellow musicians.

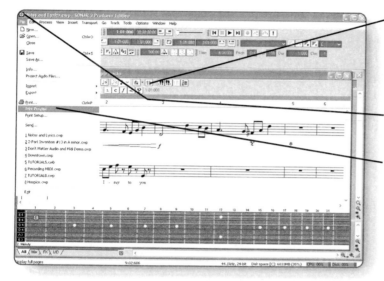

1. Click on the **Pick Tracks button** and use the dialog box to choose the correct track. These are the tracks that will be printed.

2. Click on **File**. The File menu will open.

3. Click on **Print Preview**. The Print Preview window will appear.

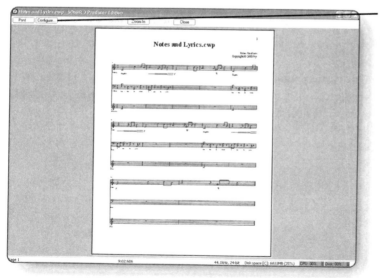

4. Click on the **Configure button**. The Staff View Print Configure dialog box will appear.

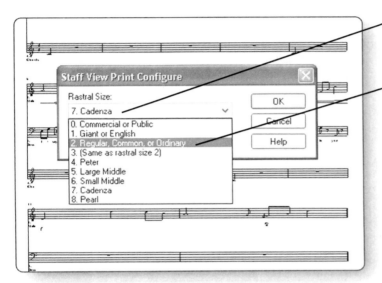

5. Click on the **Rastral Size drop-down list box**. The list will open.

6. Click on the desired **rastral size**. The list will close and display your choice.

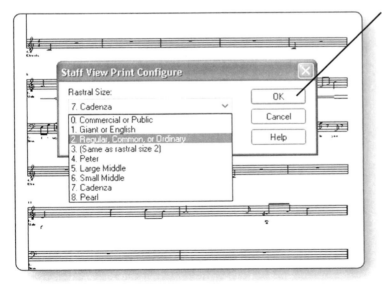

7. Click on **OK**. The dialog box will close, and the preview will be updated to reflect your choice.

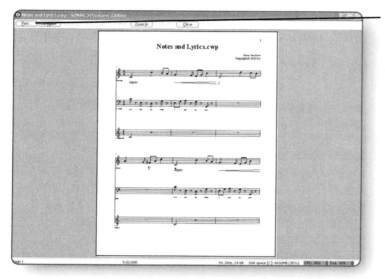

8. **Click** on **Print**. The Print dialog box will appear, and the score will be printed as soon as you **click** on **OK**.

THE RIGHT RASTRAL

The various rastral sizes will allow you to fit more or less music onto each printed page. SONAR's documentation describes the choices in detail, but ultimately you'll want to print some test pages to find the right rastral size for your current needs.

21

Using Drum Maps and the Drum Grid

Face it, drums are just different from most instruments. (Drummers are different, too, but that's another book!) Most drum sounds don't have pitches in the usual sense, and the duration of their tones is usually short and/or fixed. As a result, synthesizers deal with drums differently, and so does SONAR. Two tools—drum maps and the Drum Grid—let you manage MIDI drum information in ways uniquely suited to percussive instruments. In this chapter, you will learn how to:

- ● Assign a MIDI drum track to a drum map
- ● View and customize the Drum Grid
- ● Use the Drum Grid's editing tools
- ● Customize a drum map

Assigning a Track to a Drum Map

A SONAR drum map is a special way of viewing MIDI drum tones. Synthesizers ordinarily assign drum sounds to a single patch, with snare assigned to one note, kick to another, and so on. SONAR lets you organize these tones into a manageable set, ignoring sounds you don't need and even reassigning note numbers for ease of playing or displaying your drum kit. Before you can use the Drum Grid, you need to assign a track to a drum map.

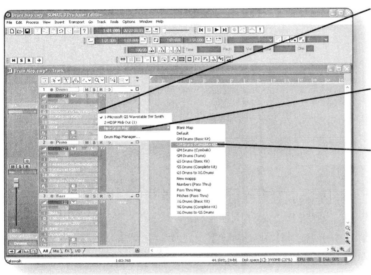

1. Click on the **down arrow** at the right of the **MIDI Output field**. The MIDI Output menu will open.

2. Point to **New Drum Map**. The New Drum Map submenu will open.

3. Click on the **name** of the desired **drum map**. The menu will close, and the chosen drum map will be displayed as the track's MIDI output.

CHANNEL, BANK, PATCH

Once you have assigned a track to a drum map, its Channel, Bank, and Patch fields are inactive. This is because the drum map takes care of those assignments automatically.

Viewing the Drum Grid

The Drum Grid is really just a special case of the Piano Roll view whose display has been customized for dealing with drums. As with any SONAR editing view, you can control how the Drum Grid appears, allowing you to see information in the way that is most efficient and useful.

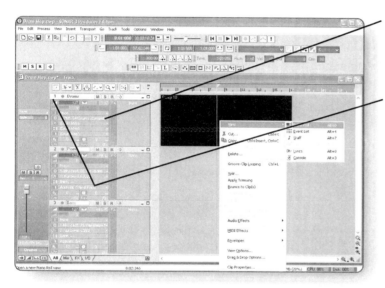

1. If necessary, **assign** a **MIDI track** to a **drum map** as described in the preceding section.

2. **Click** on the **track number**. The track will be selected.

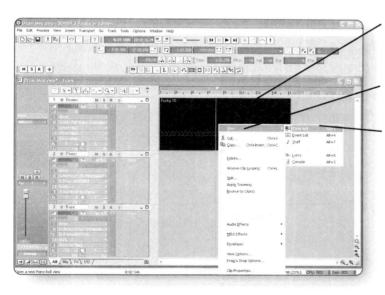

3. **Right-click anywhere** on the **track**. The context menu will open.

4. **Point** to **View**. The View submenu will open.

5. **Click** on **Piano Roll**. The Drum Grid will appear.

TRY AGAIN

If you open the Piano Roll view before assigning the track to a drum map, it will retain its Piano Roll appearance until you close the view and re-open it.

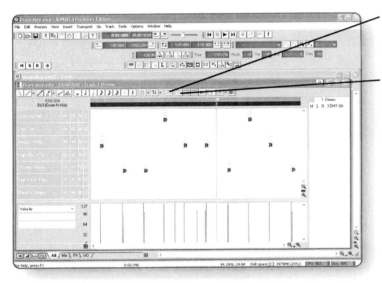

6. Click on the **Show/Hide Controller Pane button**. The Controller pane will be hidden.

7. Click on the **Show/Hide Track Pane button**. The Track pane will be hidden.

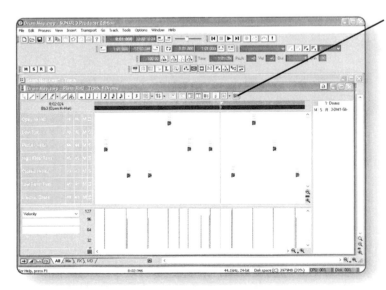

8. If necessary, **click** on the **Show Durations button**. The display format of the notes will change.

DRUM DURATIONS

Showing note durations is unnecessary when working with drums, because when you hit a drum it rings and stops, unlike a clarinet tone that is sustained by the player. In fact, most MIDI drum patches completely ignore Note Off messages! Showing durations in SONAR's Drum Grid will ordinarily just make the view more cluttered, so leave durations off.

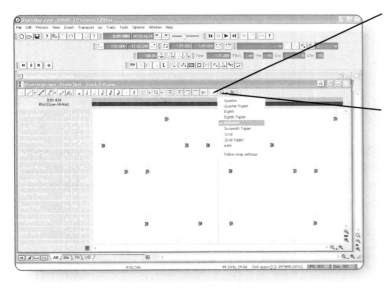

9. If necessary, **click** on the **Show Velocity Tails button**. The button will be highlighted, and each note will display a small ladder that indicates its velocity.

10. If necessary, **click** on the **Show/Hide Grid button**. The button will be highlighted, and a rhythmic grid will be displayed in the Notes pane.

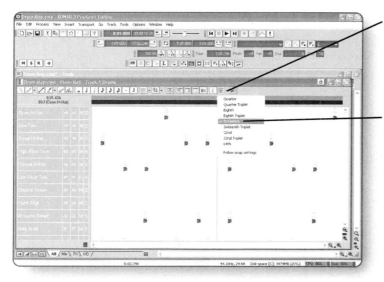

11. **Right-click** on the **down arrow** at the right of the **Show/Hide Grid button**. The Grid drop-down list box will open.

12. **Click** on the desired **grid resolution**. The displayed grid will reflect the specified resolution.

Editing in the Drum Grid

Editing in the Drum Grid is similar to editing in the Piano Roll view, but you have a couple of drum-specific functions at your disposal now. You will also find the Pattern Brush to be more interesting in this view.

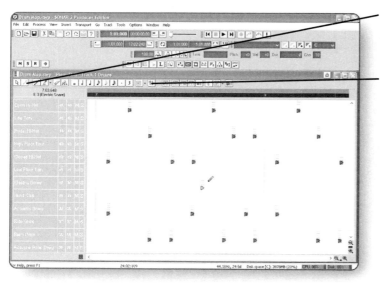

1. **Click** on the **Draw Tool button**. The mouse pointer will appear as a pencil.

2. Optionally, **click** on the **Snap to Grid button**. The button will be highlighted and drawing and editing will be rhythmically constrained to the grid.

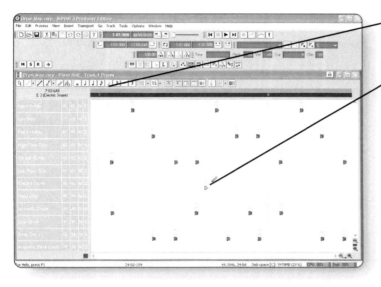

3. Click on a desired **rhythmic value button**. The button will be highlighted.

4. Click in the **Notes pane**. A new note of the specified rhythmic value will be created where you click.

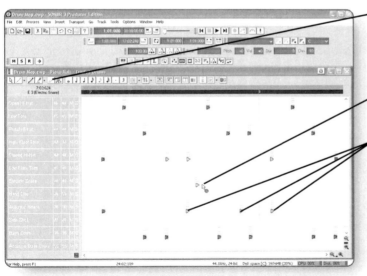

5. Click on the **Eraser Tool button**. The mouse pointer will appear as an arrow with a slashed circle.

6. Click on a **note**. The note will be erased.

7. Drag across **multiple notes**. The notes will be erased.

FAMILIAR TECHNIQUES

Other editing functions you remember from working in the Piano Roll view apply here as well, such as dragging notes with the Select tool, Ctrl+dragging to copy, and lassoing notes to move, copy, or delete them as a unit.

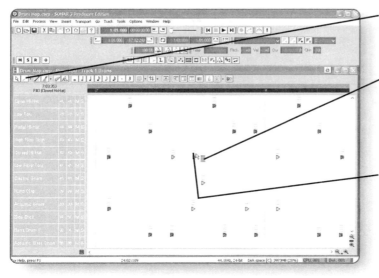

8. Click on the **Draw Tool button**. The mouse pointer will appear as a pencil.

9. Point to a note's **velocity tail**. The mouse pointer will sprout a velocity tail of its own, indicating that it is ready to edit the note's velocity.

10. Click and **drag up** or **down**. The note's velocity tail will grow longer or shorter, indicating increased or decreased velocity, respectively.

PERFECT VIEW

Now you see the power of the Drum Grid. Everything is laid out according to a visible rhythmic grid, notes are identified by name instead of their equivalent keyboard pitch, irrelevant duration information is hidden, and velocity is easily edited right at the note level. Getting familiar with this view will definitely help you produce better drum tracks more quickly.

Editing Drum Maps

The drum map is responsible for how those notes are displayed along the left edge of the Drum Grid. SONAR allows you to customize a drum map in almost infinite ways, from limiting what notes get displayed to changing their order regardless of pitch. You can even build a drum map that triggers different hardware and software synthesizers on different notes—the ultimate drum kit! It's a deep and powerful tool, and these steps will get you started.

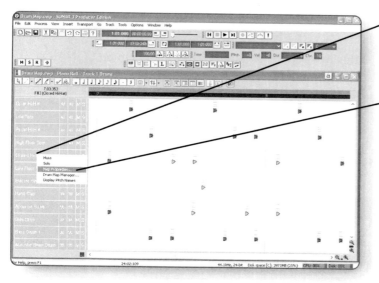

1. **Right-click** on the **note** you wish to modify in the **Drum Map pane**. The context menu will open.

2. **Click** on **Map Properties**. The Map Properties dialog box will appear.

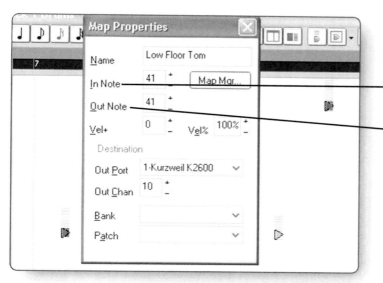

3. **Edit** the note's **parameters** as desired. Key parameters include

- **In Note.** This is the pitch you will play to trigger this note.

- **Out Note.** This is the pitch SONAR will send to the synthesizer when this note is triggered.

SO FAR, SO GOOD

If this remapping of notes were the *only* thing SONAR's drum maps did for you, it would still be extremely cool. This allows you to reassign the various notes of a drum kit to notes that are easy to play from your master keyboard or to make a Kurzweil drum patch respond to the General MIDI arrangement of drum tones.

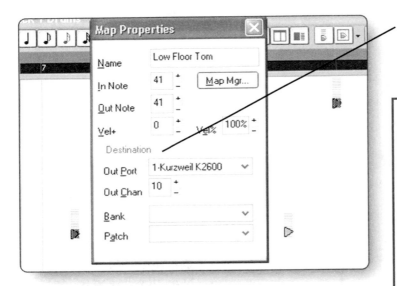

- **Destination.** These settings specify which synthesizer will be triggered when you play this note.

OUTPUT PORTS

Theoretically, each note of a drum map can trigger a different synthesizer. In this dialog box, the Out Port setting lists instruments as assigned in the Assign Instruments dialog box. (Refer to the section "Assigning Instruments" in Chapter 15, "Mastering MIDI's Ins and Outs," for details.)

4a. **Click** on the **Close button**. The dialog box will close.

OR

4b. **Click** on the **Map Mgr. button**. The Drum Map Manager dialog box will appear.

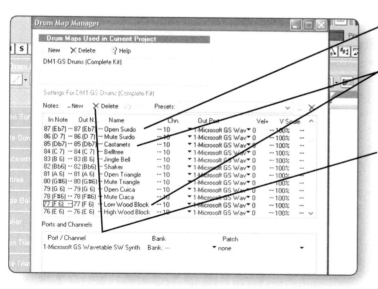

5. **Click** on a **note**. The note will be highlighted.

6. Optionally, **Ctrl+click** or **Shift+click** to **select additional notes**. The notes will be added to the selection.

7. **Click** on the **Delete button**. The notes will be deleted from the drum map.

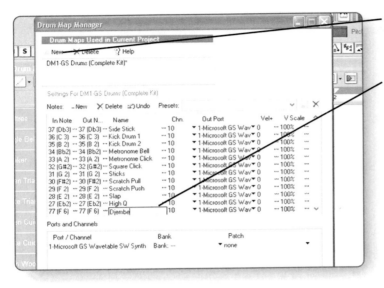

8. **Click** on the **New button**. A new note will be created in the drum map.

9. **Double-click** on any **note parameter**. The parameter will be highlighted for editing.

10. **Type** a **value** and **press Enter**. The parameter will be changed.

ALL ACCESS

The parameters available in the Drum Map Manager are the same as those in the Map Properties dialog box, except that the Drum Map Manager gives you access to all notes in the map simultaneously. The Out Port field lists MIDI outputs rather than instruments, but it's referring to the same thing as the Map Properties dialog box.

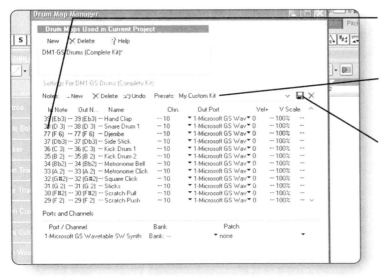

11. Drag a **note** to a new location. The order of notes will be changed.

12. Type a **name** in the **Presets field**. The name will be displayed.

13. Click on the **Save button**. The current drum map will be saved for future use.

ROLL YOUR OWN

Take the time to configure a drum map that uses only the notes that you regularly use. Arrange them in an order that is easy to read, and assign input notes that make it easy to play. Choose output ports that take advantage of the best sounds you have on your various synthesizers, and then save your new drum map as a preset so you can recall it whenever you are creating drum parts.

22

Grooving with Cyclone DXi

Cyclone DXi is a virtual instrument included with both the Producer and Studio Editions of SONAR 4. It represents a major step forward in manipulating audio loops, allowing you to go beyond mere triggering to the point of actually playing loops like an instrument. In this chapter, you will learn how to:

- Work with Cyclone's pads
- Edit individual slices
- Trigger sounds with MIDI
- Trigger individual slices

Using Cyclone's Pads

Like many drum machines, Cyclone uses a set of pads to trigger its sounds. You can load a complete audio file or just a fragment on each pad and trigger them independently to build complex beats.

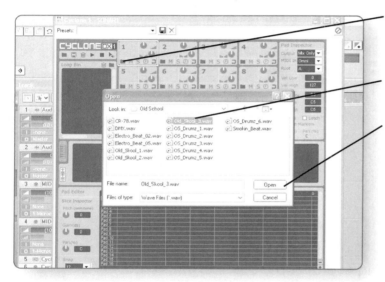

1. Click on a pad's **Load button**. The Open dialog box will appear.

2. Click on an **audio file**. The file will be highlighted.

3. Click on **Open**. The dialog box will close, and the file will be loaded into Cyclone and assigned to the pad.

READY TO GO

When you first load a file onto a pad, the file will be displayed in the Loop view and Pad Editor, ready for editing and manipulation.

4. Click on the **pad**. The audio file will start to play and will loop when it reaches its end.

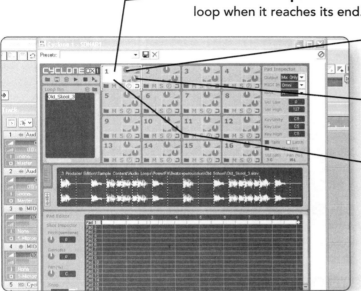

5. Drag the pad's **volume knob**. The volume will change accordingly.

6. Drag the pad's **pan knob**. The pad's pan position will change accordingly.

7. Click on the **pad**. Playback will stop.

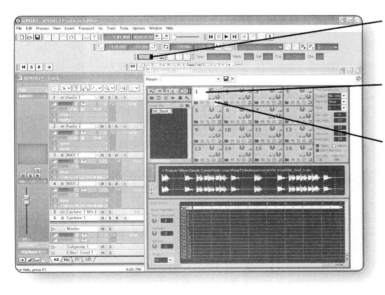

8. Double-click in SONAR's **Tempo field** and type a new tempo.

9. Click on the **Cyclone pad**. The file will play at the new tempo.

10. Click on the pad's **Sync button**. The file will play at its original tempo, ignoring SONAR's tempo.

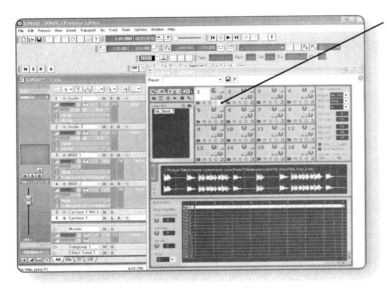

11. Click on the pad's **Loop button**. The file will stop without looping when it reaches its end.

LOOP AND SYNC

You can synchronize multiple loops within Cyclone. Simply assign each loop to a different pad, make sure each pad's Loop and Sync buttons are enabled, and trigger the pads.

Editing Individual Slices

When you import groove clips into Cyclone, its individual slices will be displayed in the Loop view and Pad Editor. You can use the Slice Inspector to change the pitch, gain, and pan of each slice.

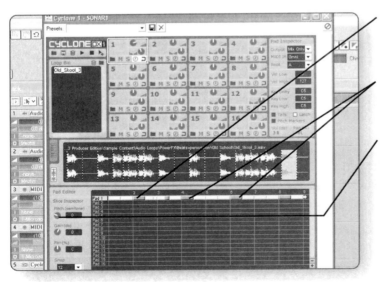

1. Click on a **slice** in the Pad Editor. The slice will be highlighted.

2. Optionally, **Shift+click** on **additional slices**. The slices will be added to the selection.

3. Click and **drag** on the **Pitch, Gain,** or **Pan knobs** in the Slice Inspector. The parameters of the selected slice(s) will be modified.

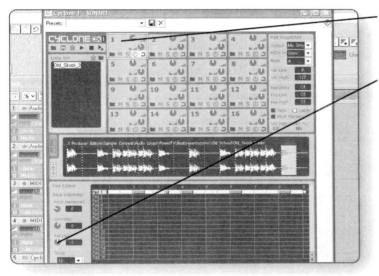

4. Click on the **pad**. The playback will reflect the modifications.

5. Optionally, **change parameters** during playback. The changes will be heard as soon as the file loops.

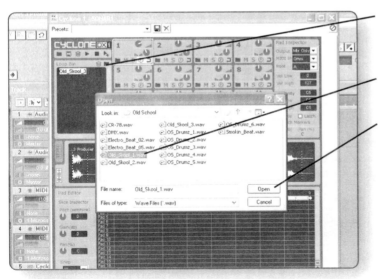

6. Click on the **Load button** in the Loop Bin. The Open dialog box will appear.

7. Click on an **audio file**. The file will be highlighted.

8. Click on **Open**. The dialog box will close, and the file will be loaded into Cyclone without being assigned to a pad.

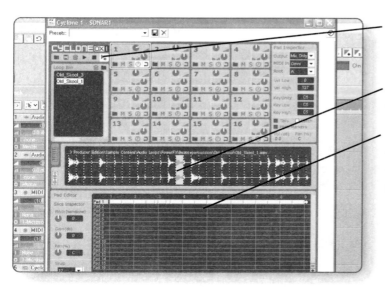

9. Click on the **Auto Preview button**. The button will be highlighted.

10. Click on a **slice** in the Loop view. The slice will play.

11. Drag a **slice** from the Loop view and drop it on a slice in the Pad Editor. The new slice will replace the old slice.

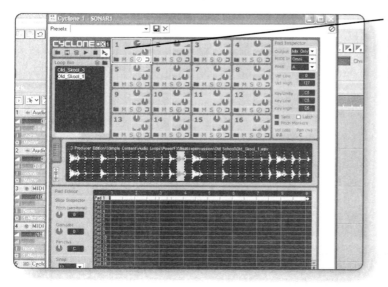

12. Click on the **pad** to audition the change. The loop will play back with the new slice in place of the original slice.

REPLACING SOUNDS

This is a great way to replace drum sounds. If you've got a drum loop that feels right but doesn't have the sound you're after, drag the right sounds from a different loop onto the corresponding beats of the original loop. The loops are not permanently changed by this process.

Using MIDI to Play Cyclone

Everything about Cyclone can be controlled via MIDI. That means also that you can record MIDI tracks to play Cyclone, and then apply all of your MIDI editing knowledge to those tracks to achieve a perfect performance.

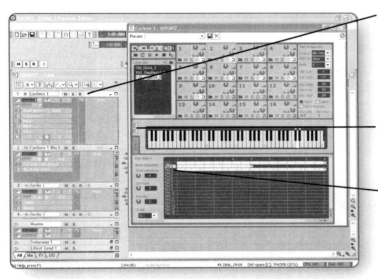

1. If necessary, **click** on the **Input Echo button** on the Cyclone's MIDI track. The button will be highlighted, indicating that MIDI input will be sent to the Cyclone to be played.

2. Click on the **Key Map View tab**. The tab will come to the front.

3. Click on a **track** in the Pad Editor. The MIDI note that is assigned to trigger that pad will be highlighted in the Key Map view.

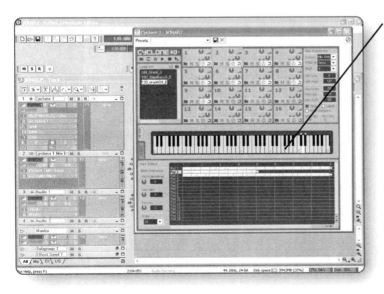

4. On your MIDI keyboard, **play** the **note** that is assigned to trigger the pad. The pad will play.

5. Play the **same note** again. The pad will stop playing.

LATCH

By default, Cyclone's pads toggle between play and stop at each Note On message, ignoring Note Off messages entirely. You can change this behavior on a pad-by-pad basis by selecting a pad and deselecting Latch in the Pad Inspector.

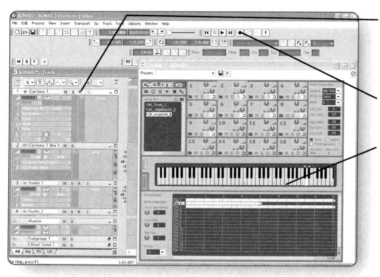

6. **Click** on the **Record Arm button** on a MIDI track assigned to Cyclone. The button will be highlighted.

7. **Click** on the **Record button**. Recording will start.

8. On your MIDI keyboard, **play** the **MIDI note** assigned to the pad repeatedly. Playback of the pad's loop will start and stop accordingly.

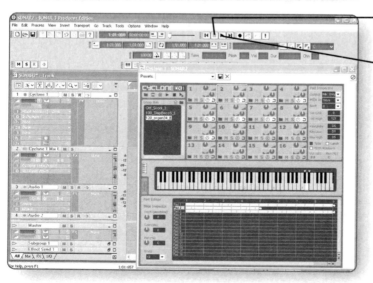

9. **Click** on **Stop**. Recording will stop.

10. **Click** on **Play**. The sequence of events you recorded will play back, starting and stopping the pad's loop in the same way.

PLAYING LOOPS

This is another way to build a track out of loops, instead of rolling them out in audio tracks. This method has the advantage of letting you replace or alter individual slices of the loops, as you've seen. It also lets you "play" the loops, building the arrangement by ear instead of by eye.

Triggering Individual Slices

Another Cyclone technique involves assigning each slice of a loop to a separate pad. If you play all the pads at once, you will hear the loop in its original form, but if you play only some of the pads you will hear only parts of the loop. Its feel will be the same, but you can create variations by subtracting notes this way.

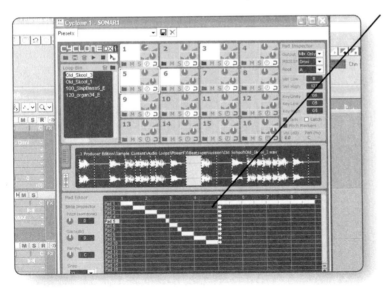

1. **Drag** the **track handle** to the **beginning** of **measure five**. The loop is now four bars long.

ODD LOOPING

You can actually create complex and interesting odd-meter loops by dragging the track handles of different loops to locations other than downbeats. By having different track-handle positions for multi-ple loops, you can set up interesting rhythmic counterpoints.

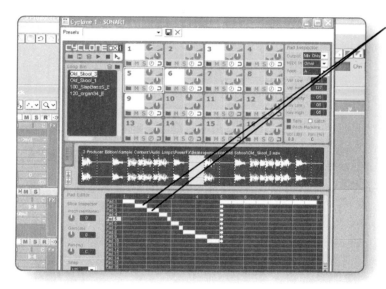

2. Shift+drag each **slice** to a **separate track**. Because each track corresponds to a pad, each slice is now assigned to a separate pad, and because Shift locks each slice in time, the loop's rhythm is maintained.

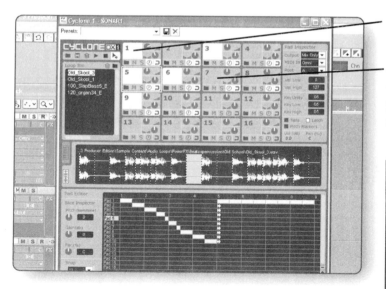

3. Click on **every pad**. The loop will play in its original form.

4. Click on **various pads**. The various slices will be silenced as you click pads off and reintroduced as you click pads back on.

MIDI CONTROL

Of course, you can trigger the pads from your MIDI keyboard and record your variations to a MIDI track, then copy/paste and edit them.

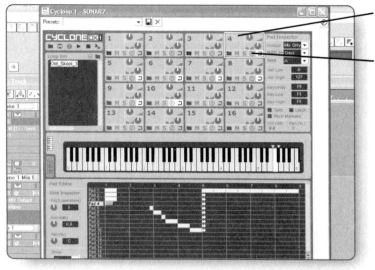

5. Click on a **pad**. The pad will be selected.

6. Click on the pad's **Sync button**. The button will be grayed out.

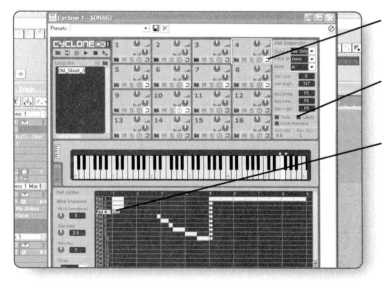

7. Click on the pad's **Loop button**. The button will be grayed out.

8. Click on the **Latch button** in the Pad Inspector. The button will be grayed out.

9. Drag the **pad's slice** all the way to the **beginning** of **bar one** in the Pad Editor. The slice will be repositioned so it will trigger without delay.

10. Repeat these steps for the remaining pads.

11. After making sure that Input Echo is enabled for the MIDI track, **play** the various **MIDI notes** to trigger the pads. Each slice will be triggered immediately when its MIDI note is played.

IT'S A DRUM KIT!

You just turned a loop into a sampled drum kit! You can now play all of the sounds that make up the loop as though they were regular MIDI notes in a drum patch, playing them in any order and rhythm you desire. Of course, you can record your performance to a MIDI track, too.

PLAYING SONAR'S OTHER VIRTUAL INSTRUMENTS

For more information about using virtual instruments in SONAR 4, including the DreamStation DXi, see this book's companion Web site.

23

Getting More Efficient

Having made it this far, you've got a good idea of how SONAR 4 works and how to do most anything you want. The next thing for you to do is to become so efficient with operating SONAR that you can focus on your creativity rather than all this cool technology. SONAR includes a number of features that are designed to help you do just that. You can create custom templates that have all the tracks and buses you need for the way you work, and you can assign virtually any function to a keyboard command to save time fumbling through menus. In this chapter, you will learn how to:

- Create and use custom project templates
- Use and customize key bindings
- Use the Patch Browser
- Use the Track/Bus Inspector
- Use the Track menu to assign inputs and outputs

Using Templates

Every time you create a new SONAR project, you choose from a list of templates. Each template holds a particular arrangement of tracks, I/O configurations, tempo, meter, key, metronome settings, and more information designed to save you time and effort in setting up a project. You should definitely spend some time exploring the existing templates to see which of them are appropriate for your needs. Some of them even provide good object lessons in SONAR signal flow, such as the various mixer templates at the top of the list.

Creating Your Own Templates

Sooner or later, you'll want to create one or more templates that are customized to your needs. It's as simple as saving a project—if you save it the right way and in the right folder, it will appear in your list of templates every time you start a new project.

1. **Create** a **new project** and **customize** it with one or more of the following steps.

2. **Create audio** and **MIDI tracks**.

3. **Assign inputs** and **outputs**.

4. **Assign MIDI ports, channels, drum maps, banks,** and **patches**.

5. **Create buses** and **sends**.

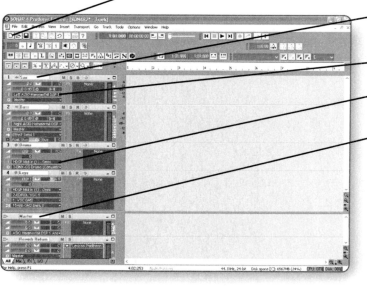

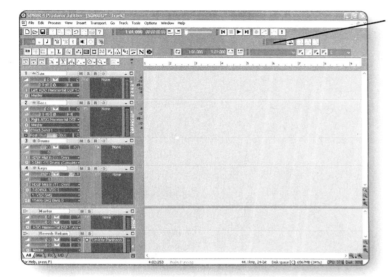

6. Set the **tempo**, **meter**, and **key**.

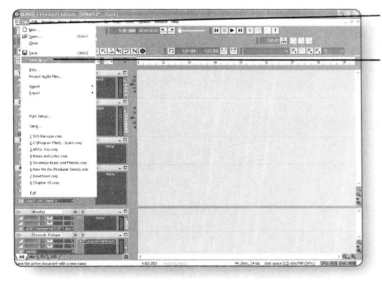

7. Click on **File**. The File menu will open.

8. Click on **Save As**. The Save As dialog box will appear.

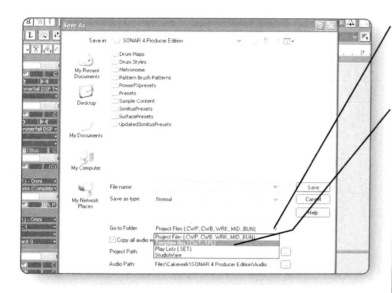

9. Click on the **down arrow** at the right of the **Go to Folder drop-down list box**. The list will open.

10. Click on **Templates (CWT, TPL)**. The list will close, and the window will display the contents of the Templates folder.

WHERE ARE THEY?

By default, the Templates folder is C:\Program Files\Cakewalk\SONAR 4 Producer Edition\Sample Content. (If you have SONAR 4 Studio Edition, the path will reflect that instead of Producer.) Note that you can change the folder for storing templates from the Global Options dialog box.

11. Type a **name** for your template in the **File name field**. SONAR will add the appropriate file extension.

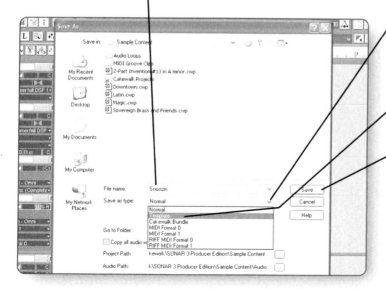

12. Click on the **down arrow** at the right of the **Save as Type drop-down list box**. The list will open.

13. Click on **Template**. The list will close.

14. Click on **Save**. The dialog box will close, and your project will be saved as a template.

A RUNNING START

The next time you create a new project, your template will be listed alphabetically among the available templates. When you base a new project on this template, you will start with all of the tracks and other settings you just configured, saving you valuable time.

Creating a New Default Template

The default template is the one called "Normal" that is already highlighted every time you create a new project. It is also the file that opens if you bypass the Quick Start dialog box that greets you each time you start SONAR or use Ctrl+N to create a new project. It is a regular template, so making one of your templates the default is as easy as renaming it.

1. **Open** the desired **template** or **configure** a **project** as you want the default template to appear.

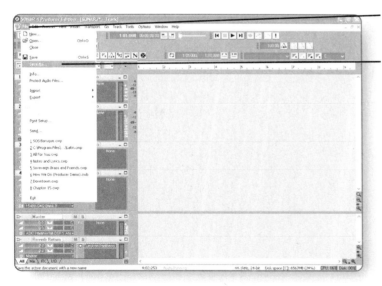

2. **Click** on **File**. The File menu will open.

3. **Click** on **Save As**. The Save As dialog box will appear.

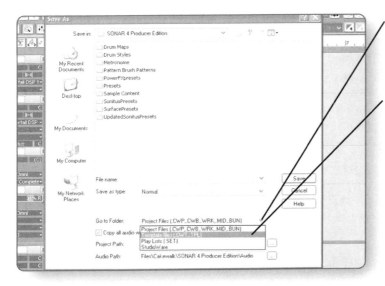

4. **Click** on the **down arrow** at the right of the **Go to Folder drop-down list box.** The list will open.

5. **Click** on **Templates (CWT, TPL).** The list will close, and the window will display the contents of the Templates folder.

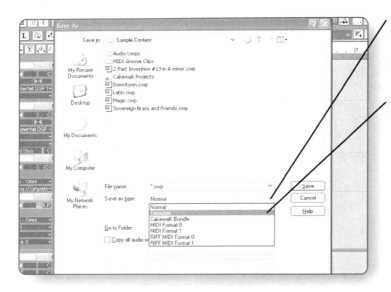

6. **Click** on the **down arrow** at the right of the **Save as Type drop-down list box.** The list will open.

7. **Click** on **Template.** The list will close, and the window will display template files.

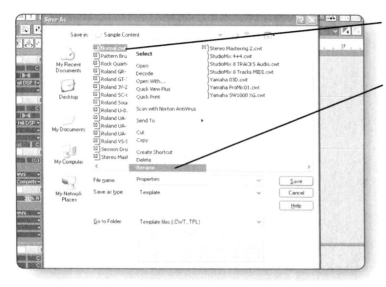

8. Right-click on the file **Normal.cwt**. The context menu will appear.

9. Click on **Rename**. The menu will close, and the file name will be highlighted and outlined.

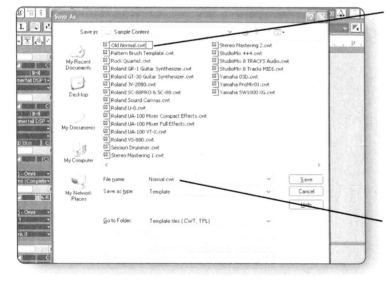

10. Type a **new name** for the old default template. The name will be displayed within the outline box.

11. Press Enter. The outline box will close, and the old default template will be renamed, creating a backup should you wish to use it or reassign it as the default at a later date.

12. Type the name **Normal** in the **File name field**. SONAR will add the appropriate file extension.

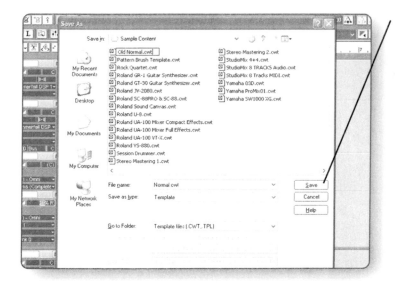

13. **Click** on **Save**. The dialog box will close, and your project will be saved as the default template.

Using Key Bindings

SONAR's key bindings allow you to assign virtually any SONAR command to a key on your computer or MIDI keyboard. For example, you could open the Drag and Drop Options dialog box, or turn the metronome on or off with a single keystroke and never have to delve into the menus. SONAR lets you use the Shift, Alt, and Ctrl modifier keys as well as the F1–F12 keys for hundreds of possible key bindings! For most of us, that's way more than we'll ever need, but any time you find yourself menu-diving for a function more than occasionally, you can save time by creating a key binding for that function.

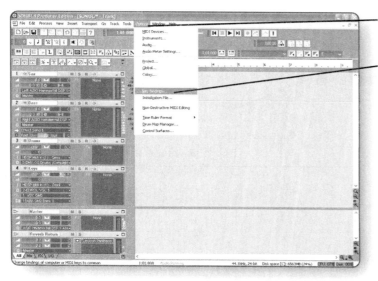

1. Click on **Options**. The Options menu will open.

2. Click on **Key Bindings**. The Key Bindings dialog box will appear.

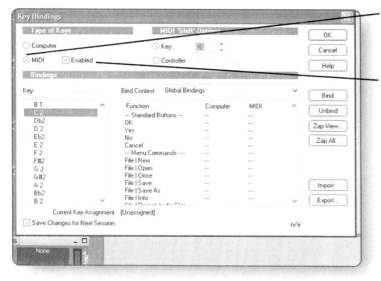

3. Click on the desired **Type of Keys option**. The option will be highlighted.

4. Click on **Enabled**. A ✔ will appear in the check box, and key bindings will be active.

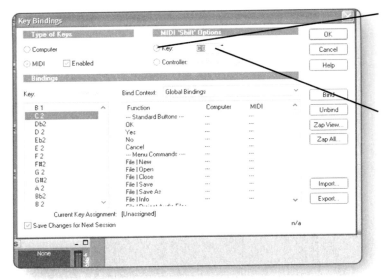

5. If you chose MIDI keys in Step 3, **click** on the desired **setting** under **MIDI 'Shift' Option**. The option will be highlighted.

6a. **Type** the desired **key** in the **Key text box**. This is the note that will be used as the MIDI Shift key.

OR

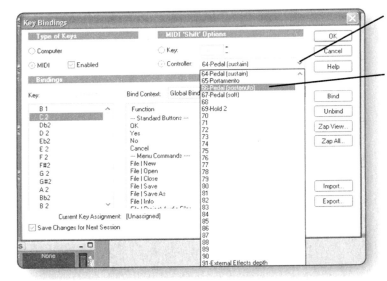

6b. **Click** on the **down arrow** at the right of the **Controller drop-down list box**. The list will open.

6c. **Click** on the desired **controller**. The list will close, and the chosen controller will be used as the MIDI Shift control.

WHAT NOTE IS SHIFT?

The MIDI Shift option alerts SONAR that you're no longer sending MIDI note and controller data but instead want to trigger a key binding. Good choices include the highest or lowest note on your keyboard or an un-used pedal.

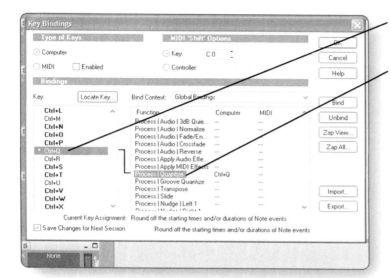

7. **Click** on a **key** in the **Key list**. The key will be highlighted.

8a. **Click** on a **function** in the **Function column** of the pane on the right. The function will be highlighted.

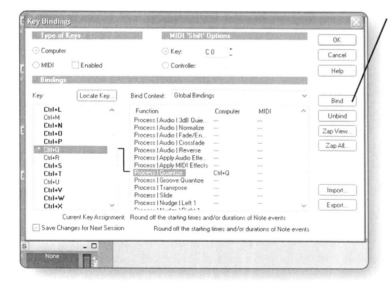

8b. **Click** on **Bind**. The key will be bound to the function. The binding will be indicated by a line connecting them.

OR

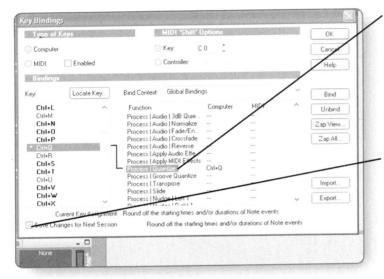

8c. Double-click on a **function**. The key will be bound to the function. The binding will be indicated by a line connecting them.

9. Repeat this **process** for other keys and functions.

10. Click on **Save Changes for Next Session**. A ✔ will be placed next to the option, and your key bindings will be remembered for future projects.

ONE AT A TIME

You can create both MIDI and computer-keyboard key bindings, but you can only use one set at a time. SONAR will remember each set of bindings, so you can switch back and forth whenever you want without losing any bindings.

Using the Patch Browser

Instead of choosing a MIDI track's sound by using the Bank and Patch settings, SONAR's Patch Browser lets you choose from a comprehensive list of all patches in all banks. When you choose this way, the Patch Browser assigns the bank and patch automatically. It also lets you sort and do simple text searches.

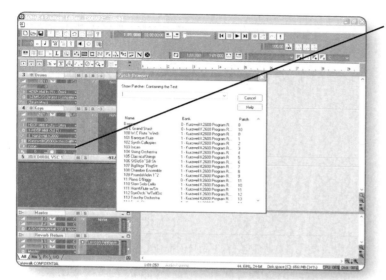

1. Right-click on a MIDI track's **Patch field**. The Patch Browser dialog box will appear.

THIS WAY OR THAT

You can also open the Patch Browser from the Bank/Patch Change dialog box (Insert, Bank/Patch Change), but that will create a bank/patch change event at the current Now time rather than as the default bank/patch for the track.

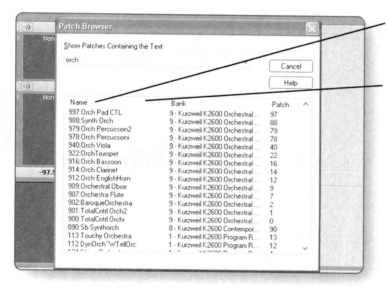

2. Click on **Name**. The list of patches will be sorted by patch name in alphabetical order.

3. Click on **Name** again. The list of patches will be sorted by patch name in reverse alphabetical order.

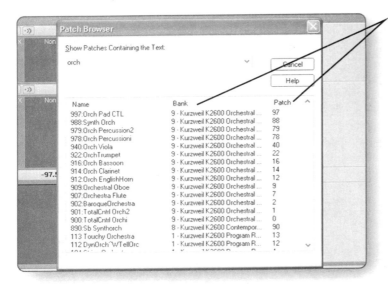

4. Click on **Bank** or **Patch**. The list will be sorted according to bank number or patch number, and the order will reverse if you click again.

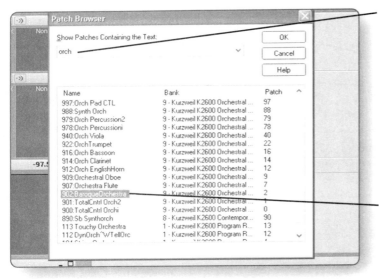

5. Type a **whole** or **partial word** in the **Show Patches Containing the Text field**. The list will be filtered to show only those patches whose names contain the text you typed.

6. Clear the **Show Patches Containing the Text field**. The complete list will be displayed again.

7. Click on a **patch name**. The patch name will be highlighted.

8. Click on **OK**. The dialog box will close, and the patch you chose will be assigned to that track.

Using the Track/Bus Inspector

The Track/Bus Inspector provides an exploded view of a track's or bus's parameters in the Track view. The Inspector allows you to keep your track height small so you can fit more tracks onscreen and still be able to adjust volume, pan, and other settings.

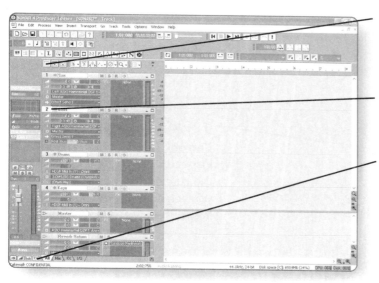

1. If necessary, **click** the **Show/Hide Inspector button**. The Track/Bus Inspector will be displayed.

2. Click on any part of a **track** or **bus**. The Inspector will display parameters for that track/bus.

3. Click on the **display buttons**. The display of sends, effects, volume, and EQ will be changed.

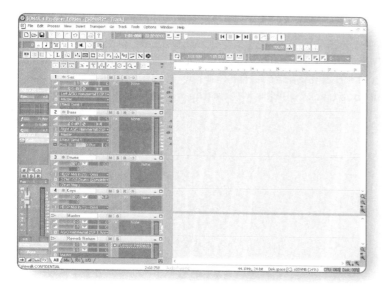

4. Adjust desired **parameters**.

THINK ABOUT IT. . .

It's so simple you may overlook just how powerful the Inspector really is. Without the Inspector, you would constantly be resizing tracks so you can see their parameters and make adjustments. Think of the Inspector as a tiny window into the Console view that lets you see one selected track at a time.

5. **Click** on the **track name** within the Inspector. The Track/Bus menu opens.

6. **Click** on the desired **track**, **bus**, or **main out**. The Inspector will be updated to reflect that element's parameters.

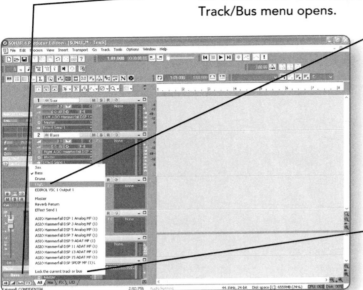

THE ONLY WAY

This is the only way you can display main outs in the Track view.

7. Optionally, **click** on **Lock the Current Track or Bus**. The Inspector will continue to display the current track or bus even if you select a different track or bus in the Track view.

Assigning I/O from the Track Menu

The Track menu enables you to assign inputs and outputs on multiple audio and MIDI tracks all at once. It's not very efficient for making changes to a track or two, but for setting up numerous tracks quickly it's just the ticket.

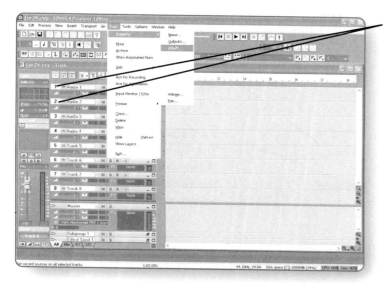

1. Select multiple tracks. The tracks will be highlighted.

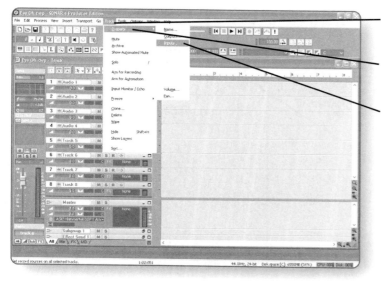

2. Click on **Track**. The Track menu will open.

3. Point to **Property**. The Property submenu will open.

4. Click on **Inputs**. The Track Inputs dialog box will appear.

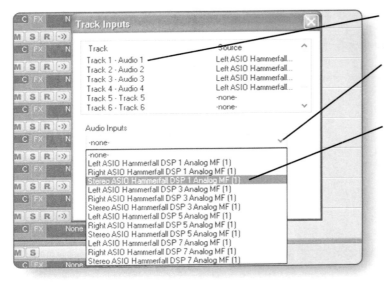

5. **Click** on a **track name**. The track name will be highlighted.

6. **Click** on the relevant **Input drop-down list box**. The list will open.

7. **Click** on the desired **input**. The list will close, and your choice will be displayed next to the selected track name in the Source column.

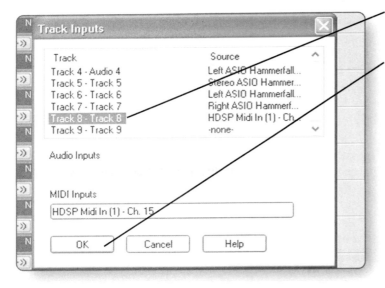

8. **Repeat the process** for other tracks.

9. **Click** on **OK**. The dialog box will close, and the track inputs will be assigned according to your specifications.

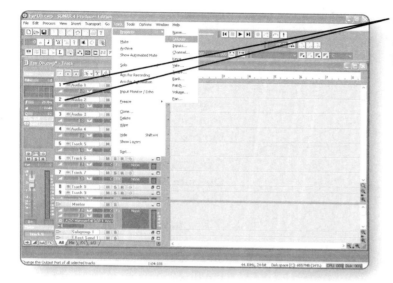

10. **Select** one or more **audio** or **MIDI tracks**. The tracks will be highlighted.

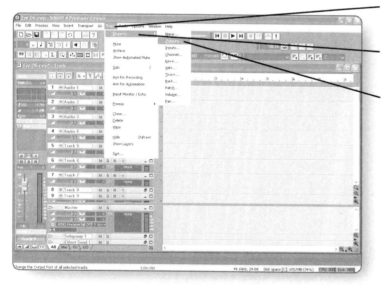

11. **Click** on **Track**. The Track menu will open.

12. **Point** to **Property**. The Property submenu will open.

13. **Click** on **Outputs**. The Track Outputs dialog box will appear.

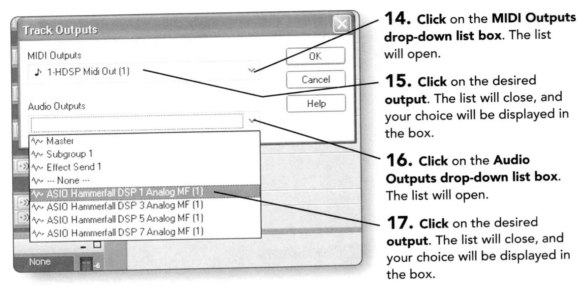

14. Click on the **MIDI Outputs drop-down list box**. The list will open.

15. Click on the desired **output**. The list will close, and your choice will be displayed in the box.

16. Click on the **Audio Outputs drop-down list box**. The list will open.

17. Click on the desired **output**. The list will close, and your choice will be displayed in the box.

18. Click on **OK**. The dialog box will close, and the output assignments of all selected tracks will be updated.

PART VII

Appendixes

A
Setup and Troubleshooting

SONAR works with many different types of audio hardware, from stock sound cards to professional-caliber audio interfaces. This appendix will guide you through the general aspects of getting SONAR and your interface to work together, as well as some preferred settings for best performance. If you have severe problems getting your system to run properly, contact the tech-support folks at Cakewalk and at the manufacturer of your audio interface.

Audio Drivers

A *driver* is a piece of software that manages the interaction between software and hardware. In the case of your audio interface, the driver tells SONAR what resolutions are possible, how many channels are available, and how the interface is configured. Follow these steps to choose and configure your drivers under SONAR.

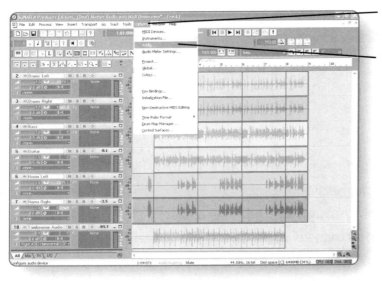

1. **Click** on **Options**. The Options menu will open.

2. **Click** on **Audio**. The Audio Options dialog box will appear.

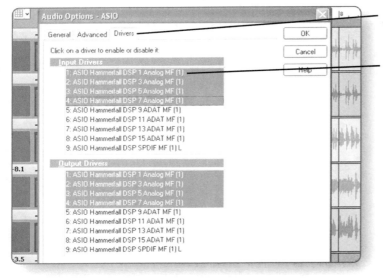

3. **Click** on the **Drivers tab**. The tab will come to the front.

4. **Click** on one or more **drivers**. The driver(s) will be highlighted. If necessary, **click** again to deselect the driver(s).

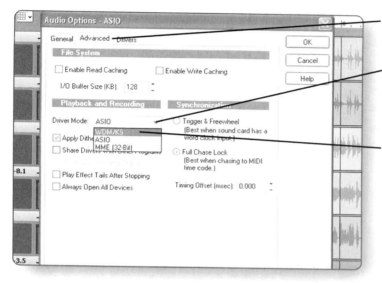

5. Click on the **Advanced tab**. The tab will come to the front.

6. Click on the **down arrow** at the right of the **Driver Mode drop-down list box**. The list will open.

7. Click on the desired **driver mode**. The list will close.

WDM/KS

If your audio card supports it, use the WDM/KS driver mode. This will ordinarily result in the best performance. ASIO should be your second choice and MME should be your third.

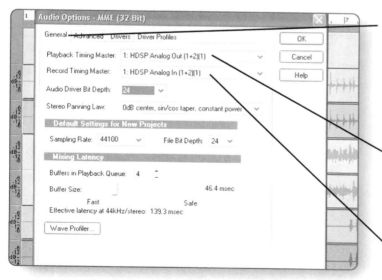

8. Click on the **General tab**. The tab will come to the front.

9. Choose desired **options** from number boxes and drop-down lists. The most important options are

- **Playback Timing Master.** If you have both a sound card and a high-quality audio interface, this should be set to your audio interface.

- **Record Timing Master.** If you have both a sound card and a high-quality audio interface, this should be set to your audio interface.

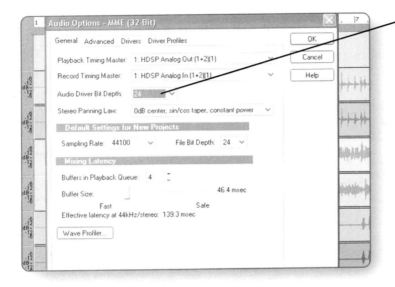

- **Audio Driver Bit Depth.** This should be set to 24 (bits) if your interface supports it.

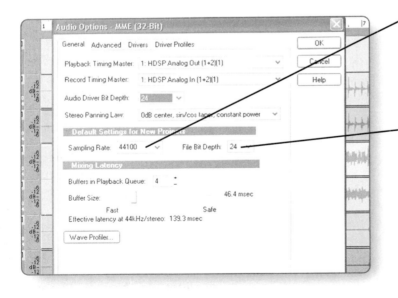

- **Sampling Rate.** This should be set to 44,100 or higher. If your interface supports it, you should consider using a 96,000 Hz sample rate for higher fidelity.

- **File Bit Depth.** This should be set to 24 if your interface supports it.

RESTARTING

Many of the audio options require quitting and restarting SONAR before changes will take effect, and sometimes changing multiple settings requires more than one restart. Fortunately, once you get everything set correctly, you won't have to fuss with the settings any more.

Wave Profiler

Unless you are using ASIO drivers, SONAR needs to profile audio hardware before it can use it properly. Ordinarily this only has to be done when you install SONAR or install a new audio interface, but if your settings get corrupted you can restore them by forcing SONAR to run the Wave Profiler.

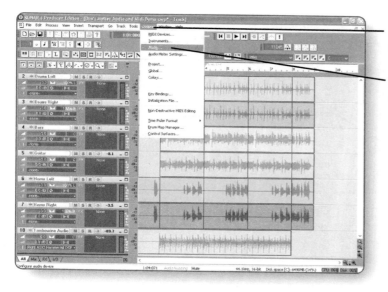

1. **Click** on **Options**. The Options menu will open.

2. **Click** on **Audio**. The Audio Options dialog box will appear.

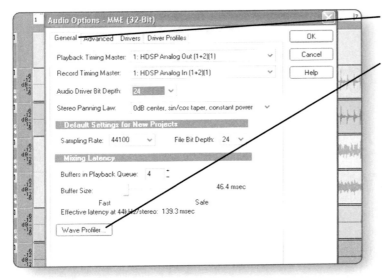

3. **Click** on the **General tab**. The tab will come to the front.

4. **Click** on the **Wave Profiler button**. The Wave Profiler confirmation window will appear.

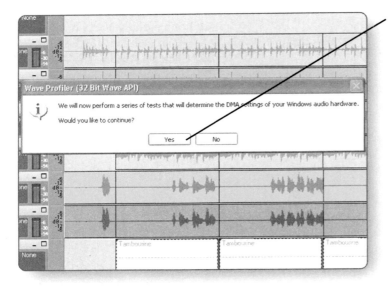

5. **Click** on **Yes**. The Wave Profiler progress window will appear.

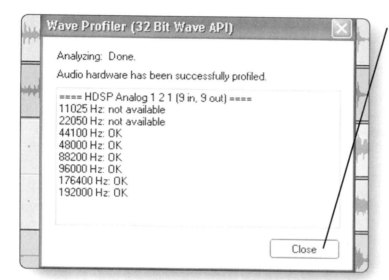

6. When the Wave Profiler has finished, **click** on **Close**. The window will close and return you to the Audio Options dialog box.

7. **Click** on **OK** in the Audio Options dialog box. The dialog box will close.

Managing Audio Latency

It takes a finite amount of time for audio to be digitized, travel through your computer, and be converted back to an analog sound so you can hear it. This is called *latency*, and if it's larger than a few milliseconds it can become a serious obstacle to getting any work done. Too much latency can also make the response of virtual instruments sluggish.

Latency is a result of the way audio is buffered at the CPU. Therefore, you can control latency by using the smallest buffer size and the fewest buffers you can get away with. With good WDM drivers and a fast computer, you can set the buffer size and number so low that you don't notice the latency at all.

As you experiment with these settings, listen carefully for any distortion or dropouts. Such sonic mayhem is an indication that your buffers are not large enough or numerous enough for smooth and consistent audio recording and playback. Once you reach that point, reset your buffer settings to the last known distortion-free setting.

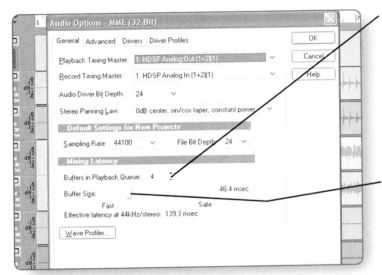

1. Click on the **plus (+)** or **minus (−) buttons** on the Buffers in the Audio Options dialog box's **Playback Queue number box**. The lower the number, the less the latency. Low numbers also increase the likelihood of distortion and dropouts, however.

2. Drag the **Buffer Size slider**. The further left, the smaller the buffer and the lower the latency. **Click OK** to confirm the new settings.

CONTROL PANEL

For the lowest latency, you will likely need to open your audio interface's control panel and set its buffer size to the smallest practical value. This buffer size is related to but independent of SONAR's Buffer Size setting. Once you have changed the interface's buffer size, you will need to run the Wave Profiler again before SONAR will recognize the change.

SITUATIONAL LATENCY

The more plug-ins and virtual instruments you are running, the harder your computer has to work to maintain low latency. It's common practice for engineers to use a very low latency setting while *tracking* (recording) and a higher latency while mixing.

THE DIRECT WAY

Most audio interfaces also feature a "direct monitor" or "hardware monitor" mode that effectively eliminates latency by bypassing the software. Audio coming in a record-armed input is immediately funneled back to the monitor outputs, so there is no delay. You should be able to enable this mode from your interface's control panel. Be sure that you don't use SONAR's Input Echo when you are using direct-monitor mode, or you will hear an annoying echo.

B

Understanding Audio and MIDI

SONAR 4 provides a unified environment for working with MIDI and audio. This makes it very easy to deal with the two types of musical material, but it also invites confusion between the two. This appendix provides general information about what makes each unique.

What Is MIDI?

MIDI is a language designed to control synthesizers. The term is an acronym for Musical Instrument Digital Interface, and it is pronounced *mih-dee*. MIDI uses 8-bit digital messages to turn notes on and off, to set volume and pan, and to modify patch parameters. Most MIDI messages have 128 possible values: 128 patches per bank, 128 note numbers, volume values from 0–127, and so forth. These messages can be recorded, edited, and played back from within SONAR to control external hardware synthesizers or software-based virtual instruments such as the Cakewalk TTS-1.

Because MIDI is simply a set of control messages, it's very easy to edit a MIDI performance in ways that you simply can't with traditional audio recording. For example, if you speed up a tape recording of someone speaking or singing, you get the classic "chipmunk" effect. This is, in fact, exactly how the voices of a number of famous cartoon characters are created. When you speed up the playback of MIDI notes, however, you get the same notes but at a faster tempo. Conversely, you can easily transpose a MIDI performance by telling SONAR to redefine which notes are to be triggered, and when you play the transposed performance it will sound as though it were recorded that way.

MIDI uses *channels* to organize its messages. As you've seen, SONAR requires that you specify a MIDI channel for each track. Each channel has its own patch—although you can change a patch in the middle of a track using the Insert Bank/Patch Change command, you can only have one patch per channel at any given time. Similarly, pan and volume information are channel-specific. Each MIDI device can have up to 16 channels with which to work. The Cakewalk TTS-1, for example, lets you play 16 different instruments, each one on a different channel. This is called *multitimbral* operation. The DreamStation DXi, by contrast, is not multitimbral and can only play one patch at a time. Fortunately, you can run multiple DreamStations (or TTS-1s!) simultaneously to achieve multiple timbres.

What Is Digital Audio?

Sound is simply a variation in air pressure within a range of frequencies and amplitude our ears can perceive. Digital audio is a method of describing that variation numerically. The most common type of digital audio, *pulse code modulation (PCM)*, measures the air pressure many times each second and assigns a binary number to each of those measurements. On playback, these measurements describe the variation of air pressure over time that recreates the sound. There's more to the process, of course—the air pressure needs to be converted to voltage first, and then the measurements really describe a voltage pattern that moves a speaker that moves the air—but this translation of air pressure to binary numbers is the essence of PCM digital audio.

Digital audio can capture and reproduce sounds quite realistically if the measurements are taken often enough and accurately enough. The speed of measurement is called the *sample rate*, and it is expressed in kilohertz (kHz)—or thousands of samples per second. Typical sample rates for professional audio production are 44.1 kHz (the sample rate of CDs), 48 kHz, and 96 kHz. The accuracy of measurement is determined by the bit depth, which determines how many units are available to measure the amplitude. Professional recording is done at 16 bits (the bit depth of CDs) or 24 bits. In general, the higher the sample rate and bit depth the more realistic the reproduction.

The down side of recording at high sample rates and bit depths is that it takes up a lot of space on your hard disk. Recording at CD-quality resolution (16 bits, 44.1 kHz, stereo) requires 10 megabytes per minute of audio. If you record eight stereo tracks at that resolution, your three-minute song eats up 240 megabytes. The same song at 24 bits and 96 kHz devours almost 800 megabytes. Clearly, you're going to need a big hard disk for recording and lots of CDs or DVDs to back up your songs!

Comparing MIDI and Digital Audio

Of course, there's a good reason that SONAR lets you use both MIDI and digital audio in your projects. Each one has its strengths, so you'll use MIDI for some things and digital audio for others. The two factors that you want to consider in deciding which to use are file size and flexibility.

MIDI can pack a lot of instructions into a tiny amount of space. That same three-minute song would take up only a few dozen *kilobytes* if it were all MIDI data. For this reason, it's common for electronic musicians to keep their MIDI tracks as MIDI tracks for as long as possible and commit them to audio tracks (remember "Recording External Synth Parts" from Chapter 19, "Capturing Your Mix for CD and the Internet"?) only when they're ready for a final mix and export.

MIDI also beats digital audio for flexibility. If you get to the final stage of a project and suddenly discover that you misjudged your lead vocalist's highest notes, wouldn't you want to be able to use Process, Transpose to lower the key? If you had recorded all of your synthesizer parts straight to audio tracks, you would have a lot harder time. Similarly, a last-minute tempo change would be much easier to accomplish with MIDI tracks than digital audio tracks.

However, once you've recorded an audio track it will sound the same every time in any studio because it precisely captured the sound of the original performance. A MIDI track is dependent on the quality of an available synthesizer, so if you don't have exactly the instrument you want you will not get the results you're after. A fantastic MIDI performance played back through a cheap synthesizer is a big let-down.

Most projects end up being a combination of audio and MIDI tracks. For example, you might have a MIDI drum track playing through the Cakewalk TTS-1, a MIDI bass track playing through the DreamStation DXi, and audio tracks with vocals and guitars. SONAR integrates all these elements seamlessly.

Managing Your CPU Resources

Your computer's CPU has to calculate the sound of a virtual instrument while calculating velocity offsets and equalization effects, all while drawing waveforms and controls onscreen. Sooner or later, even the fastest computer hits the wall. This appendix shows you how to keep the wall at bay a bit longer and what to do when you run out of gas.

The CPU and Disk Meters

In the lower-right corner of the SONAR window, there are two meters that have absolutely nothing to do with audio amplitude. The CPU meter tells you how much of your CPU's attention is currently being utilized, and the Disk meter tells you how much of your hard disk's read and write capacity is currently being utilized. If either meter hits 100 percent, SONAR will stop. Once that happens, you need to do something to free up resources.

Every virtual instrument and plug-in effect you assign will cause the CPU meter to increase. Every audio track you record or play will send the Disk meter higher. Use these meters as a guide to managing your resources. If your CPU meter is almost maxed out, you're not going to have any luck firing up another soft synth, and if your Disk meter is close to 100 percent, you're going to want to do something to fix that before you try to record a six-piece horn section and end up crashing every few measures.

Lightening the Load

There are several tricks you can use to free up CPU resources. One of the biggest is to make sure that when you run SONAR you *only* run SONAR. Other open applications consume processor cycles and memory that SONAR could be using on your music, so close them all. In particular, anti-virus programs, especially the ones that continually scan for harmful activity, tend to distract the hard disk and wreck great performances, so turn them off before starting SONAR. Look at your System Tray at the right end of your Windows Taskbar—if you've got more than a couple of icons there, you're wasting valuable system resources that SONAR needs. Disable as many of them as you can.

Using File-Based Effects

When you use Process, Apply Audio Effects (remember Chapter 16, "Using Audio Effects"?) to "print" your effects to the audio clips, you eliminate the need to run processors on those tracks. Similarly, any processing you apply from the Audio Effects context menu are part of the audio clips themselves and require no CPU resources during playback.

Using Group Effects

Reverb plug-ins tend to eat up more CPU resources than any other effect plug-ins. Because of this—and because of historical and aesthetic reasons—reverbs are ordinarily applied to groups of tracks by using buses. For example, if you wanted to add reverb to your background vocals you *could* insert a Lexicon Pantheon on each track. You could, but you shouldn't. Even if your system has the CPU resources to do that, it probably won't give you quite the sound you're after.

Instead, create a new bus and then create sends on all of your background vocal tracks that point to this new bus. Insert a Lexicon Pantheon or other reverb on the bus. Now a copy of each vocal track is being routed through the bus with the reverb, and you can balance the reverberated bus against the original audio tracks. Be sure to set the reverb to 100 percent wet. This is the standard way of routing reverb (as you learned in Chapter 17, "Mastering Audio's Ins and Outs"), and it only uses one instance of the plug-in rather than needlessly eating up CPU resources with a reverb on every track.

Submixing Audio Tracks

In the heyday of the ADAT and other eight-track recorders, it was a common practice to *bounce* six tracks of drums to two tracks and then re-use those original tracks for recording additional parts. This *ping-ponging* of tracks allowed engineers to get a lot more than eight tracks of music onto a tape with only eight tracks. In SONAR, submixing tracks this way will not only free up CPU cycles from any effects that had been on the tracks originally, but it will also enable you to get more tracks of playback and recording out of your hard-working hard disk.

The Edit, Bounce to Track(s) command is similar to the File, Export Audio command, except that it automatically brings the bounced audio into an audio track. A typical application would be to solo all of your drum tracks, select them through the entire song, and bounce them to a new track. Once you've got the new track, select and archive the original drum tracks. All of their settings will be saved for future reference, but they will no longer use disk and CPU resources. Note that simply muting a track does not stop it from consuming disk and CPU resources.

Freezing Tracks and Synths

SONAR 4 introduces a powerful new way to maximize your CPU cycles—freeze. Freezing a track or synth (virtual instrument) is equivalent to bouncing the output of the track with effects and then deactivating the original. This effectively substitutes a processed audio clip for the original unprocessed audio plus effects, allowing you to use your CPU for something new.

We covered the process for freezing a track in Chapter 18— the process for synths is virtually identical. Select the track or tracks you want to freeze, and then choose the command from the Track menu. If you decide to tweak the track some more, you can unfreeze it to get the original back.

Index